Case studies in organizational behaviour

Case studies in organizational behaviour

Edited by
Chris W Clegg, Nigel J Kemp and Karen Legge

P·C·P
Paul Chapman
Publishing Ltd

First published 1985
by Harper & Row Ltd

Reprinted 1989, 1990
by Paul Chapman Publishing Ltd
144 Liverpool Road
London N1 1LA

British Library Cataloguing in Publication Data

Case studies in organizational behaviour.
  1. Organizational behaviour——Case studies
  I. Clegg, Chris W.   II. Kemp, Nigel J.
  III. Legge, Karen
  302.3'5'0722   HD58.7

  ISBN 1 85396 089 6

B C D E F   5 4 3 2 1 0

Typeset by Inforum Ltd, Portsmouth
Printed and bound by Athenaeum Press Ltd, Newcastle upon Tyne

Contents

SECTION 3: INDUSTRIAL RELATIONS

Preface

During the summer of 1983 one of us innocently remarked that we needed a book of case studies for our teaching. Here it is – 27 cases by 40 authors who between them have enormous experience of research and problem-solving in organizations using and developing ideas and theories in the field of organizational behaviour. We are extremely grateful to all our contributors for the skills and forbearance they have displayed over the last few months. Our thanks also go to the managing editor, Marianne Lagrange, for her commitment to the project and for her practical support at all times.

The book is aimed at students – at undergraduate, graduate or post-experience levels – who are taking courses with a significant Organizational Behaviour component, including Personnel Management and Industrial Relations. We firmly believe that people enjoy problem-solving, in particular when they are working with well prepared and rich case material which presents concrete and practical situations. We hope the cases are fun as well as being useful and academically stimulating. A companion volume – a teacher's manual – is also available for use with this set of cases.

To our contributors, secretaries, colleagues and families we extend our heartfelt thanks. We have enjoyed editing this collection. We hope it will both entertain and inform.

CWC, NJK, KL
October 1984

Notes on the Contributors

Chris Brotherton is a Lecturer in Psychology in the Department of Psychology, University of Nottingham

Dr John Burgoyne is director of the Centre for the Study of Management Learning, University of Lancaster

Chris Clegg is a Senior Research Fellow at the MRC/ESRC Social and Applied Psychology Unit, University of Sheffield

Professor Cary Cooper is Professor of Organizational Behaviour at the Department of Management Sciences, University of Manchester Institute of Science and Technology

Leela Damodaran is a Co-Director of the Human Sciences and Advanced Technology Research Centre, University of Loughborough

Sandra Dawson is a Senior Lecturer in the Department of Social and Economic Studies, Imperial College of Science and Technology

Dr P.K. Edwards is a Principal Research Fellow at the Industrial Relations Research Unit, University of Warwick

Dr Mike Fitter is a Senior Research Officer at the MRC/ESRC Social and Applied Psychology Unit, University of Sheffield

Dr Robert Goffee is a Lecturer in Organizational Studies at the London Graduate School of Business Studies

Dan Gowler is a Fellow of Templeton College, Oxford, and Lecturer in Management Studies at the University of Oxford

Richard Graham is a consultant in interactive skills with the Huthwaite Research Group Ltd

Dr David Guest is a Senior Lecturer in Industrial Relations at the London School of Economics and Political Science

Dr Jean Hartley is a Research Fellow at the ESRC Industrial Relations Research Unit, University of Warwick

Professor Andrew Kakabadse is Professor of Organizational Behaviour at Cranfield School of Management, Cranfield Institute of Technology

Dr John Kelly is a Lecturer in Industrial Relations at the London School of Economics and Political Science

Mike Kelly is a Senior Lecturer at the Centre for Educational Development and Training, Manchester Polytechnic

Dr Nigel Kemp is a Research Fellow at the MRC/ESRC Social and Applied Psychology Unit, University of Sheffield

Karen Legge is Reader in Organizational Behaviour at the Department of Social and Economic Studies, Imperial College of Science and Technology

Joyce McNally was formerly a Research Officer in the Department of Behaviour in Organizations, University of Lancaster

Professor Iain Mangham is Professor of Organizational Behaviour at the School of Management, University of Bath

Mick Marchington is a Senior Lecturer in Industrial Relations at Lancashire Polytechnic

Linda Marsh is a consultant in interactive skills with the Huthwaite Research Group Ltd

Dr Nigel Nicholson is a Senior Research Fellow at the MRC/ESRC Social and Applied Psychology Unit, University of Sheffield

Dr Roy Payne is a Senior Research Fellow at the MRC/ESRC Social and Applied Psychology Unit, University of Sheffield

Dr Riccardo Peccei is a Research Fellow in the Department of Industrial Relations, London School of Economics and Political Science

Susan Pomfrett is a Research Associate at the Human Sciences and Advanced Technology Research Centre, University of Loughborough

Dr Bill Reddin is an independent consultant with W J Reddin and Associates Ltd

Sheila Rothwell is Director of the Centre for Employment Policy Studies, The Management College, Henley

Paul Routledge is Labour Editor of The Times

Professor Richard Scase is Professor of Sociology in the Faculty of Social Sciences, University of Kent

Hugh Scullion is Scottish Development Manager, Employment Relations, University of Strathclyde

Professor Sylvia Shimmin is Professor of Organizational Behaviour in the Department of Behaviour in Organizations, University of Lancaster

Dr Rosemary Stewart is Dean and a Fellow of Templeton College, Oxford

Roger Undy is a Fellow of Templeton College, Oxford

Dr Toby Wall is a Senior Research Fellow and Assistant Director at the MRC/ESRC Social and Applied Psychology Unit, University of Sheffield

Professor Don Wallis is Professor and Chairman of the Department of Applied Psychology, University of Wales Institute of Science and Technology

Dr Paul Willman is a Lecturer in Industrial Relations at the London Graduate School of Business Studies

Dr Barry Wilkinson is a Lecturer in Organizational Behaviour at the School of Management, National University of Singapore

Pauline Wingate is an independent researcher

Dr Stephen Wood is a Lecturer in Industrial Relations at the London School of Economics and Political Science

Introduction

Karen Legge, Nigel Kemp and Chris Clegg

This book consists of 27 teaching case studies, each of which has been derived from empirical research employing the case study method. Each case addresses a specific issue or range of issues and the book overall provides broad yet detailed coverage of the field of organizational behaviour, including personnel management and industrial relations. Clearly the book speaks of some commitment to the case study method as an approach to both teaching and research.

In this introduction, we first describe the book and its structure; second, we offer guidance on how it can be used most effectively; and in the third part we consider some of the strengths and limitations of the case study method.

Description of the Book

This book arose because we felt a need to collect a set of good case study material for use in a teaching environment. We have found that most students actively enjoy working with and learning from well prepared and rich case material. To the student there are two major advantages to the approach. In the first place most people enjoy the descriptions of practical problems and are more comfortable working from the concrete and specific to the abstract and general rather than vice versa. Secondly, people like solving problems, especially when the situation is not threatening: they can develop, experiment with and debate their own ideas with little or no risk.

To the teacher there are two further benefits from the use of case studies. The first is that practical problems resist compartmentalized thinking and action. Read any one or more of the cases which follow and the sense of overlap or interrelatedness is recognized very quickly! Indeed the very nature of many of the cases, where a systems perspective is adopted, makes it unavoidable that issues, problems and solutions coexist and overlap. Secondly, practical problem-solving provides an excellent arena for testing out and developing theories. Here we are thinking of the cases being used either deductively or inductively (see Bennis 1968; Walton 1972).

Deductively, the cases can be tested by students against the theories that have been presented to them via lectures or through readings. Thus, the cases will highlight the theories which are useful in diagnosing problems or formulating solutions or, even, those which are contradicted by the case data. Used inductively, the cases can be presented to the students for them to generate issues, problems and solutions and to attempt to explain the behaviour described in the text. Importantly of course, the use of either of these approaches will influence whether detailed readings, presentations or lectures are given before or after the students read the cases!

For both students and teachers we believe that Lewin's aphorism, 'there is nothing so practical as a good theory' (Lewin 1951), remains as true today as ever. In the field of organizational behaviour above all perhaps, we are reminded of the Maoist doctrine that the theorists should go out into the community to test the usefulness of their ideas. A final advantage to all parties is also well worth mentioning: in our experience well prepared case material provides for stimulating and lively classes to the advantage of all involved.

Our commitment to the case study method then is very strong. What we have found as teachers is that while good material exists, there is no single text that fits our needs. Certainly books of case studies in the area of organizational behaviour do exist – but the texts providing the coverage we sought are all American, written by and for Americans. Although the topics covered may be very similar, the perspectives adopted can be quite different, the most obvious examples being in the area of industrial relations, where our history, culture and legal initiatives are more European than trans-Atlantic. In short we wanted a collection of British cases.

This book is aimed at people on courses with a significant organizational behaviour component. Certainly we believe it has its place for those studying personnel management, industrial relations, business studies, management studies, management science, and occupational psychology. We would also like to think it will be suitable for the increasing numbers of engineers and technologists for whom organizational behaviour is an important subsidiary subject.

The book is also aimed at people studying at different levels and with different needs. Thus it should be appropriate for undergraduates, people studying for diplomas in management studies and in personnel management, masters and doctoral students, students in further education colleges, and people on post-experience courses – indeed the full range of courses for which problem-solving in organizations is relevant.

One of our major problems was to choose the topics we wanted to include. Any selection is of course difficult. In part we have been guided by our own experiences and those of our immediate colleagues as well as by the content of relevant courses elsewhere in the UK. On the other hand, it is also true that we have been influenced by what we knew to be available in the field. In each instance we have insisted that contributions are by experienced researchers with a specialist interest in and detailed knowledge of their area. All of the cases reported are the result of their detailed first-hand knowledge of particular situations and of careful research into it. We have also tried to ensure that the problems are set in a range of organizations. Some are large, some small; some are privately owned and others public; and some are in manufacturing and others in service industries. For all that, there inevitably remain some gaps. For example we have no cases set within schools or voluntary or charitable organizations, yet clearly these are significant kinds of organization in which our discipline is relevant.

In the end our basic choice was to provide coverage of three major subdisciplines, namely organizational behaviour, personnel management and industrial relations. The book is organized in these three main areas. Within each we have identified a number of major topics which we believe require inclusion in courses in these areas. Furthermore, we decided to organize the cases within each area working broadly from the 'micro' to the 'macro', since in each instance the level of analysis can be different. Not surprisingly perhaps, many cases in practice incorporate individual, group and company-wide issues. As a result we have finally settled on the 27 topics summarized in Table 1. Unfortunately limitations of space have restricted the range of areas covered. We have not, for example, been able to include cases on organizational culture or employment law, although issues related to these topics pervade a number of the cases.

Let it also be said that the way in which we have structured the material is only for convenience. It reflects our current perceptions of the field and its subdisciplines, but it is arbitrary. The first case on job design, for example, while raising issues concerning employee motivation, job satisfaction and performance, also includes related topics such as stress, supervisory behaviour, information and control systems, turnover, training and skills, as well as more 'macro' issues, such as payment systems and equal opportunities. This, however, is not a weakness either of our ability to provide a taxonomy for the discipline or of the cases themselves. Rather it is a strength. Our view is that any course requires some basic organization of material: but this will be inherently problematic. We hope that our chosen structure for the material is useful to teachers and fits well with course designers. One of our aims in compiling this book has been to demonstrate to students the interrelatedness of the topics we are covering and the arbitrariness of this or any other structuring of the material.

Use of the Book

Each case is quite short, 4000 words being the maximum length. The authors have been encouraged to provide background information giving the *context* within which their problems occur. At the end of each case the writers ask some very *specific questions* which the students should answer. In most instances students can work alone, in pairs or in small groups to answer the questions, before coming together for class discussion. Guidance is also given on how long some of the questions require for discussion. Some, for example, only require one or two hours whereas others may be suitable for sessions spread over several days. Some cases also incorporate experiential, role-playing activities. At the end of each case, two reading lists are provided. The first comprises a very short list of *essential reading*. This should be done by the student or the basic ideas covered in presentation by the teacher. The longer list comprises some *additional reading* that can be undertaken. In addition, of

Table 1 Structuring of material

	Section 1: Organizational behaviour	Section 2: Personnel management	Section 3: Industrial relations
Micro →	1 Job design	12 Absence and turnover	20 Negotiating behaviour
	2 Man–machine interface	13 Selection and recruitment	21 Collective bargaining
	3 Stress	14 Training and skills	22 Industrial disputes
	4 Supervisory behaviour	15 Health and safety at work	23 A 'lock-out'
	5 Managerial style and appraisal	16 Redundancy	24 Strike organization
	6 Information and control systems	17 Management development	25 New technology
	7 Decision making	18 Payment systems	26 Participation and communication
	8 Power and politics	19 Equal opportunities	27 Trade union democracy
	9 Organizational consulting and development		
	10 Small businesses		
Macro	11 Organizational structure		

course, a teacher may wish to add further questions and references.

A key, distinctive feature of this book is that there is also a separate teacher's manual in which the case authors have provided four sets of information (in about 1000 words) for use by the teachers. First they provide some notes on the appropriate *theoretical background* to the case. Essentially these are the ideas which the case study writer found useful in understanding the problems encountered. Secondly, they describe what *actually happened* in the case study they undertook. This is particularly useful where organizations actively tried to resolve their problems. Thirdly, they provide a set of *answers* to the questions they set. Finally, they add a further reading list, for example covering the theoretical work which the teacher can draw upon and any fuller descriptions of the case that may be available elsewhere. We should make it clear that these notes are not designed to give *definitive answers* to the questions set in the book. The hope is that teachers and students will develop and explore their own ideas from their own perspectives. But the notes do provide some specific guidelines prepared by the researcher who undertook the case. They are given to provide the busy teacher with a structure and a start. After that . . .

It is also important to recognize that each case (along with its notes in the teacher's manual) stands in its own right. We are not expecting people to work through from Case 1 to Case 27. There may be a host of reasons why people should select from amongst the cases and decide upon their own sequencing. To help in this process we provide an index to the cases in the form of a matrix (see Table 2). In this we show the major topic covered but also indicate the range of subjects embraced by each case. For example the teacher looking for material on the theme of job design would look down column 1 in the matrix and see that this is the major theme in Case 1 but also is relevant to Cases 2, 3, 4, 6, 12, 14, 15, 18, 21 and 25. Looked at the other way, by looking across row 1, the user of Case 1 would see that it is principally about job design but also raises other themes such as stress, supervisory behaviour, information and control systems, absence and turnover, training and skills, payment systems and equal opportunities at work. We hope such cross-referencing is useful.

It is of course also possible that teachers may wish to develop their own questions and answers from a number of cases, and build up their own cross-references. It would be possible, for example, to reinterpret several of the cases in terms of the methods by which individuals and organizations cope with and respond to uncertainty, or the ways in which individuals and organizations cope with change. We hope the material is flexible enough to handle such an approach – it should be!

Above all we hope people enjoy the book. It has been fun collaborating with the authors and we find the cases a good read in their own right. If the book entertains and teaches, it will have succeeded.

The Case Method

What is a case study? As far as research goes, Denny's (1978) definition would appear to capture the understanding implicitly held by many of our contributors: 'an intensive or complete examination of a facet, an issue, or perhaps the events of a geographic setting over time' (Denny 1978, p. 2). While the focus may differ, from

Table 2 is a matrix. The columns are the eleven cases (numbered 1–11); the rows are the twenty-seven topics (numbered 1–27). A solid circle (●) marks the principal topic of a case and an open circle (○) marks a subsidiary topic.

Cases (columns 1–11)

No.	CASE	TOPIC	SETTING
1	Fab Sweets Ltd.	Job Design	Confectionery Firm
2	Oilco	Man-machine Interface	Marketing and Distribution Division of Oil Company
3	Stress amongst Crane Drivers	Stress	Construction Companies
4	Photoproducts UK	Supervisory Behaviour	'Greenfield' Film Processing Factory
5	Administrators in the NHS	Managerial Style and Appraisal	National Health Service
6	Tewes Ltd.	Information and Control Systems	Confectionery Firm
7	British Rail	Decision-Making	Nationalised Industry
8	TVN	Power and Politics	Independent Television Company
9	John Player and Sons	Organizational Consulting and Development	Cigarette Manufacturing and Distribution
10	J. & S. Nicholson Ltd.	Small Businesses: Family firms and management	Construction Company
11	Gamma Appliances	Organizational Structure	Manufacturing and Marketing of Electronic Office Equipment

Matrix of topics (rows) × cases (columns)

Topic	1	2	3	4	5	6	7	8	9	10	11
1 Job Design	●	○	○	○		○					
2 Man-machine interface		●		○							
3 Stress			●	○							
4 Supervisory Behaviour	○			●		○					
5 Managerial Style and Appraisal				○	●	○			○	○	○
6 Information & Control Systems	○	○		○		●					
7 Decision-Making					○	○	●	○			○
8 Power and Politics					○		○	●		○	○
9 Organizational Consulting & Development								○	●	○	○
10 Small Businesses: Family Firms & management										●	
11 Organizational Structure		○		○	○		○	○	○	○	●
12 Absence & Turnover	○										
13 Selection & Recruitment			○								
14 Training and Skills	○	○	○	○							
15 Health & Safety at Work			○								
16 Redundancy											○
17 Management Development					○			○	○		
18 Payment Systems	○										
19 Equal Opportunities	○										
20 Negotiating Behaviour							○				
21 Collective Bargaining							○				
22 Industrial Disputes							○				
23 A Lock-Out											
24 Strike Organization											
25 New Technology		○		○		○					
26 Participation & Communications		○	○		○	○		○			
27 Trade Union Democracy											

Table 2 Matrix of cases and topics

Table (rotated 90°). Far-left vertical group labels: **PERSONNEL MANAGEMENT** (cases 12–19) and **INDUSTRIAL RELATIONS** (cases 20–27). Matrix columns numbered 1–27 (○ = open circle, ● = filled circle).

	CASE	TOPIC	SETTING	1	2	3	4	5	6	7	8	9	10	11	12	13	14	15	16	17	18	19	20	21	22	23	24	25	26	27
12	The Absentee Bus Crews	Absence and Turnover	Coal Valley Bus Company	○			○		○						●	○													○	
13	HAL	Selection and Recruitment	Manufacturing and Distribution of Electronics		○				○							●				○	○	○							○	
14	Royal Navy	Training and Skills	Naval Training Establishments	○	○										○	○	●											○		
15	Texchem	Health and Safety at Work	Textile, Chemical and Plastics Manufacturing Factory	○	○				○						○		○	●											○	
16	Office Engineering Company	Redundancy	Manufacturing Company			○					○			○					●						○					
17	British Rail	Management Development	Nationalised Industry								○	○		○						●	○	○								
18	Mayfly Garments Ltd.	Payment Systems	Manufacturing Company	○			○				○	○		○		○	○				●	○	○	○					○	
19	Champion Oils Ltd.	Equal Opportunities	Refining and Production in a Process Plant						○		○				○	○	○				○	●								
20	Micklethwaite Brewery Plc.	Negotiating Behaviour	Brewing Industry							○													●	○	○					
21	Car Co.	Collective Bargaining	Vehicle Manufacture and Assembly	○			○	○			○												○	●	○					○
22	Small Metals Factory	Industrial Disputes	Engineering Factory	○							○												○		●	○				○
23	Times Newspapers Ltd.	A Lock-Out	Fleet Street				○	○	○		○												○	○	○	●	○			○
24	Steel Strike	Strike Organization	Rotherham, S. Yorkshire Strike Committee					○			○												○	○	○	○	●	○		○
25	'RM' Division	New Technology	Manufacturing Company	○	○						○					○	○				○		○	○	○	○	○	●	●	○
26	Kitchenco	Participation and Communications	Manufacturing Company					○		○	○			○		○	○				○		○	○					●	○
27	Union Government and Union Democracy	Trade Union Democracy	Transport and General Workers Union						○	○	○			○										○					○	●

naturally occurring experiments to slices of everyday organizational life, the emphasis of all contributors is on dynamic naturalistic settings and the importance of context (however conceptualized) in generating explanations for observed attitudes and behaviours. The methods of data collection employed range from naturalistic observation, use of existing records and unobtrusive measures, informal discussions and meetings to structured interviewing and use of questionnaires, depending on the theoretical and epistemological stance of the researcher.

Clearly, the functions of the case study in research and teaching differ. The aim of a *research* case study is to identify and examine phenomena and meanings, in order to establish relationships and configurations, with an eye to generation or (loosely speaking) testing of a hypothesis. In teaching, the aim is to present these studies in a form that will stimulate the development of critical questioning, insight and understanding. As a result it is inevitable that a teaching case study will differ from a report of case study research. But when a teaching case is *based* on case study research, it is necessary to look first at its limitations as well as its strengths as a research method in order to appreciate the nature of the material which will be available to the case writer.

The popularly attributed limitations of the case method in research centre around the issues of verification and generalizability: of internal and external validity to use Campbell and Stanley's (1966) classic terms. Let's take the question of verification first. Many commentators have made the criticism that a single, one-off case, particularly if of relatively short duration, does not afford the possibility of establishing causal inferences among the variables which it encompasses. Because a one-off case offers no variation in either the presumed effect or the possible causes, there is no immediate empirical basis for eliminating or establishing a preference for any one of the possible causes. Plausible rival hypotheses cannot be accepted or rejected as, in principle, they can be when experimental or quasi-experimental designs are used. If causal inferences are drawn, in practice they rest on the implicit comparison 'with other events casually observed or remembered' (Campbell and Stanley 1966, p. 6), or reference to other knowledge.

Secondly, critics claim that case study as a research method is inevitably subjective. Thus the data selected and presented and the interpretations which direct this selection and presentation may be both idiosyncratic and partial. Hence case studies 'too often present[s] processed information that the reader must take on faith. Writer biases or errors in judgement cannot easily be detected' (Guba and Lincoln 1981, p. 377).

Turning to the question of generalizability, there is the problem that one-off cases may be precisely that – opportunistic and unique, rather than representative of a larger population. As such, it is argued, they do not allow for scientific generalization.

If one accepted these criticisms of case study research one might hesitate to use any of its findings for teaching, or any other legitimate purpose. For the criticisms would imply that no relationships between cause and effect could be validly inferred from the findings, that the findings, such as they were, could not be generalized, and that in any case they would likely be idiosyncratic, biased and unreliable.

Not only do we reject most of these criticisms but, as far as they are valid, we suggest that very similar criticisms can be raised about so-called more 'rigorous', 'objective' research methods.

Taking these criticisms together, we observe that they all assume a commitment to positivism – and an old fashioned positivism at that. It is a positivistic position that believes that the important research question is establishing the real causes of real events, the effects of real intervening 'variables' and so on. Those holding a phenomenological view (e.g. Filmer et al. 1972) would of course argue that such an ontological and epistemological position is inappropriate for studying human action, given its reflexivity. A more valid enterprise is to aim at recreating the socially constructed world that individuals enact through developing shared meanings and taken-for-granted understandings – an enterprise which demands ethnographic case study research! But, even if we accept the legitimacy of an emphasis on causal inference, can any research method objectively and unequivocally establish caus-ation? If the case study method makes causal inferences on the basis of implicit subjective comparisons, or appeals to other knowledge, are the inferences made as a result of quasi-experimentation in practice much different? As Campbell (1974) himself has pointed out, even the positivist has to take on trust common-sense beliefs about the world in order to experiment at all. In order to test a particular hypothesis, the plausibility of all the other hypotheses entering the experiment have to be assumed. The ratio of the doubted to the trusted is always a very small 'fraction'. *Quantitative* testing *has* to depend on *qualitative* judgement. It is, finally, a judgement about the plausibility of one causal explanation over rival explanations that dictates its acceptance as a scientific 'truth'; furthermore, such judgements inevitably reflect the prevailing values of the scientific community.

As even Campbell (1979), learning from the classic ethnographers, has now come to recognize, the one-off case study can test causal hypotheses by a process of pattern matching. The theory which the researcher uses to explain an observation also generates predictions or expectations about other relationships he or she might observe if that theory held water. If multiple case observations cannot substantiate the pattern demanded by the theory, then the researcher ends up having to admit that his or her prior beliefs and theories are wrong. This is precisely the situation which many famous case study researchers (e.g. Becker 1970; Wax 1971) have admitted to having experienced – along with the satisfactions of successful pattern matching. And if, for the positivist, this sails close to the practice of induction (indeed, it is sometimes termed 'analytic induction' – see Denzin 1978), we should not forget that in 'normal' science the part played by falsification is larger in theory than in practice (Kuhn 1970) and, in any case, is philosophically suspect (Rescher 1978).

If case studies can be criticized on the grounds of subjectivity and hidden selectivity, let us be clear in what sense, if any, this is a problem. It is well known that 'subjective' and 'objective' can be understood in two contrasting senses, the quanti-tative and the qualitative (Scriven 1972). In its quantitative sense, 'objective' refers to what a number of people experience, and what is therefore amenable to inter-subjective agreement, whereas 'subjective' refers to what is experienced by one individual. In this sense the case study researcher may produce a subjective report, in so far as it is based on observations that are unique to him or her, and non-replicable. But 'objective' and 'subjective' can also be understood in a qualitative sense, that is, as referring to the quality of the observation regardless of the number of people making it. It is in this sense that 'subjective' denotes unreliability and bias, whereas 'objective' denotes reliable, factual and unbiased. But the two senses do not necessarily coincide. An observation can be quantitatively objective but qualitatively subjective – for example there are some cultural biases to which a group is more susceptible than an individual (e.g. racial prejudice or jingoism). Conversely, 'one would be more inclined to accept the reports of one magician standing in the wings during another magician's performance than the reports of a large audience, all of whose members were being systematically deluded' (Guba and Lincoln 1981, p. 125).

If we take subjectivity in the latter sense, suggesting partiality, selectivity and so forth, two points can be made. First, *all* research methods, including the quasi-experimental, are selective in that all observations are theory laden (Kuhn 1970). Indeed, the different world views presented by different perspectives and epistem-ologies are not just alternative interpretations of the same empirical data since the data themselves are products of the paradigmatic lenses through which we view the world. Second, taking bias in the derogatory sense of unreliability, there is no reason why a case study researcher, even one using participant observation, should be more biased than the quasi-experimentalist adopting an 'objective outsider' role. There are many techniques available in case study research whereby checks may be made on the validity and reliability with which the research is conducted. These chiefly involve strategies of triangulating sources and methods (Jick 1979) such as survey feedback and the agreeing of interview notes, and various forms of external 'anchor-ing' of data collection and analysis procedures (see, for example, Wax 1971; Spradley and Mann 1973; Hammersley and Atkinson 1983; Legge 1984, pp. 131–139).

There is still the problem of generalization. We suggest that, if this criticism is being made comparatively, it is weaker than it might appear. Can one always generalize any better from quasi-experimental research and surveys than in practice from case studies? It should be remembered that positivistic designs' claims to generalization rest upon designs involving either random assignment (exceptionally rare in organizational research) or various forms of sampling. Leaving aside the likelihood that, in practice, survey groups – and experimental and control groups – may well be corrupted by selection effects, confounded treatment effects and situ-ational effects, the ability to generalize is almost inevitably undermined by differential mortality. This is the differential loss of subjects across comparison groups leading, first, to problems of representation and generalization and, second, to difficulties with respect to the explanation of time and treatment effects (see Campbell and Stanley 1966; Cook and Campbell 1979). Furthermore, statistical inferences drawn from such studies can, in theory, only be extended to material in an identical frame (Deming 1975). Taking all these points together, if the non-case study researcher wishes to generalize, strictly speaking he or she is in the business of applying subjective, if expert, judgement on the extent to which the findings are generally applicable given sampling limitations and the study parameters. Such expert judgement can just as well be applied in generalizing case studies – and the same, of course, holds for the sampling – along time, people, or context – which occurs *within* a case study.

In some case study research, for example, where the emphasis is phenomenological, it must be recognized that it is epistemologically inappropriate for the researcher to attempt to generalize his or her findings. But even here, it is perfectly appropriate and possible for them to *be generalized* by their audiences, who can share the meanings they embody and identify them with their own experiences and settings.

However, if the supposed limitations of case study research are either mis-attributions or shared by the so-called more rigorous methods, its strengths in its own right, and as the basis for teaching material, are real and, some might argue, unique. A good case study can provide rich 'thick description' (Geertz 1973); it can be holistic, and convey a feeling of what it is like to experience an organization, or a problem, from the 'inside'. It can explain attitudes and behaviours in context and from their actors' own frames of reference. Above all perhaps, even allowing for its pattern-matching approach to hypothesis testing, par excellence, it is the research method which allows the '*discovery* of grounded theory' (Glaser and Strauss 1967).

As with all research, of course, the claimed advantages of this method depend largely on how well the research is conducted. Furthermore, although these strengths are usually claimed for all well conducted case studies, it should be borne in mind that the nature of the 'rich' data, the conceptualization of 'context' and so forth will very much depend on the *type* of case study conducted. For example, at one end of the continuum, we can think of ethnographic case studies with a phenomenological focus on the meanings of a particular community or subculture which are taken for granted (e.g. Spradley 1970; Pollert 1981). At the other end, perhaps more characteristic of organizational research, we can think of research comprising comparative case studies based on structural-functionalist, systems or Marxist perspectives (e.g. Lupton 1963; Warmington et al. 1977; Wilkinson 1983). Some studies labelled 'case studies' rely on structured questionnaire instruments as a chief means of data gathering (e.g. Clegg and Fitter 1981). In all cases the data produced may be rich in detail but the nature of the richness will depend on the perspective adopted. What perspectives predominate in this selection of cases?

In answering this question we need to consider the differences between the case method in research and teaching and how this might affect the end product – the written case study. The functions that cases have been identified as serving in teaching impose some constraints on the presentation, for teaching, of research material.

Briefly, a 'good' teaching case study should aim to develop a range of skills in a student, from the analytical, application and creative skills that come from diagnostic problem solving, to the social and communication skills that arise from group discussion and presentation of solutions, and even the self-analysis skills that emerge when disagreements occur in discussions over value judgements (see Easton 1982 for a useful discussion). In the writing up of research material for teaching, we emphasized to our contributors that they should aim at an account which would allow the application of a range of different theories and approaches in the analysis of the situation or 'problem', and also a range of alternative strategies for tackling the issues presented, each with a different set of costs and benefits. As far as the writing of the case studies goes – leaving aside for the moment how they might be used to develop social skills – we emphasized to contributors that material should be presented in a way which would allow critical analysis of an issue and creative problem-solving.

Returning to the question 'what perspectives predominate in this selection of cases?', it is clear that the teaching requirements outlined have inevitably placed some constraints on how material derived from a specific research perspective is presented. The perspectives most readily applicable to the 'problem-solving' aspect of teaching objectives are those contained in what Burrell and Morgan (1979) term the 'regulative-objective' paradigm (e.g. structural-functionalist, systems, pluralist, action frames of reference). Not surprisingly, most of the research cases on which the teaching cases are based have, in fact, adopted one or other of these perspectives – systems and pluralist perhaps predominating. However, there are cases (and we leave readers to identify which!) where the research perspective owed far more to critical theory or symbolic interactionism than might be apparent in the account rendered for teaching purposes. For while such perspectives are excellent in providing material that will foster *critical analysis*, they can present problems if the aim is also for the student to suggest strategies of *problem-solving*. Given that we expect this collection to be used on undergraduate, postgraduate and post-experience courses, it is expected that students will largely be encouraged to see problem-solving from a managerial perspective – be that 'manager' a company *or* union bureaucrat! Perspectives which argue such radical 'solutions' as system over-throw may not be found helpful – although we would hope that teachers (and the teaching manual) would at least encourage this alternative perspective to surface, particularly in cases dealing with issues of power, labour process, conflict and so forth. Similarly, given this problem-solving perspective, *fully-blown* phenomeno-logical cases cannot be presented, as their nominalist ontology, by implicitly contending that there is no objective world to act upon, does not allow the managerially realist definition of, and approach to, problem formulation and solution.

Teaching objectives may influence how research material is presented in other ways. Although most of the cases included here present their account in as veridical a form as possible, a small number might be termed 'fictionalized documentaries' in that, while true to the findings of the case study research on which they are based, they represent an amalgam of several situations, or introduce peripheral issues or red herrings realistic to the context, but not present in the specific organization on which the case is based. 'Gilding the lily' in order to highlight a problem, complicate an issue or whatever has not been discouraged, as long as the resulting account is consistent with the body of research from which it is drawn and 'rings true' to related research findings. The guiding principle here has always been, 'Will the resulting account enhance the development of critical awareness to a greater extent than an "unvarnished" account?' Needless to say the usual liberties have been taken with names and some quantitative data in order to protect the guilty! (The editors and an author received notice of the truthfulness of one case, which was withdrawn following the threat of legal action.)

We feel that the use of teaching cases derived from research case studies offers the student two important opportunities. The 'thick description' of an organization and an issue which its members confront allow a student to experience the reality of a real problem in a real setting. Information is not complete, but then neither is it for the manager or any other organizational member. And, if the author's own brand of 'thick description' (from whatever perspective) is well presented, we anticipate that being placed figuratively within real organizations, confronted by a range of different 'facts', opinions and hypothesized relationships, may enable students themselves to embark on a process of discovery. We hope that they may come to appreciate that issues can be analysed from different perspectives, that depending on perspective there are many alternatives and no definitive answers to problems and that, in developing such answers, new questions are inevitably raised.

References

Becker H S (1970) Sociological Work, Aldine

Bennis W G (1968) The case study, Journal of Applied Behavioral Science 4: 227–243

Burrell G Morgan G (1979) Sociological Paradigms and Organizational Analysis, Heinemann.

Campbell D T (1974) Qualitative knowing in action research, Kurt Lewin Award Address, Society for the Psychological Study of Social Issues, meeting with the American Psychological Association, New Orleans, 1 September 1974

Campbell D T (1979) 'Degrees of freedom' and the case study, in Qualitative and Quantitative Methods of Evaluation Research, edited by T D Cook and C Reichardt, Sage, pp. 49–67

Campbell D T Stanley J C (1966) Experimental and Quasi-experimental Designs for Research, Rand-McNally

Clegg C W Fitter M J (1981) Organizational and behavioural consequences of uncertainty: a case study, Journal of Occupational Behaviour 2: 155–175

Cook T D Campbell D T (1979) Quasi-experimentation, Rand-McNally

Deming W E (1975) The logic of evaluation, in Handbook of Evaluation Research, Vol. I, edited by E L Struening and M Guttentag, Sage

Denny T (1978) Story-telling and educational understanding, address delivered at a national meeting of the International Reading Association, Houston, Texas, May 1978

Denzin N K (1978) The Research Act: A Theoretical Introduction to Sociological Methods, 2nd edition, McGraw-Hill

Easton G (1982) Learning from Case Studies, Prentice-Hall

Filmer P Philipson M Silverman D Walsh D (1972). New Directions in Sociological Theory, Collier-Macmillan

Geertz C (1973) Thick description: toward an interpretive theory of culture, in The Interpretation of Cultures, Basic Books

Glaser B Strauss A (1967) The Discovery of Grounded Theory, Aldine

Guba E G Lincoln Y S (1981) Effective Evaluation, Jossey-Bass

Hammersley M Atkinson P (1983) Ethnography, Principles in Practice, Tavistock

Jick T D (1979) Mixing qualitative and quantitative methods: triangulation in action, Administrative Science Quarterly 24: 602–611

Kuhn T S (1970) The Structure of Scientific Revolutions, Chicago University Press

Legge K (1984) Evaluating Planned Organizational Change, Academic Press

Lewin K (1951) Field Theory in Social Science, Harper and Brothers

Lupton T (1963) On the Shop Floor, Pergamon Press

Pollert A (1981) Girls, Wives, Factory Lives, Macmillan

Rescher N (1978) Pierce's Philosophy of Science: Critical Studies in his Theory of Induction and Scientific Method, University of Notre Dame Press

Scriven M (1972) Objectivity and subjectivity in educational research, in Philosophical Redirection of Educational Research, edited by L G Thomas, Chicago University Press

Spradley J P (1970) You Owe Yourself a Drunk: An Ethnography of Urban Nomads, Little, Brown

Spradley J P Mann B J (1973) The Cocktail Waitress, John Wiley

Walton R F (1972) Advantages and attributes of the case study, Journal of Applied Behavioral Science 8: 73–78

Warmington A Lupton T Gorfin C (1977) Organizational Behaviour and Performance, Macmillan

Wax R (1971) Doing Fieldwork, University of Chicago Press

Wilkinson B (1983) The Shopfloor Politics of New Technology, Heinemann

SECTION 1: Organizational Behaviour

In this section we include 11 separate cases ranging from relatively micro-scale issues concerned with the design of jobs and of a man–machine interface, through to macro-scale issues focusing on the planning of a large-scale piece of organizational change, the evolution of a small family business and the restructuring of a company.

It will become clear that our 'definition' of organizational behaviour is both loose and broad – it embraces study of the behaviour, attitudes and feelings of individuals and groups within an organization, as well as the behaviour of the organization itself. Pervading the cases are the issues of motivation, satisfaction and performance along with those of control and commitment. But it is also clear that perceptions, attributions and meanings vary within the cases both according to the actors as individuals and to their places in the organization. If there is a single message from this collection it is that organizations and the people in them are complex, inter-related and, often, highly differentiated.

We have tried to order the cases from the micro-scale to the macro-scale for ease of use but in practice such a progression is not neatly maintained. For example, the early cases amply demonstrate the role of some of the wider organizational issues, as do the later ones the role of certain key individuals. In the same way none of the cases addresses a single discrete issue – the matrix in the Introduction (Table 2) demonstrates the major interdependencies within the book as a whole but even this fails to capture the richness of the overlap. Again we stress that we see this as healthy rather than as evidence of some conceptual malaise.

The first case by Nigel Kemp, Chris Clegg and Toby Wall (Case 1) presents a description of work organization in a factory department along with the types of production and interpersonal problems encountered. The circumstances are appropriate for job redesign and the case involves working out details of how the change should be undertaken, what the new jobs should entail, and how the new work organization fits into the wider organizational systems.

In Case 2 Leela Damodaran and Sue Pomfrett describe the problems arising from the introduction of an electronic mail system and its man–machine interface in an oil company. The problem here is to decide what to do following an unsuccessful field-trial. This involves studying the factors influencing 'acceptability' of the new system, including the hardware and software interfaces along with analysis of the opportunities for office automation more generally.

Case 3 by Cary Cooper and Mike Kelly examines the links between individual stress and accident levels amongst mobile crane operators in the construction industry. Questions are raised concerning the quality of evidence linking stress and accidents and the appropriate action the companies should take. Issues here range from work organization through to supervisory and managerial practices.

Sheila Rothwell in Case 4 highlights the issues affecting supervisors in a new factory introducing a computerized materials management system. This case requires analysis of supervisory relationships and roles along with their training needs. The basic issue here is what to do about the 'problem' of supervision.

In the fifth case, Rosemary Stewart and Pauline Wingate (Case 5) examine the style of a senior manager working in the National Health Service. The emphasis here is on examining the effectiveness of this manager when there are no easily measurable outputs and on the strategies that could be adopted to improve it.

In Case 6 Mike Fitter and Chris Clegg describe an information and control system in a production environment. The principle tasks are to develop a set of design criteria and then use them to redesign the system in a way that will remove the dysfunctional consequences as well as improve departmental performance and promote satisfying work. The case also raises more general problems of information and control system design.

Riccardo Peccei and David Guest, in Case 7, focus on decision-making processes in a large bureaucracy. The case highlights the protracted and 'messy' nature of organizational decision making along with the need to understand the context within which it takes place, the complexity of the issues and the influences impinging on the key actors and groups.

Case 8 by Iain Mangham looks at issues of power and politics within a senior management team in a television company. The case requires analysis of the respective roles of two particular individuals. The problem here is to decide what action to take to resolve the interpersonal conflicts between two powerful individuals working in a complex organization.

Roy Payne and Bill Reddin (in Case 9) examine the issues surrounding the design of a major piece of planned organizational change in a large tobacco company. The case is unusual in its focus on the development of a relationship between the company and an external consultant. It also examines the objectives for the change programme and asks for an assessment of the likelihood of their achievement.

Case 10 by Robert Goffee and Richard Scase describes the development of a small family firm with particular attention given to the respective roles and relationships amongst the founding family members and their senior managerial staff. The central task is to understand the factors accounting for the firm's current managerial problems and to decide how to resolve them. Important issues here include management style and succession, and organizational restructuring.

The last case in this section, Case 11 by Andrew Kakabadse, is also concerned with organizational structure. The case requires analysis of the problems faced by a large manufacturer and supplier of office equipment. The problem is to consider whether the current organization structure is appropriate and to decide how any changes should be managed.

CASE 1

Job Design: Fab Sweets Ltd.

Nigel Kemp, Chris Clegg and Toby Wall

Organizational setting

FAB Sweets Limited is a manufacturer of high quality sweets. The company is a medium-sized, family-owned, partially unionized and highly successful confectionery producer in the north of England. The case study is set within a single department in the factory where acute problems were experienced.

Background to the Case

The department (hereafter called 'HB') produces and packs over 40 lines of hard-boiled sweets on a batch-production system. It is organized in two adjacent areas, one for production staffed by men and one for packing staffed by women. The areas are separated by a physical barrier, allowing the packing room to be air conditioned and protected from the humidity resulting from production. Management believed this was necessary to stop the sweets from sweating (thus sticking to their wrappers) during storage. Each room has a chargehand and a supervisor who reports to the departmental manager, who himself is responsible to the factory manager. In total 37 people work in the department (25 in production, 12 in packing), the majority of whom are skilled employees. Training takes place on the job, and it normally takes two years to acquire the skills necessary to complete all the production tasks. Figure 1 presents an outline of the physical layout of the department and the work-flow.

The production process is essentially quite simple. Raw materials, principally sugar, are boiled to a set temperature, with 'cooking time' varying from line to line. The resulting batches are worked on by employees who fold and manipulate them so as to create the required texture, while adding colouring and flavourings ('slabbing' and 'mixing'). Different batches are moulded together to create the flavour mixes and patterns required ('make up'). The batch, which by now is quite cool, is then extruded through a machine which cuts it into sweets of individual size. Some

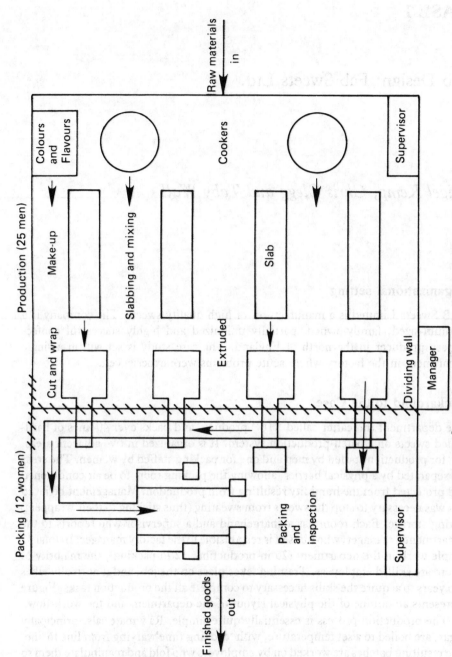

Figure 1 The HB department: physical layout and work flow.

products at this stage are automatically wrapped and then passed by conveyor belt to the packing room where they are inspected, bagged and boxed ready for despatch to retail and wholesale outlets. Other products progress unwrapped into the packing room where they are fed into a wrapping machine, inspected, bagged and depatched. Several different product lines can be produced at the same time. The most skilled and critical tasks occur early in the process; these include 'cooking' mixtures for different products and 'make up' (e.g. for striped mints). These skills are gradually learned until the operator is able to 'feel' the correct finish for each of the 40 lines. All the tasks are highly interdependent such that any one individual's performance affects the ease with which the next person down the line can successfully achieve his/her part of the production process. Although the work appears quite simple and the management of the process straightfoward, the department nevertheless experienced acute problems. These are outlined below.

The Problem

In objective terms the problems in HB were manifest in a high level of labour turnover, six new managers in eight years, production which consistently fell below targets based on work study standards, and high levels of scrap. The department was known as the worst in the factory and its problems were variously characterized in terms of 'attitude', 'atmosphere' and 'climate'. Moreover, employees had few decision-making responsibilities, low motivation, low job satisfaction, and received little information on their performance. Finally there were interpersonal problems between the employees in the production and packing rooms, between the two supervisors and also amongst the operators, and there were a number of dissatisfactions relating to grading and payment levels.

Experience of the Method of Working

To understand how HB works and how people experienced their work it is necessary to recognize the strong drive throughout the organization for production. Departmental managers are judged primarily in terms of their production levels (against targets) and the efficiency (against work study standards) at which they perform. In HB this pressure was transmitted to the two supervisors. In practice, production levels were the number of batches of sweets processed, and efficiency was the ratio of batches produced to hours used by direct labour.

The production supervisor responded to the pressure for production in a number of ways. First, in an attempt to maximize production, he always allocated people to the jobs at which they performed best. He also determined the cooker speeds. In effect, this set the pace of work for both production and packing. Buffer stocks were not possible in production because the sweets needed processing before they cooled down. If he was falling behind his target, the supervisor responded by speeding up the pace of work. In addition, he regarded his job purely in terms of processing batches, and ignored problems in the packing room which may in fact have resulted directly from his actions or from those of his staff. The supervisory role thus involved allocating people to tasks, setting machine speeds (and hence the pace of work), organizing reliefs and breaks, monitoring hygiene, safety and quality standards, maintaining discipline and recording data for the management information systems. The chargehand undertook these responsibilities in the absence of a supervisor, spending the rest of his time on production.

The men in production complained that they were bored with always doing the same jobs, especially as some were physically harder than others (for example, 'slabbing' involved manual manipulation of batches of up to 50 kilograms). Several claimed that their greater efforts should receive financial recognition. Furthermore, this rigidity of task allocation was in direct conflict with the grading system which was designed to encourage flexibility. To be on the top rate of pay in the department, an operator had to be capable of performing all the skills for all the lines, and hence be able to cover any job. Training schedules matched this. In practice, however, people rarely used more than one or two of their skills. The others decayed through disuse. All the staff recognized that the grading system was at odds with how the department actually worked and tended to be dissatisfied with both. The production supervisor's strict control over the pace of work also proved suboptimal in other ways. For example, he sometimes pushed the pace to a level regarded as impossible by the staff. Whether this was true or self-fulfilling is a moot point – the net result was an increase in the level of scrap. Also he ignored the wishes of the staff to work less hard in the afternoon when they were tired: again scrap resulted. In addition the feeling was widespread amongst the men in production that management and supervision organized the work badly and would do better if they took advice from the shop floor. Their own perceived lack of control over the job led them to abrogate responsibility when things went wrong ('We told them so'!!). And finally, although the processes of production were highly interdependent, operators adopted an insular perspective and the necessary cooperation between workers was rarely evident, and then only on the basis of personal favours between friends.

The equivalent pressure on the packing supervisor was to pack the sweets efficiently. As her section could pack no more than was produced, her only manipulable variable was hours worked. Thus to increase her efficiency she could only transfer the packers to 'other work' within her room (e.g. cleaning) or to another department.

The packers for their part resented being asked to work flat out when HB was busy, only to be moved elsewhere when things were slacker. As described above, their own work-flow was basically controlled by the speed at which the men were producing. When in difficulty, direct appeals to the men to slow down were unsuccessful and so they channelled their complaints through their supervisor. Because of the insular perspective adopted by the production supervisor (in rational support of his own targets), her approaches were usually ignored ('It's my job to produce sweets'), and the resulting intersupervisory conflict took up much of the departmental manager's time. In addition the packing room was very crowded and interpersonal conflicts were common.

Finally, production problems throughout the factory were created by seasonal peaks and troughs in the market demand for sweets. These 'busy' and 'slack' periods differed between production departments. In order to cope with market demands the production planning department transferred staff, on a temporary basis, between production departments. In HB this typically meant that, when they were busy, 'unskilled' employees were drafted in to help, whereas when demand was low HB employees were transferred to other departments where they were usually given the worst jobs. Both of these solutions were resented by the employees in HB.

This description of the department is completed when one recognizes the complications involved in scheduling over 40 product lines through complex machinery, all of it over 10 years old. In fact breakdowns and interruptions to smooth working were common. The effects of these on the possible levels of production were poorly understood and in any case few operators were aware of their targets or of their subsequent performance. More immediately the breakdowns were a source of continual conflict between the department and the maintenance engineers responsible to an engineering manager. The department laid the blame on poor maintenance, the engineers on abuse or lack of care by production workers in handling the machinery. Much management time was spent in negotiating 'blame' for breakdowns and time allowances resulting since this affected efficiency figures. Not surprisingly, perhaps, the factory-wide image of the department was very poor on almost all counts, and its status was low.

Participants' Diagnoses of the Problems

Shopfloor employees, chargehands, supervisors, the department manager and senior management were agreed that much was wrong in HB. However, there was no coherent view of the causes and what should be done to make improvements. Many shopfloor employees placed the blame on supervision and management for their lack of technical and planning expertise, and their low consideration for subordinates. The production supervisor favoured a solution in terms of 'getting rid of the trouble-makers', by transferring or sacking his nominated culprits. The department manager wanted to introduce a senior supervisor to handle the conflicts between the production and packing supervisors and further support the pressure for production. The factory manager thought the way work was organized and managed might be at the core of the difficulties.

Case Study Tasks

Imagine you are the production director, with overall responsibility for sweet production at the factory.

Your objective is to decide what action to take to solve the production and interpersonal problems in HB. In so doing you should consider both the process and content of change. You should also keep in mind the practical limitations likely to be involved. Your budget, for example, is limited to £30 000, which precludes any major investment in new machinery. Also important is to locate your actions within an appropriate theoretical framework. The more specific questions and issues outlined below reflect many of the factors involved and answering them will provide first steps towards an overall 'solution'. Questions 1–4 are appropriate for teaching sessions of one or two hours. Questions 5–7 require longer time periods to answer. It will help if students work in pairs or small groups to solve the problems in HB.

1 What do you think of the solutions offered by
   a shopfloor employees
   b the production supervisor
   c the department manager
   d the factory manager?
2 How would you improve motivation and morale in the department?
3 What would be the effect of your solution on
   a productivity and quality
   b employee absence and turnover?
4 What would you do about the style and structure of supervision and management in the department?
5 What would you do about
   a selection and training in the department
   b target and feedback systems for the operators
   c the pay and grading systems
   d the technology and the physical layout of the department
   e interpersonal and communication problems
   f relationships between the department and other departments, e.g. maintenance engineering and production planning?
6 How would you manage and organize the process of change in the department?
7 What would you anticipate would be the wider organizational ramifications of your changes on, for example, manpower planning, employee participation and management information systems?

Essential Reading

Wall T D (1978) Job redesign and employee participation, in Psychology at Work, 2nd edition, edited by P B Warr, Penguin pp. 264–285
Child J (1984) Organization: a guide to Problems and Practice, 2nd edition, Harper & Row

Additional Reading

Blackler F H M Brown C B (1978) Job Redesign and Management Control, Saxon House
Davis L E Taylor J C (eds) (1979) Design of Jobs, 2nd edition, Goodyear Publishing
Hackman J R Oldham G R (1980) Work Redesign, Addison-Wesley
Handy C B (1976) Understanding Organizations, Penguin, pp. 306–322
Katz D Kahn R (1978) The Social Psychology of Organizations, 2nd edition, John Wiley
Kelly J E (1982) Scientific Management, Job Redesign and Work Performance, Academic Press
Klein L (1976) New Forms of Work Organization, Cambridge University Press

CASE 2

The Man–Machine Interface: Oilco

Leela Damodaran and Susan Pomfrett

Organizational Setting

'Oilco' is a UK oil company that exists within a multinational group. It is in the business of supplying, refining and marketing oil and oil-based products. It is the marketing function that is the focus of this case. Marketing and the other divisions are served by an information services group. A new unit was set up within this group and made responsible for office automation and administrative methods.

The marketing and distribution function in the company is organized largely on a regional basis, there being seven geographic regions. In every region there is a regional office and also a network of representatives and engineers (fieldstaff) who work from their homes. There is a functional division in each region between 'commerical' and 'retail' staff, although there are some administrative personnel who serve both the commercial and retail divisions, e.g. credit management staff. Simply, 'commercial' can be thought of as dealing with mainly industrial customers and 'retail' as dealing with garages whether they be company-owned or privately owned.

Within the commercial and retail divisions in each region, there is a further geographic split into a number of 'areas'. In addition the regional office staff and fieldstaff work closely with the distribution terminals in the region whose function is to distribute the oil or oil-based products. Outside the regional system, there are two central offices: a head office in London and an accounts centre near Manchester.

Background to the Case

One of the first main tasks of the office automation group was to undertake a study in one of the regions to look at how the quality, speed and cost effectiveness of the regional office services could be improved. The study concentrated on textual information and included an examination of the local information flow via telephone, telex, mail and other paperwork.

The results of this study showed that 86% of the mail received was sent from other Oilco staff; 57% of the mail received was copied between two and five times and passed on, stressing the role of the office as focal point for the region. The majority of telephone calls were also made internally.

There was also found to be a specific communication problem. This was between staff at the regional office and the fieldstaff working from home. If the fieldstaff were doing their jobs well, then it was not possible to contact them during office hours, as they were at or on their way to customers' premises. It was usually *possible* for fieldstaff to contact the office but this was frequently inconvenient (e.g. requiring permission to use a customer's telephone).

The study looked at word-processing and concluded that, although word-processing is generally the first step towards office automation, the acquisition of word-processing hardware could not be justified simply as a replacement for type-writers. Word-processing could, however, play a major role in electronic mail systems. This conclusion coupled with the findings on information flow and communication problems increased the importance of investigating electronic mail. The examination of the regional office also concluded that there was a case for electronic filing and retrieval but that this could only be justified as an extension of an electronic mail system.

Electronic mail seemed to be the key, but would such a system help with regional communication and would it be acceptable to the users? If the man–machine interface was acceptable and the concept of such electronic systems was also accept-able, then the introduction of office automation more generally might also be possible. A good way of phasing in office automation would be to start with electronic messaging. On the other hand, if there were problems with the man–machine interface, it was important to know; otherwise a complete office automation programme could be in jeopardy. It was as much to answer these questions of acceptability as it was to answer the more obvious questions of technical feasibility that an experiment was set up in one region (the North-Eastern Region) to invest-igate electronic mail.

Electronic mail usually assumes that each participant has access to a computer terminal: a keyboard and a screen and/or printer which can be connected directly, or using a telephone, to a computer. There is a directory listing all the participants on a particular 'network'. The idea is that these individuals regularly 'look into their mailbox', by contacting the computer.

In this particular case, this involved dialling the telephone number of the computer and then, when the connection was made, either placing the receiver in a special 'acoustic coupler' attached to the terminal or pressing a button on the phone. (There are special telephones which can be connected to a terminal.)

After the computer introduces itself, the user identifies himself with a password and the system will display a summary of any messages that have been sent to him which he has not yet read. The user can read one or more of the messages if he wishes or he can send a message to someone else. Alternatively, he may wish to look through his files to check the detail of a message he sent or received in the past, etc. To send a message, the user types his composition into the terminal and types in the name of the recipient, say Fred Bloggs. When he is happy with what has been 'input', he 'sends' the message by pressing the appropriate key(s). Then, the next time Fred Bloggs contacts the computer, it tells him there is a message for him.

The combination of features making up electronic communication means that it is very different from any of the conventional means of communication and has many far-reaching ramifications for organizations choosing to use it. One thing is certain; the acceptability of the man–machine interface is crucial to the success of any such systems.

The experiment set up in North-Eastern Region involved the following groups having access to the electronic mail system:

a   all the fieldstaff in one of the 'retail' areas and one of the 'commerical' areas within the region

b   the administrative groups at the regional office

c   regional managers for 'retail' and 'commercial'

d   key personnel at the head office, in London

e   some administrative offices at the accounts centre near Manchester

f   two of the regional distribution terminals

g   a number of individuals acting in a support capacity to help with any problems in using the system.

In some cases, office-based staff were to use terminals which were already used in the office. These terminals had a screen like a television screen and a keyboard. Otherwise, special portable terminals were used. These did not have a screen but just a keyboard and a paper printout. The paper was heat sensitive so that text could be printed very quietly by heat instead of impact.

Everyone involved was told of the experiment and it was made clear that if, at the end of the trial period (six months), the system was found to be unacceptable, then it would be withdrawn. If it was a success, it would remain and be developed.

The equipment was distributed at each training session. Fieldstaff were trained individually at their future 'work station' in their own homes. At least one user in each office section was trained in the use of the system. Typically this operational training lasted about two hours. With training complete, the experiment was started.

The Problem

It was expected that, over the period of the experiment, use of the system would vary. It was anticipated that at the beginning use of the system would steadily increase as more and more people received their equipment and learned how to put it into practice. In these early stages usage would be higher than 'normal' because people would 'play' a lot. This would be partly because of novelty and partly for purposes of familiarization and learning. Then, the system would be used less as these play and practice sessions were no longer needed. Finally a plateau of 'normal' usage would be reached with only minor fluctuations.

It was a surprise to the project team to discover that this pattern of usage was not being followed. To begin with everything went as expected in the sense that usage increased rapidly and then began to decline, but no plateau was reached. Usage went on declining steadily as the months went by.

The group which was most concerned about this finding was the office auto-mation group responsible for the experiment. If there were such severe problems with the man–machine interface that the system was gradually slipping into disuse, then there would be serious ramifications not only for hopes of a solution to the communications problem but also for 'office automation' policy generally.

On investigation it became clear there were many reasons why the system was being used less and less; some were general and some specific to certain groups of users. Thus, for any specific task, there were a number of factors which determined whether or not the message system would be used. If the communication was 'too long', required discussion, required urgent (same day) action and/or a reply, involved numbers or pictorial information, or if the recipient was believed to be unlikely to check into the system, then the electronic message system would not be used.

For example, communication between users on this particular 'network' often included a lot of figure-work, e.g. prices, amounts, dates, etc. The technical performance of the system was not good enough to be able to rely on the accuracy of such communications. Using ordinary telephone lines meant that there was always the possibility of the signal travelling down the line being corrupted by 'crackle', etc., on the telephone line; for example, YOU HAVE 4 NEW MESSAGES was transformed to YOU \ HA6\ T EN ME3SAGES.

Also, there were many problems for the users at the accounts centre. Their telephone exchange was not good and so the service was not very reliable; this resulted in a good deal of nonsense being sent and received. It was sometimes so bad that the line would be completely lost and the entire procedure would have to be started again (very annoying if this happened after half an hour of inputting messages before getting a chance to 'send' them). Also, many of the groups at the accounts centre did not get the equipment out at all because they had no need to initiate communication with anyone else on the network. There were, however, occasions when other users wanted to contact *them*. Usage at the accounts centre was also low because the training and support provided was not good enough. It had been thought that it was the office staff (especially at the regional office) who had most to gain from the system (and therefore the most motivation to use it). Also, the office staff had previous experience of using computer systems. For these reasons, early support and training resources were concentrated on the fieldstaff at the cost of the office staff. The result of this was that some offices (especially at the accounts centre) felt very ill-equipped to use the system and therefore did not use it or used it infrequently.

There were also concerns about using the equipment at home, e.g. use of the terminals caused interference with television and radio and in one case neighbours complained. Furthermore, although the portable terminals used by fieldstaff in their homes were relatively small and quiet, to be used comfortably they had to be placed on a flat surface of reasonable height, close to a telephone and preferably close to a 13 amp socket (otherwise an extension lead was required). Frequently there was not a great deal of spare space in the home of the representative or engineer. If he was lucky, he could use a desk, but in some cases an occasional table in the bedroom was the only solution and working postures were not ideal. There were also fears on the part of the fieldstaff about 'Big Brother' and the extent to which control over fieldstaff could be increased by using the system.

There were some difficulties in using the keyboard due to a lack of typing skills. The portable terminals used by the fieldstaff took quite a long time to set up each time they were used. It was also difficult sometimes to set up the equipment correctly. This entailed putting the telephone receiver into two tightly fitting rubber cups at the back of the terminal. After having spent some time doing this, the telephone line to the computer was sometimes engaged or not working properly. Because most of the hardware problems were concerned with the portable terminals and the link between these and the telephone, there were few hardware problems in the offices (which could use their standard VDUs).

Although the computer commands were thought on the whole to be quite easy to use, some of them repeatedly caused problems. The edit and file commands were found to be particularly difficult to use. Information given to the user by the system was also found to cause problems. For example, if the user told the computer he had finished, the system would let the user know if he had forgotten to 'send' any messages he had written, but the system would then disconnect without allowing the user to go back and send the messages. Also, if a command was typed incorrectly, the computer would inform the user by displaying an 'error message', but these were often very confusing, e.g. 'too many arguments' (referring to the syntax of the command not disagreements!).

It also became clear that communication systems with a 'network' of users need a 'critical mass' of these users to contact each other regularly for the network to be maintained. Because the system in the experiment was used *only* for sending messages, there was no routine reason for contacting the computer other than to send a message or to see if one had been sent. This led to yet another reason for the steady decline in usage. If Fred sends a message to Joe and, for one or more of the reasons listed above, Joe does not often 'look in his mailbox', then Fred's message will not be read promptly. Perhaps three weeks go by and Fred assumes Joe has acted on his message. He then finds out that this is not the case, e.g. Joe did not visit a customer when he should have done. Fred then becomes disillusioned not with Joe as a user but with the effectiveness of the message system as a whole and starts to use it less frequently himself. Then Harry sends a message to Fred and the story is repeated. If the 'critical mass' of users is not maintained, the network will break down.

User Opinions at the End of the Experiment

A large sample of the users were asked if they would prefer to work with the system or without it. Twenty said they would prefer to work with it and 15 without, three being unsure. The same sample was then given a more complex hypothetical choice for the future:

a   no electronic message system to be used (*preferred by three users*)
b   the electronic message system to be used but with all regions joining in (*preferred by four users*)
c   this electronic message system to be used as in the experiment until a better system is introduced (*preferred by 14 users*)
d   no electronic message system to be used until a better system is found (*preferred by 12 users*)
e   this experiment to be continued for a limited period (*not preferred by any users*)
f   other (*preferred by two users*)

Two users could not make up their minds between options **c** and **d**.

Case Study Tasks

Imagine you are the manager of the office automation group with overall responsibility for the development of office automation throughout the UK. Your objective is to decide what action to take with regard to (a) the experiment in the North-Eastern Region and (b) office automation company-wide. In making your decision, it should be recognized that users of the electronic mail system in the various roles listed below will have a variety of diverse and sometimes conflicting needs as a result of their differing functions and locations: the head office, the accounts centre, the regional office, area management (home-based) and fieldstaff (home-based). Part of your decision-making process should therefore include some consideration of the different user requirements and characteristics.

Questions 1–5 are appropriate for teaching sessions of one or two hours. Questions 6–7 require longer time periods to answer. It will help if students work in small groups to solve the problems presented here.

1   List the combination of characteristics of *electronic* communication that differentiate it from conventional communication methods.
2   List the problems or issues that have been identified from the experiment under the follow headings: task match, ease of use, user support and indirect consequences.
3   What would be your suggestions for improving the immediate man–machine interfaces for the users in the trial (the hardware and software interfaces)?
4   What would be the effect of introducing another office automation facility (such as word-processing or information retrieval facilities) in conjunction with the electronic mail facility?
5   Could the system have been used more successfully by users with different needs and/or characteristics to those in the experiment? If so, specify the profile of such a user population.
6   a   In the light of user responses in the experiment, which, if any, of the options presented to the users in the survey would you action?
    b   What are the implications of your answer to Question 6a for office automation policy throughout the company?

7   What action is required to
    a   make electronic mail succeed
    b   promote office automation in the company generally?

Essential Reading

Damodaran L (1981) Measures of user acceptability, in Health Hazards of VDUs?, edited by B G Pearce, John Wiley

Additional Reading

Armbruster A (1983) Ergonomic requirements, in New Office Technology: Human and Organizational Aspects, edited by H J Otway and M Peltu, Frances Pinter (Publishers)
Bailey R W (1982) Human Performance Engineering, Prentice Hall
Damodaran L Simpson A Wilson P A (1980) Designing Systems for People, National Computer Centre
Jensen S (1983) Software and user satisfaction, in New Office Technology: Human and Organizational Aspects, edited by H J Otway and M Peltu, Frances Pinter (Publishers)
McCormick E (1976) Human Factors in Engineering and Design, 4th edition, McGraw-Hill.

CASE 3

Stress: Stress among Crane Drivers

Cary Cooper and Mike Kelly

Organizational Setting

The case focuses on the jobs of mobile crane operators in four major construction companies, and a number of small enterprises in the same industrial sector. Their activities range from building motorway bridges, the construction, maintenance and repair of sewage plants, quarry work, and small-scale industrial construction through to a 10–15 year programme of construction of an atomic reactor. The enterprises are all sizes, from small ,plant-hire concerns to large multinational construction companies. The majority of firms operate across the United Kingdom, either through their hiring activities, or because of their size and the nature of their construction work and expertise.

In general, many members of the labour force on construction sites move from job to job, and from firm to firm and are often contract-based, though this applies less to the mobile crane operators. These are more often likely to be long-term employees who have gained promotion from general labourer employment into the crane operation end of the enterprise. However, they are generally seen to be at most semiskilled, and largely trained on site by another operator. They rarely belong to a union, and work in an environment where production deadlines are quite strictly enforced – transferring 100 tons of liquid, quick-setting cement from transporters at ground level to a half-built motorway bridge 50 feet high cannot wait until after lunch, or through a pay-rate negotiation.

Background to the Case

Basic Construction Activities

The mobile crane operator is primarily concerned with the lifting and handling of heavy and/or awkward objects. Mobile cranes can be hydraulic telescopic boom machines on wheels or tracks, or lattice boom machines, also on wheels or tracks. Most common are those of the former type, able to lift various maximum weights up to 100 tons, though some of the lattice boom cranes can lift up to 400 tons. No formal differentiation is made between operators using cranes at different heights or of different weight capacity. Typical basic activities involve lifting and handling concrete 'shutters' or ribs for bridges, steel girders, pipes and chambers, and other basic construction materials. The operator works from his cab (no female operators were seen or reported to be employed in the United Kingdom), usually with a co-worker, or 'banksman', giving oral or signalled information on the task in hand. Part of the expertise in the job involves assessing the security of the ground support for the machine, both beneath the wheels or crawler track treads and beneath the outrigger floats (which widen the base of the crane), the weather conditions, particularly wind strengths, and other operating parameters such as the jib radii required for the job, general site conditions and geography, the lift weights and the degree of slewing involved. It is also not uncommon for operators to be working while unable to see, at least directly, the load being carried by the crane. His 'banksman' will often be a relatively permanent colleague, and is often, but not necessarily, an aspirant to crane driving himself. In perhaps one-third of cases, he will merely be the nearest available person on the site.

Tasks and Roles of the Mobile Crane Operators

The job of operating the mobile cranes falls into three main areas; first, the operator has to set up and 'ground' his machine securely, and in an appropriate location for the work to be done, and generally in what are perhaps best described as 'building site conditions'. Second, he lifts and moves a variety of construction materials. Third, he keeps his machine in good order – generally he is allowed around 10% of his weekly hours for this greasing, checking and maintaining function.

Once set up, it is his task to enable the construction operation involving the various skilled and unskilled teams of other workers on the site to be carried forward. In the work with large and heavy materials, he is a lynch-pin in the enterprise, and works alone in his cab, involved in sometimes very delicate adjustments and some-times 'on hold', both for long periods at a time. In setting the crane up, he has to satisfy himself of the safety of the ground support of the crane and its outriggers, and, where appropriate, of the ropes and slings on the crane and its loading. Common accidents involve such things as the overturning of the crane, the loss of its load, and/or damage or destruction of property (and people) in the immediate environment. It appeared from the literature, and to some extent from the investiga-tion, that such accidents were related to practices common in the industry involving penalty clauses for missing deadlines and delays in construction. Though crane operators generally have a more secure and steady employment than the bulk of unskilled and semiskilled workers in the construction industry, their wages and bonus payments are related in at least some companies to completions and deadlines, though such relations are much looser than, say, piecework systems. However, because of their key role as a 'lynch-pin' in the building process, other workers much more closely tied to 'payment by results' systems are often dependent upon them and their work for their own remuneration levels.

The Research Investigation

Once entry into the organization and the construction site had been achieved, through managers, supervisors and safety officers, the crane operators were asked to help with an enquiry into the types and degrees of stress involved in hazardous jobs in the construction industry. There followed in-depth interviews with operators using a wide range of mobile cranes to diagnose stress factors in the job, and their potential for causing accidents on the site.

Eight main factors were isolated in the interviews, and followed up in a large-scale investigation using questionnaires. Only 9% of those interviewed or completing a questionnaire felt there was *never* any stress attached to the job of mobile crane operation. Some 75% felt it was stressful *now and then*, with 16% feeling that it was *often* or *always* stressful. Stress was defined as feeling 'very physically or mentally tired' *or* 'very frustrated' *or* 'uptight' *or* 'anxious' *or* any combination of these.

The stress areas identified were seen to fall into three groups or problem areas: those related to the demands of the job, those connected with interpersonal relationships, and those arising from the crane operator's personality.

Demands of the Job   Many crane operators showed themselves to be very concerned about the risks to persons and to property inherent in the job of lifting and handling large, heavy and/or awkward loads, often in confined spaces, and sometimes with other workers and members of the public close by. In addition, 80% of drivers mentioned work pressures, including technical problems to do with the job to be done, deadlines for completion, and changes in work schedules consequent upon such things as weather problems, breakdowns, intractable ground conditions and so on. Some complained of physical stress related to the cab design, while most felt that the stop–start aspects of the job, and boredom arising from waiting for deliveries, or 'holding' patterns of work, also contributed to stress.

Interpersonal Relationships   Significant numbers of respondents mentioned the lack of awareness of danger on the part of co-workers as a problem. Also a lack of sympathy with their problems among both co-workers and superiors, combined with a tendency to blame hold-ups upon the crane drivers, was seen as leading to insensitive co-worker relationships. In some cases this was exacerbated by 'off the job' problems in the drivers' lives, and by isolation and loneliness in the cab. This was mentioned by over half the operators and was sometimes seen as having a 'dislocating' effect from reality.

Personality Factors   Scores from the anxiety/depression measures on the questionnaire showed nine out of 10 of the crane operators displaying low levels of personal anxiety and depression, when compared to the normal distribution in the population at large. The other 10%, however, scored significantly higher on the items than both the norm scores and those of a control group of psychiatric outpatients. In addition, the section of the questionnaire dealing with job satisfaction among the operators showed some correlation on two sets of responses: firstly, one in 10 checked AGREE or STRONGLY AGREE with the statement 'Most of the time I have to force myself to go to work' and almost one in five gave the AGREE or STRONGLY AGREE response to the statement 'Each day of work seems like it will never end'.

Finally, further confirmation of the general stressfulness of the occupation and the effects of personality was found when 12 statements, taken from drivers who were interviewed, were proposed in the questionnaire. Some 84% rated the statement 'There's more pressure on the driver now than ever before' to be ALWAYS/OFTEN TRUE, and 47% rated in the same way the statement 'It can get really bad towards the end of the day – you get very tired, but you've still got to concentrate the same'.

The Problem

Links Between Stress and Accident Levels

It was generally believed, throughout the industry, that stress levels among mobile crane operators might be higher than the average for construction workers in general due to the nature and context of the job. It was felt that this in turn might be linked to higher than average accident levels connected to mobile crane operation. In one of the very few studies of accident levels in this sector of the industry, Butler (1978) considered 472 incidents involving cranes over the period 1974–6. These incidents were about one-sixth of the total number of incidents reported to the Factory Inspectorate in that period, and included statistics for tower cranes as well as for mobile cranes. Tower cranes accounted for 13% of the incidents and 14% of the repair costs, and have been excluded from this discussion. Of the 87% of the incidents caused by mobile cranes, 46% were attributed to *human error*, the rest being due to machine or other technical defects. These 219 incidents took up 72% of the crane repair and associated costs (£719 219), and involved three out of the four fatal accidents, and 28 out of the 31 personal injuries covered by the 472 incidents. According to general industrial accident levels reported to the Factory Inspectorate, these are significantly above average, particularly taking into account the relatively low number of employees involved in individual construction site operations.

Research indicates that the linkage between stress levels and accidents may be all the stronger in particular industrial contexts and activities. Modes of operating machinery, isolation, accident-proneness, and the cumulative 'flashpoint' effect of multiple stressors have all been investigated to ascertain the part the stress chain has to play in any theory of accidents.

Employer and Employee Views of the Problem

Against this research evidence, the managers, supervisors and safety officers on site, as well as the crane operators themselves, while agreeing that there were the variety of stressors inherent in the job described above, had varying and ambivalent views on the levels of accidents associated with cranes. When the questionnaires were analysed, there appeared to be a strong correlation in the responses between the levels of stress and those of accidents. A specific example follows, which may serve to indicate the source of variance and ambiguities amongst staff involved.

John, a 37-year-old mobile crane operator, lived with his wife and three small children at his parents' home in a small northern town. He was involved in the construction of a pit for storage tanks by the side of a major trunk road, next to a school playground. On the day in question, there had been early rain, and the particular job was moving full concrete skips from the side of the road, across the corner of the playground, down into the pit, at intervals of about 40 minutes, to supply four labourers and one supervisor in the pit. The operation involved setting the crane outriggers on his telescopic boom crane to give stability, lifting the skips from the carriers on the road, turning through 140° across the corner of the playground to the pit, and lowering and tipping the skips into the concrete shutters which made up the lining of the pit. Due to the breakdown of his crane on the previous day, the work continued non-stop once a convoy of carriers arrived and involved two periods of four-hourly continuous activity in the day with a half-hour break for lunch. For John, actual crane operation and movement was in a pattern of 10 minutes on, 20 minutes hold, 10 minutes on, with four or five changes of position on the edge of the pit during each four-hour delivery session. The ground around the pit was uneven and rarely much wider than the crane with outriggers in place. For the last five minutes in each cycle, John had to operate and manoeuvre with only a partial view of the skips, working with the help of hand signals from his banksman.

Towards the middle of the day's second delivery of concrete, John lifted a full skip, with his boom over the front end of the crane's chassis, slewed through 110° into an 'over the side' position, and toppled into the pit, killing the supervisor and injuring one of the labourers. He himself suffered minor bruising to the body and head.

Case Study Tasks

It is recommended that you work on the tasks individually, in pairs, or in small groups of up to five members. You are a group of directors or senior managers in one of the construction companies in the case, concerned with the twin tasks of lowering costs (human and financial) and improving the quality of working life of your employees. One group member might take on the role of an experienced crane operator co-opted to the group to contribute his views. You have been asked, in particular, to address five questions. Questions 1–3 are intended to be the basis of one to two hours work, whereas Questions 4 and 5 are likely to take longer.

1   Consider the specific example.

   a   What kinds and degrees of stress were operating upon John?

   b   Did stress contribute to the accident?

c More generally, does the case establish a link between stress and accidents?

2 How clear and appropriate were the definitions of stress used in the case? What would you add or delete?
3 What measures could realistically be taken to prevent accidents resulting from crane operations?
4 What action would you take to overcome 'resistance to change' on the part of the crane operators, their co-workers, supervisors and managers?
5 What will be the wider implications of your proposals to reduce stress and accident levels? In particular what may be the impact on production levels, quality, work organization, management style, and communications generally?

Essential Reading

Cooper C L Payne R (eds) (1978) Stress at Work, Wiley
Kakabadse A (ed.) (1982) People and Organisations, Gower
Warr P B (ed.) (1978) Psychology at Work, Penguin

Additional Reading

Beckhard R Harris R (1977) Organisational Transitions: Managing Complex Change, Addison-Wesley
Butler A J (1978) An investigation into crane accidents, their causes and repair costs, Cranes Today 62: 24–31; 63: 28–34; 65: 25–27
Crump J H Cooper C L Smith M (1980) Investigating occupational stress: a methodological approach, Journal of Occupational Behaviour 1: 3
Jarvis I L (1979) Stress and Frustration, Harcourt Brace
Kay H (1978) Accidents: some facts and theories, in Psychology at Work, edited by P B Warr, Penguin
Poulton E C (1978) Blue collar stressors, in Stress at Work, edited by C L Cooper and R Payne, John Wiley
Quick J C Quick J D (1979) Reducing stress, Human Resource Management, Autumn, 15–23
Speroff B Kerr W (1952) Steelmill 'hotstrip' accidents and interpersonal desirability values, Journal of Clinical Psychology 8: 89–91

CASE 4

Supervisory Behaviour: Photoproducts UK

Sheila Rothwell

Organizational Setting

Photoproducts is the UK subsidiary of an American-owned multinational company manufacturing and distributing photosensitive materials. Its operations are spread over several different sites in the UK, mainly in the south, but two are in the north, and the case study factory 'Greenfields' (which opened in 1981) is in the Midlands. There are about 10 000 UK employees with 350 employees at the factory in the study. The company has had a paternalistic 'human relations' philosophy, but in recent years has attempted to move towards a more participative style. Although trade unions were not recognized until about 15 years ago, the workforce is now about 75% unionized.

The last few years have seen many changes. A major international rationalization and efficiency programme relocated and integrated product manufacture in the UK, Europe and the USA, resulting in fewer products and longer production runs in each plant and each country, eliminating any duplication. The UK company remains highly aware of the need to improve its competitive position or risk losing part of its manufacturing operations.

Background to the Case

Greenfields factory was built to meet the demands of the expanding European market and the opportunity offered by a fresh site was utilized by management to organize the plant along different lines from existing factories, to introduce computerized information systems, and to try to develop a better industrial relations climate from that of the 'Brownstone' factory in the south.

Greenfields was custom-built on a flexible modular basis, on a new site, previously part of a mining area. It receives bulk film from film-producing units elsewhere in the country and 'finishes' it by 'spooling' it or putting it into cassettes and packing it into boxes. Six lorries a day then transport the finished product to the comprehensive computerized customer ordering system that processes and controls incoming goods and customer orders at Brownstone. This system (initiated by the US parent) is now linked via the central mainframe computer with the new materials management system being introduced at Greenfields for controlling production (minicomputers), inventories and finished goods. The movement of materials is tracked through the factory using magnetic card technology, replacing a manual card system. Considerable savings are being realized through reductions in stock-holding and in work-in-progress time as well as through improved speed and accuracy of information – clerical staff numbers are minimal.

The factory has a clean modern atmosphere and VDUs are in evidence in the offices of the security guards at the entrance as well as in the warehouse (where fork-lift truck operators access them directly) and production supervisors' offices. Nevertheless, the nature of the film spooling process demands that the major work be done in darkness and that operators' teams keep the semiautomated machines (six per team) running (except for major repairs or maintenance) in conditions of 'pit-pony' gloom, from which eyesight takes several minutes to adjust. The task of inserting film, changing spools, and adjusting and monitoring machines is, however, varied by quality inspection of the finished product outside the dark area, placing it for packing, obtaining new supplies and inputting data and receiving instructions from the VDUs. The packing lines (mainly automated) put the finished product into containers with instruction leaflets, pack these into outers, then load and bind them on to pallets. The computer pallets are then moved to the loading bay, with magnetic cards, and put on trucks for the distribution centre in the South. Some of the operators at Greenfields are female, but about 85% of the workforce is male.

The factory is organized into six departments, the heads of which report directly to the factory manager. The head of production is the senior supervisor, and there are three group supervisors (one per shift) to whom six line supervisors report (two per shift) and through them, on each shift, seven team leaders and 60 operators. On each shift there are also two shift engineers (with their craftsmen) who also report to the group supervisor (see Figure 2).

The supervisory team grew from the transfer from the Brownstone factory of four personnel who had already had some supervisory experience. 'New style' line supervisors were created from leading hands and senior operators, most of whom had also transferred from Brownstone (like one-third of Greenfields employees), so that the majority have only been supervisors for one or two years. Their previous experience related to a much more authoritarian, 'progress-chasing' style of super-vision. The necessity for a 'new style' supervisor arose from the creation of shopfloor teams of operators who have taken over some traditional supervisory responsibilities as well as undertaking a more flexible mix of tasks between them than the old style 'one task–one operator' approach of the Brownstone factory. Every operator has been given training to perform the whole range of tasks.

Most of the supervisors have therefore 'worked their way up', although one had previously been a training officer and another a quality technician. The majority are aged 35–45 years, although the ages range from 31 to 60 years.

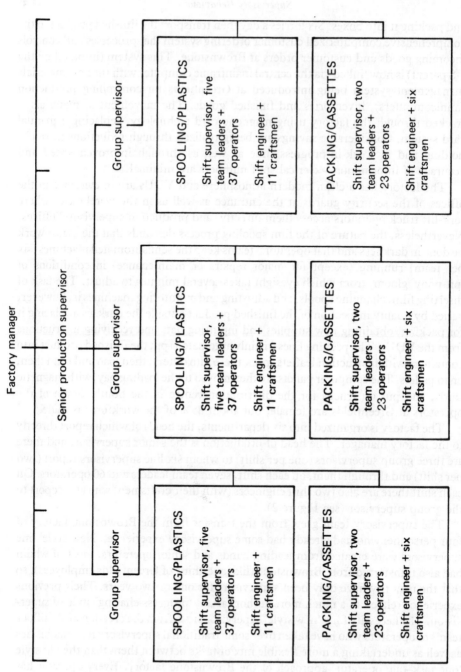

Figure 2 The Greenfields production group.

The Problem

The Basic Difficulties

The supervisors are the main production line management of the factory and as such they are seen as having prime responsibility for increasing productivity. There is constant emphasis on this by the senior supervisor and the factory manager, yet it is part of the current company philosophy (intiated in the USA) that operator teams should be given more autonomy and encouraged to develop responsibility and problem-solving skills. Operators have been given some training in this and now resent any apparent reversion to traditional interventionist or 'authoritarian' supervision. The position of the 'team leader' is also particularly sensitive.

Supervisors are criticized by managers for making insufficient use of the new information now available to them through the computer system with regard to the reports which they make and in diagnosing and resolving problems.

Supervisors therefore feel that they are under increased and often contradictory pressures from various sources, to an extent which is not fully understood or appreciated by management. The factory works on a three-shift – 24 hour – continuous system and there is some ambiguity over the relationship between the production supervisors and the shift engineers. These are not now entirely separate functions, since both engineering and production supervisors report to a group supervisor who works on site with his shift. A long-established engineering supervisor found problems of coordination in that 'senior supervision was not keeping both engineers aware of what was taking place on both sections. This may well have been due to the fact that they were not engineering types of supervisor'.

Some Detailed Information

Industrial relations at Greenfields have generally been good and noticeably better than those at the Brownstone factory. There is some concern, however, that the early substantial commitment to a new site may be beginning to wear off. The factory management has from the beginning tried to communicate at a personal level. Trade union structures have not been highly developed: the trade union branch (of the Transport and General Workers Union) has remained that of Brownstone, although it is likely that a new Greenfields branch will be set up shortly, rather than joining with a local Midlands branch.

Single status was introduced at the beginning (unlike other sites) and continual attempts have been made to negotiate out the incentive bonus from the payment system as 'inappropriate for modern working conditions and automation'. A few managers, however, saw the incentive bonus as a 'cheap form of supervision', and would have liked to keep it. It now represents about 10% of earnings.

Factory output is recorded daily to encourage productivity awareness. While some team rivalry is encouraged, weekly production targets and achievements are published on a group, not a shift, basis to encourage cooperation, in case competition between shifts results in all the 'hard' jobs being left for the next shift.

The computerized materials management system has been phased in gradually over a 2½ year period, starting with presentations to the whole workforce over two days. Management's stated aim was wide supervision and employee involvement but in practice, after an initial presentation and some discussion with supervisors, most of the basic design and detailed decisions were made by systems specialists. Immediately prior to implementation, working practice procedures and manuals were discussed with the operators concerned before finalization. Classroom training and practice sessions were organized for each shift for six weeks before the system went live: overtime payment was made for this.

Implemetation was carefully staged in three phases. Phases I and II involved warehouse data input of goods received, affecting about 15 storemen (a combined 'stores clerk' and 'fork-lift truck operator' role) and four work planners. Information was recorded first for the advisory system and then for the planning process by feeding magnetic cards into 'Factman'. Phase III involved process teams, who had previously had to walk across to a central shopfloor work planning office, collect a workcard for the next batch of product and then annotate and return it when they had completed the task. With the new system the operator uses work station terminals sited in the spooling area, so that the 5–10 minutes needed for their eyesight to adjust from the white light to the dark area can be minimized.

Much of the training was done directly by the systems specialist, but the inclusion of one supervisor (with some responsibility for keeping others briefed) in the system implementation team (together with a senior shop steward) meant that there was some supervisory involvement. As each phase 'went live' this team 'lived with' each one of the three shifts during the first month of operation. The supervisors' main responsibility, however, was to ensure that output levels were maintained, and they tended to feel left out of the technicalities of the new system. Management said that supervisors had been unwilling to take up opportunities for training in it.

Team leaders and operators had also, over the same period, been given a series of one-day team-building workshops to clarify their roles and facilitate personal involvement through understanding their responsibilities for equipment, safety, quality, recording, fault communication and team member support. Team leaders as working members of the team have responsibility for coordinating all team activity and tasks, chairing team meetings, acting as spokesmen for their groups, monitoring group performance and setting the 'climate'. They do not have disciplinary or administrative responsibilities.

Management decided that supervisors would benefit from attending discussions later on during these workshops because they would then be able to work out a 'contract' with their teams. Supervisors were keen to do so. (Each team was devising its own 'constitution' or working norms at these workshops.) A special three-day course tailored more to supervisors' needs was also designed, with a course manual using material on motivation, teamwork and leadership which had been produced in the USA. These topics clearly related to the Greenfields' concept of what the new supervisory role should be, although this was largely emerging through trial and error: group supervisors' objectives are set in terms of key result areas – machine continuity; quality; low overtime; safety; industrial relations grievances. Aims in each area are set and activities listed to be carried out to achieve these aims.

Maintaining a good relationship with shop stewards by investing much of their time (and patience) on communications is regarded as important. Over-communication is encouraged to 'err on the safe side'. Shop stewards try to bypass first-line supervisors, and second level supervisors have to try to help solve this problem. Implementation of the new materials system was generally free of industrial relations problems until the final stage, when a short strike was experienced over pay and grading. This arose from management's refusal to increase the grading of spoolers' jobs because of a fear of 'knock-on' claims from packers and then from storemen. The company was determined to avoid pay increases in association with the introduction of new technology, and thus to maintaining existing grade differences despite avowed objectives of greater workforce flexibility. Supervisors tend to feel that 'we are not handling the unions in the best way possible for management and workforce'; 'some agreements made with the unions left much to be desired and at times put us in an awkward situation'.

Monthly team meetings are held and supervisors from each shift join these meetings towards the end, to resolve problems directly. Supervisors at both group and first line levels also respond to team development workshops by helping teams achieve their action programmes. Dealing with women operators in some teams is seen as an additional problem by some supervisors.

Otherwise, individual or collective grievances at Greenfields are generally fewer than at Brownstone. Computerized systems facilitate management control but people seem less resentful of being blamed for faults which are clearly theirs than for those which are partly at least the responsibility of others. Disciplinary action is at times taken over incorrect data entry (or for not reporting or correcting errors) since the implications of this for other departments, and even other sites, can now be considerable. Management often speaks of the need for 'new discipline' in the sense of adhering to laid down procedures for obtaining supplies or logging production: this tends to mean that previous supervisory skills, often acquired through years of experience, of 'bypassing', 'fixing' or trading favours in order to 'get it out the door' are set aside.

Some rivalry between shifts and departments remains, particularly in the case of packing supervisors seeming lax over starting work times, so that engineering supervisors cannot get their people out of the canteen from tea breaks and at overlap times. The growth of the new plastics moulding section means other problems of supervisory coordination and responsibility. One supervisor was resentful of the fact that 'before handling areas that may be rather sensitive always having to check back with my boss to find how we were handling it at present'. There is now a tendency for supervisors to relate to each other more than to their managers or their work teams.

This increases managers' tendency to grumble about supervisory shortcomings and non-use of computerized information available to them, while supervisors in turn continue to feel uncertain about the many and even conflicting expectations of them. How are they to improve output, adopt a nondirective approach, not usurp the role of team leader, and also make additional analytic reports? There is a feeling that 'nobody else has problems like mine'.

Responses to a research questionnaire reflected some ambivalence. While they enjoyed many aspects of their job – 'contact with people', 'positive decision making' (production supervisors); 'dealing with machine breakdown problems', 'working as a member of the work team directly' (engineering supervisors) – they all saw some sort of man–machine balance as important in their jobs. They also all thought that their responsibilities had changed over the past year or two 'with an increased workload', dealing with 'new boss, new people', more time spent on written work and on 'ensuring I have the right information to give and have let everyone know'. Nevertheless, one supervisor found problems 'with different people making different assumptions using the same information'. They saw the changes as arising mainly out of 'new company policy' and 'increased competition'. Several also mentioned the new technology and the fact that 'one can rely too much on the technology, which can give severe problems when it fails'; 'because of labour numbers, engineering resources have been stretched, therefore existing problems have taken longer to solve, causing a certain amount of frustration'.

They were beginning to experience the benefits of 'the workforce becoming more aware of the running of their areas'. Although they 'expect to receive more detailed information on its running', this means 'I am able to spend more time doing other aspects of my job which I could not do earlier'. Another said it gave him the 'opportunity to look at my own career and potential'.

There was a widespread desire for more training. One individual was critical of the fact that he 'had been on no courses, other than those relating to projects' in the four years he had been a supervisor. Some specifically wanted training in 'problem-solving', 'basic psychology', 'man-management' or 'report writing'. One supervisor said he would value contact with other 'people who have been working the "team working" concept longer than we have', while another merely thought 'all training is very useful'.

Job satisfaction was probably higher among the younger, newly created supervisors than the older ones who found it more difficult to adjust to change. This was reflected in the comment of one who had been in the position for just on a year: 'I have worked hard for 12 years as a mechanic and I have got a just reward in being made a supervisor. I suppose, before I got made up, after eight hours I went home and forgot the job until I came back, but now I will make sure my fellow supervisors have all the information I can give them to help them sort out problems while I am off duty'. Managers may still have to work at maintaining that level of commitment, however, rather than taking it for granted.

Case Study Tasks

Imagine you are the factory manager. Discussions with various specialist managers and the senior production supervisor have reinforced your awareness that there is a supervisory problem.

Your task is to decide what to do about it in terms of structural reorganization and/or selection, training and development. (Questions 1–4 and 6–7 are suitable for one- or two-hour teaching sessions, whereas Question 5 may require a half-day.)

1 Are there too many levels of supervision?
2 Can anything be done about the problems of relationships between production and engineering supervisors?
3 How would you define the supervisory role at Greenfields? What should be the selection criteria for new supervisors in future?
4 Are the perceived supervisory shortcomings largely those of 'skills' or of 'attitudes'? How do these relate to the literature on 'leadership style'?
5 What sort of training or development programme would you plan to meet some of the needs: preparation, length, place, content (theoretical and/or practical), tutors, methods, evaluation?
6 Can you suggest any other ways of improving supervisory motivation?
7 To what extent do you think the supervisory problems were a result of technological or of organizational change? What problems arise in the development of any greenfield site?
8 What implications (ideas to notice or points to avoid) can be drawn from this case study for the role of supervisors in the implementation of computerized information systems?

Essential Reading

Child J Partridge B (1982) Lost Managers: Supervisors in Industry and Society, Cambridge University Press
Rothwell S (1984) Supervisors and new technology, Employment Gazette 92: 21–25

Additional Reading

Bowey A (1973) Changing status of the supervisor, British Journal of Industrial Relations 11: 393–414
Thurley K Wirdenius H (1973) Approaches to Supervisory Development, Institute of Personnel Management
Toye J (1978) Supervisors in Industry: A Survey of Research and Opinion, Industrial Training Research SY2, Industrial Training Research Unit, Cambridge

CASE 5

Managerial Style and Appraisal: Administrators in the NHS*

Rosemary Stewart and Pauline Wingate

Organizational Setting

This is a study of a district administrator (DA) in the National Health Service (NHS). The NHS is divided into geographical districts each responsible for a population of about 250 000, though some districts are somewhat smaller and others larger. Above the districts are regional authorities and regional officers. Each district is controlled by a District Health Authority (DHA) whose members are appointed, not elected as in local government. The officers are appointed by, and report to, the DHA. The chairman of a DHA receives a small, part-time salary.

The DA's job at the time of the case study had three main aspects: management of the administrative staff; secretary to the DHA and member of the district management team (DMT). Since the study a new post has been created – that of district general manager. At the time of the study the district management team had no permanently designated head but members took it in turn to act as chairman.

The district in this case study is a mixture of urban and rural, but is mainly urban. It serves a population of 300 000. The district has a full-time staff equivalent to over 4000 and a budget of over £4 million (1983 figures).

Background to the Case

The district administrator (DA) is in his early forties. He had been DA in the same district since 1975 and had worked there for two years before that.

The case study was carried out shortly after the 1982 reorganization which abolished the middle tier in the geographical structure of the NHS, that of the area. It gave each district its own District Health Authority. This meant that the DA and

*The research for this and two other case studies was financed by the King Edward's Hospital Fund for London.

other senior officers were for the first time reporting directly to a DHA, and that the DA was working directly to the chairman. The impact of these changes on the DA's job was considerable in terms of extra work and new responsibilities.

The Problem

This case is not about a particular problem but about how this senior manager saw his role and priorities and how his colleagues judged his effectiveness.

The DA's Priorities

The DA is ambitious for his district, working to build for it a progressive and dynamic reputation. He makes every effort to find people with new ideas and is always ready to offer the district as a proving ground for new schemes. He feels he needs to be seen to be making changes. He must ensure that the organization remains dynamic. This means he must seize on new ideas and opportunities – even in the middle of reorganization – and he must make them work.

He places great emphasis on publicity for the district. He contributes to the district's reputation and opportunities for development through his membership of a whole range of national and regional committees.

He is now resigning from some of his external committees because he feels the DHA must have prior claim on his time. He is the executive arm of the DMT and the DHA. This is his biggest, most serious responsibility.

The DA sees himself as an overall manager of the district rather than just the administrator and thinks his title not well suited to the role he plays. He is interested in and feels the need to keep in touch with everything that goes on in the district. He makes no distinction between hospitals and community and doesn't confine his interest simply to the work and to his own staff. He does a fair amount of visiting because it gives him a better understanding of the problems and atmosphere. He sees it as part of the overall management monitoring process.

The DA's Views of His Role in Administration

The administration must see him as the boss 'otherwise I can't exist in any meaningful sense'. This 'depends on being seen to be a winner, a man of sound judgement, someone capable of protecting their interests and of doing something about the problems'. He gets involved in issues 'if it's necessary in order for us to win'.

He delegates established administrative work to his subordinates. He expects high standards of volume and thoroughness and trusts them to get on with it. In the last year though, he has had to delegate more and be involved in operational detail less than he would like, which he finds very worrying. He still makes time for visits.

The DA attaches importance to understanding the work of different staff. For example, he spent a couple of days with health visitors to see them in action and a day in the laundry, and another two in a medical records department.

Guidelines and problems are discussed at administrative meetings: for his immediate subordinates a debriefing session immediately after the formal DMT meeting followed by an informal general debate; a more formal meeting once a quarter for a wide group of senior officers.

For day to day matters on which he is trying to keep tabs, he has an envelope on his desk for each of his senior staff and colleagues and at least once a month calls them in to discuss progress. He feels that this system is not going to be good enough in the future. Something much more specific will be needed and must be developed once they are into the new organization.

The DA has individual discussions every six months with his subordinates specifically about their career development and how effective they are in their work. This is a pilot experiment which originated with the Regional Staff Development Committee for Administrative and Clerical Staff. It is an example of the kind of innovation that the DA welcomes.

He thinks that being 'opportunistic', seizing opportunities, is one of his most significant contributions to the effectiveness of the administration.

How the DA's Subordinates See Him

The DA is seen as a man of power and influence, virtually the chief executive, because of his responsibility for the overall coordination of the organization. He uses the power that comes from (1) his position as secretary to the DMT and DHA, giving him influence over what is discussed by them and when; (2) his very wide range of contacts throughout the health service, giving him access to information and to people with money and influence; (3) the length of time he has been in the district.

He spends a lot of time on his public relations role: on his relationships with other bodies in the district, with businessmen who might donate money or services, with the media, with colleagues in other districts, and on a whole range of national and regional administrative committees. He is also the politician, 'striking the bargains with consultant staff in the corridors of the hospitals . . . negotiating between clinical specialities . . . the person with the most power to shift resources'.

His main skill was described as follows: 'negotiating, finding a way through, manipulating pressure groups, avoiding head-on collision, keeping the whole thing going in order to achieve aims . . . he uses this skill widely, between people, between districts, with trade unions, in the local population. . . . It's an ability to wheel and deal. It means being very pragmatic.'

This approach was seen to have disadvantages. The DA can be too pragmatic. Pragmatism and compromise are not inspiring: 'It would be better if he sometimes looked for the best decision as this can be needed to get commitment from people.' The district lacked leadership and a sense of direction before the arrival of the DHA and the chairman's vision of patient care in the future.

The DA was seen as very effective at representing the views of administration and protecting their interest: 'If you persuade him to do something you know he will have the clout to carry it through . . . nothing worse than a boss who hasn't.' 'He is a fighter who believes in success and he does win.'

He can delegate completely: 'He respects his senior officers. He doesn't have to watch over them. There is terrific mutual respect. That is not to say he is not interested. It is proper delegation.' 'In tackling a problem he goes directly to individuals, but he would get more commitment if he brought people together to work in teams. . . . He can also get involved in too much detail and become too personally involved.' He can bypass the formal structure in order to work with a person he needs on a project, or issue a press release which can leave their immediate boss asking, 'Shouldn't I have known . . .?'

Contact between the DA and his subordinates is usually very business-like and infrequent. The DA's style is fairly formal at administrative meetings. He 'dominates the group more than is good for other members of it'. 'Senior officers' meetings tend to be a monologue.' He is out of the office a great deal: 'I can go six or seven weeks without seeing him.' 'It is not that there is any barrier.' 'He is potentially interested in everything and can show a surprising attention to detail . . . is extremely patient. But his style and the atmosphere of his office is such that I would not wish to trouble him with mundane issues. . . . I am aware of the level at which he is operating and of what it is appropriate to tell him.'

At times people can feel the need for greater guidance on objectives and for a greater interest in their work: 'Initially, I felt quite lost . . . there is a sense of isolation.' However, 'You do grow in confidence (if you don't become despondent). You learn to manage without the encouragement. It's great if you're a self-starter . . . it gives you freedom of action.'

He is very popular and his own energy and enthusiasm can rub off on others. He can be very good at involving his staff positively in what is happening, making them feel that they are in a very go-ahead district and must live up to it. He will always take up challenges at meetings. However, 'He's bad in that he doesn't always take into account the resources available to fulfil the commitments he made on behalf of his staff. People don't like to let him down but they can wear themselves out and he is not always aware of the strain on them, or of what work was put aside or neglected for the job he wants done.'

Other People's Views on the DA as Head of Administration

There was some criticism of the efficiency of his own department, which he has not been able to improve even though he has been in the district a long time: 'There are many practical areas of administration, a lot of the underlying systems and procedures, which are very poor . . . a DA with a different approach would have given priority to ensuring that the mechanics of the administration were operating smoothly.'

He tends, it was suggested, to credit his subordinates with qualities that they do not possess: 'He can produce reports very quickly and well, dictate 30–40 letters in a day and do meetings going into the evening. Other people cannot do this . . . . He delegates very substantially . . . too readily . . . and he does not keep an overview.'

There is regret that the organization is not geared up to cope with the DA's enthusiasm to accept challenges, to seize opportunities, the flashes of inspiration which he thinks can be immediately implemented. He is less aware of the stress and strain in the organization than he might be – 'He really is too innovative.'

The Chairman's View of the DA's Role

The DA's part in seeing that the decisions of the DHA are carried out is crucial: 'He should be an effective enabler and make things happen.' He must keep the chairman fully informed and should know where to find any information. He is the link between all the disciplines and must control any complex interdepartmental planning and be the voice of the DMT to the chairman. He is very influential in projecting the image of the authority.

The chairman has an office next to the DA and shares his secretary. There is quite a bit of contact, including dropping in on each other, although the chairman feels that they do not have enough time together. The chairman gets very frustrated by delays: 'Everything takes too long, but it is not his fault. He is very under-staffed.'

The DA's View of His Role

The DA takes his responsibilities to the DHA very seriously, feeling that he has had to adjust his work style to fulfil the role required of him. This has meant that he has not been able to spend as much time with his subordinates as he would have wished since reorganization. The DA feels that he must be seen to be supporting the chairman, that he must persuade the DMT of the importance of coming to DHA meetings, that he must write good briefing papers and take action on behalf of the DHA.

He now feels the need to have some oversight of other departments so as to ensure that action is taken and to keep an eye on any possible trouble spots. This has to be done tactfully. He is aware that the DHA and the chairman see him as 'first man' – some even as chief executive. He thinks that this is mistaken but accepts that it is 'absolutely the DA's responsibility to see that the DHA's decisions are carried out'. He must also make sure that the members of the DHA are fully aware of the consequences of any decisions that they make, particularly if they are against DMT advice. He accepts that the members of the DHA see him as the voice of the DMT. Above all, the DA wishes to use the abilities of the members of the DHA and to encourage them to go on producing new ideas. He sees broadening their knowledge as part of his role.

The DA and the DMT

Organization of the DMT and the Role of the DA   The DMT recently went on a week's workshop at the suggestion of the DA. They agreed that their most pressing problem was that meetings were taking far too long; the DA mentioned one which took 15 hours over two weeks. They concluded that agenda were overloaded, badly structured and that there was a need for greater discipline in discussion. The team leaves the composition of the agenda to the DA and most of the items come through the administration. The DA has been aware of these criticisms but preferred to 'err on the side of over-communication'. He now agrees that there are other ways of sharing ideas and communicating them and cuts out half the items, particularly matters arising, which was used for a continuous updating process.

The DA plays the role of initiator of items, because most of the organization's mail comes to him, and adds items of which the team has asked to be reminded. He tends to talk to introduce each item because of time pressures and lack of administrative support. The team decided at the workshop that the DA should write a background note for each item.

There is criticism that the DMT is too slow in making decisions. The DA might be able to help them to be more decisive. However, he believes in consensus because 'you get a greater input, a wider range of debate, more ideas come out and greater commitment to the decision'. He often acts as judge of what decision the team has come to as a result of the discussion.

How Other Members See the DMT and the DA's Role   The team workshop, 'an example of very effective DA action', was considered very worthwhile because the objectives which would lead to improving the team's effectiveness had been identified and accepted. They appreciate the DA's reorganization of the agenda, particularly putting the difficult problems first. But meetings still go on too long, as the new chairman understands very well.

The DA probably talks more than anyone else 'because of his personality, definite views and involvement'. Most of the items are processed through his department: 'Those who are not officers defer to him because they don't know what is going on. They think that he is a good DA and trust him.' The DA's skill in taking the views of the team and making sense of them was valued. There is a suggestion that the DA could do more to help the team to be more decisive, but, said one of the medical members, 'I don't see why he should. They ought to do it as a team. And the DMT work happily together.'

Other members would find it helpful to have more time to prepare their own input to the meeting: 'The agenda comes out on Friday for Tuesday's formal meeting. This is not long enough to get feedback and information . . . . I need to make inquiries from my own department.' Sometimes papers were on the table for meetings, which is hopeless: 'We had all complained and the DA was more aware of the problem than anyone.'

The DMT appreciate the DA's excellent follow-up: 'We depend very heavily on the minutes. They are the bring forward system, the check-up.' 'The follow-up process takes up half the agenda . . . but it is better to be secure.' The team also appreciate the way the DA 'will gently prod the chairman or will himself suggest who will take on responsibility for action when this is not immediately clear'. 'He doesn't annoy people.'

General Comments on the Role and Personality of the DA

The DA's colleagues were united in their praise of his personal qualities and abilities: 'charming', 'gracious', 'calm', 'personable', 'a great sense of humour', 'sociable', 'enthusiastic', 'optimistic', 'involved', 'committed', 'energetic', 'a hell of a nice guy'.

They appreciated his skill in handling people: 'keeping them happy', 'making them feel he thinks their problems are important', 'calming them down', 'not upsetting them', 'drawing them out because he is a good listener', 'keeping them up to the mark'. They praised his skill and energy in and commitment to public relations, to building up a good image for the district which, they expect, will attract a better calibre of people to the district and build up the staff's and public's confidence in the district. It also helps a lot in keeping industrial relations smooth and trouble free.

The DA is not seen as a particularly strong or effective head of administration. He is excellent as a coordinator of day to day matters and never loses sight of an issue. He is not good as a coordinator of planning, ensuring that the process is properly set up and timetabled, bringing in all the other disciplines. The DA was criticized for being careless of communication, 'holding his cards too close to his chest', creating mistrust by saying 'that's all you need to know, trust me' or 'taking risks on getting things through by the back door without people noticing'. He is seen as not tough enough. He 'bows to the strongest wind' and 'tries too hard to be all things to all men'.

The DA's colleagues praised his intellectual ability ('a good brain', 'a clear, incisive thinker', 'a skilled debater', 'knowledgeable', 'a superb grasp of what is going on in the district'), his industry ('his work load is enormous'), and his personal efficiency ('very well organized . . . can use his time well . . . never wastes five minutes').

Case Study Tasks

1 What are this DA's objectives? Consider both the explicit and implicit ones.
2 What are his main focuses of attention? Are these right for the current situation?
3 Would you like to work for him? Why? Why not?
4 What is the output of the DA's job? How would you judge his effectiveness in terms of output?
5 What are his weaknesses? In what ways is he ineffective?
6 What should he look for in others to compensate for his weaknesses?
7 What else do you think that he could do to improve his effectiveness?

Essential Reading

Stewart R (1982) Choices For The Manager: A Guide to Managerial Work and Behaviour, McGraw-Hill (see Chapters 1, 2, 8, 11, 12, of which Chapters 1 and 11 are the minimum)

Additional Reading

Belbin R M (1981) Management Teams, Heinemann
Boyatzis R E (1982) The Competent Manager: A Model For Effective Performance, John Wiley
Cameron K (1980) Critical questions in assessing organizational effectiveness, Organizational Dynamics, Autumn

Drucker P E (1967) The Effective Executive, Heinemann

Kieser A (1984) How does one become an effective manager?, in Leaders and Managers: International Perspectives on Managerial Behaviour and Leadership, edited by J G Hunt, D Hosking, C A Schriesheim and R Stewart, Pergamon Press, pp. 90–94

Machin J (1981) Expectations Approach: Improving Managerial Communications and Performance, McGraw-Hill

Stewart R Smith P Blake J Wingate P (1980) The District Administrator in the National Health Service, King Edward's Hospital Fund for London, distributed by Pitman

CASE 6

Information and Control Systems: Tewes Ltd.

Mike Fitter and Chris Clegg

Organizational Setting

Tewes Limited is a manufacturer of high quality sweets. The company is a medium-sized, family-owned, partially unionized and highly successful confectionery producer in the north of England. The case study is set within a single department in the factory.

Background to the Case

The Departmental Setting

This particular department produces and packs in excess of 40 different lines of sweets and was organized in two adjacent rooms separated by a partition. In one room men produced the sweets, and in the other women packed them. Approximately 35 people worked in the department. Each room had its own supervisor responsible to the departmental manager who reported directly to the factory manager. In response to strong pressures for output the two supervisors held rigid control over the production and packing processes, allocating people to jobs, deciding the timings of breaks, determining priorities and standing in for people who needed a personal break. Above all, the production supervisor set the pace of work for both rooms by fixing the cooker speeds at the beginning of the process.

Production is organized in batches. Raw materials enter the production room and each batch is cooked to set temperatures for specified times. The hot batch is then transferred to a large table (or slab) where colours and flavours are added and where different batches are moulded together to create the required flavour mixes and patterns. The cooked batch is then extruded through a machine which cuts it into individual sweets. Some are automatically wrapped at this stage and pass on conveyors into the packing room where they are inspected, bagged and boxed ready for despatch. Other sweets arrive in the packing room unwrapped and are fed into an automatic wrapping machine prior to inspection, bagging and despatch. The essential characteristic of this process is its sequential interdependence such that any problem at any stage has an immediate impact – both on the people working 'further down the line', who may be waiting for work, and on the people 'back up the line' who must slow down to prevent making buffers of produce which cool and have to be scrapped. The technology itself is old-fashioned in that almost all the plant is over 10 years old. Usually two product lines are made concurrently for a whole day each (although changes during the day are sometimes necessary).

The Management Information Systems

The information systems operating in the firm were fairly conventional. Thus production was planned, controlled and assessed with the help of three functions: work study, production planning and management information.

Work study used work measurement techniques to determine standard times and manning levels appropriate for each product line. Such times specified the number of hours required to produce each kilogram of a given product line assuming 100% levels of efficiency. The numbers of batches required for each line varied, but on average, when the department was at full strength, 100 high quality batches per day were required to satisfy work study standards. Production planning used sales forecasts to determine the demands on the department and then used work study figures to set a daily production plan for the week, at the same time indicating the numbers of operating staff that would be needed assuming high levels of efficiency. Production planning followed seasonal peaks and troughs in the market for this department and elsewhere in the factory. The manager and his supervisors (especially the one responsible for production) adapted this weekly plan on a day to day basis to meet their circumstances, bearing in mind which product lines could and could not be made concurrently, the stock levels of materials that would be required, and any 'urgent' demands by the marketing function. It was their responsibility to draft in any extra staff that might be needed, or to transfer surplus staff to busier departments. These staff movements were fairly regular because of the seasonal nature of many lines produced in the factory.

The two supervisors provided management information daily with a wide range of statistical information which included the weight of goods produced and packed, the staff hours worked and the amount of production time lost, which was allocated to a number of categories. Some of this lost time was 'allowable' and did not 'count against' the operators when their performance was assessed (e.g. when machines broke down through no fault of the operators). Management information used these figures, along with the standards produced by work study, to compute a series of complex departmental weekly statistics which included, for example, the hours lost to production as a result of machine breakdowns, absence, scrap reclamation and cleaning. However, the principal measure for each department was the efficiency with which it produced its output that week. For example, an efficiency of 100% would mean that the operators in the department had produced in the hours available for production (i.e. excluding 'allowable' losses) exactly what would be

1 SUMMARY OF PERFORMANCES

	Actual week	Actual cumulative
(a) Overall losses		
Dept hours lost as a percentage of total hours available	C	
Non-dept hours lost as a percentage of total hours available		
Total loss of hours as a percentage of total hours available		
(b) Analysis of dept losses		
Absenteeism in hours as a percentage of total hours available		
Other dept hours lost as a percentage of total hours available		
Inefficient hours lost as a percentage of total hours available	B	
Total dept hours lost as a percentage of total hours available	C	
(c) Other performances		
Overtime in hours as a percentage of total hours available		D
Efficiency ratio – standard hours related to hours available to production		

2 ANALYSIS OF HOURS

	Actual week (hours)	Actual cumulative (hours)	As a percentage of total hours available — Week	Cumu'tive
(a) Total hours available				
Normal hours				
Overtime hours				
Total hours available	F			
(b) Loss of hours				
Dept losses				
Reclamation				
Machine breakdown				
Waiting for materials			A	
Waiting for work				
Cleaning				
Absenteeism				
Others				
Inefficiency	H		B	
Total	G		C	
Non-dept losses				
Factory allowance				
Waiting for instruction				
Meetings				
Training				
Experiments				
Unmeasured work				
Lay offs				
Total				
Total loss of all hours				
3 STANDARD HOURS PRODUCED	E			

Figure 3 Weekly report form.

expected of them if they were working at standard performance in work study terms. From a managerial point of view the aim was to achieve high levels of operator efficiency (target 100%) along with high levels of machine utilization (target 100%). Put another way the aim was to have the operators working hard on plant that was available all the time.

An example of a weekly information sheet for this department is given in Figure 3. The most important information on the sheet is marked. Thus A indicates the percentage of time lost as a result of machine breakdown giving a measure of machine utilization; B indicates the percentage of time lost as a result of operator inefficiency; C is the aggregate of all time lost for reasons within the department (including A and B); and D is an efficiency ratio computed by comparing the amount of sweets produced expressed in standard hours (E) divided by the total actual hours available to production (F), excluding time lost as a result of inefficiency ($G–H$). Thus

$$D = \frac{E}{F - (G - H)} \times 100.$$

Management information passed all the departmental performance statistics to the factory manager who, partly because of the keen emphasis in the firm on meeting production targets, adopted a management by exception philosophy. As such he pressurized those managers whose performance fell below acceptable levels, for example below 85% efficiency. This was frequently the case for this department. Unfortunately such discussions between the factory manager and the departmental manager were based on information which arrived two to three weeks after the production week in question (because of the processing time), and the figures represented a summary for a whole week. These two factors combined to make it difficult for them to diagnose exactly where and why problems were occurring. Although a more complex system giving a more detailed picture of events and problems was feasible, there seemed an implicit assumption that the optimal balance between a system giving accurate information but that was not impossible or expensive to administer, had already been reached. In practice the departmental manager talked to the supervisors and operators in order to effect control of the production process and to keep production going on a day to day basis.

The Departmental Information Systems

Within the department the supervisors and operators understood the information systems only in the very broadest terms. Emphasis on the shop floor was on 'doing' the job, information gathering being regarded as irrelevant to the process of manufacturing sweets. Information systems were seen as a managerial concern and a supervisory chore. This meant that information recording at the best of times was lax and was usually done by the supervisor at the end of the day or on the next day. In addition, when the production process was interrupted through a machine break-down, a fairly common occurrence with the old machinery, the effects were quickly felt by all the people working on that product line. Thus, if one machine in the middle of the process broke down, all the people working after that machine were soon waiting for work and the people before it had to slow down or stop working so as to prevent a pile-up of products that would quickly cool down and become 'scrap'. It was during such interruptions to the smooth flow of work that the supervisors in particular were at their busiest – working with the maintenance engineers to try to put things right. Thus, at the very time when detailed and careful recording of information by them was necessary to give an accurate picture of events which would enable problem diagnosis later, the supervisors in particular were liable to be in the thick of things directing operations wholly unconcerned with the clerical aspects of the job. Therefore, the information system was systematically inaccurate in the sense that allowable losses of production time, e.g. when a machine broke down through no fault of the operator, sometimes went unrecorded or, more often, were subsequently underestimated. Furthermore, the department only received a time allowance for the actual period for which a machine was broken down, even though after repair there might be a considerable lead time before it could be used again because of the nature of the production process.

The net result of these inaccuracies in the recording system was that the department's efficiency was unfairly depressed. Equivalently the machine utilization of plant in the department was exaggerated since the full impact of breakdowns was rarely recorded. Thus in general the information systems made the department look 'worse', and maintenance look 'better' than they really were. Furthermore there was no systematic method of feeding back information to the operators. The manager tended to post photocopies of the 'weekly report' on the department notice board. As well as being very complex and presenting too much data, these sheets were usually posted when performance looked bad and the manager was under pressure from the factory manager to make improvements. His attitude when the staff performed satisfactorily was there was no need to 'congratulate' them as they were only doing what they were paid to do.

Not surprisingly the basic message received by the staff was demotivating. Furthermore, reliance on this inaccurate system sometimes led the departmental manager to take actions which were perceived by the staff as inappropriate and unfair – in particular, criticizing people who already thought they were working hard enough. The staff felt cynical about both the information system and management's motives. At the same time they often felt unable to improve their performance because almost all the working decisions were made by the supervisors. When performance was low the supervisors came under increasing managerial pressure to tighten controls which again reflected the emphasis in the organization on meeting production and efficiency targets. Supervisors and managers were themselves evaluated on their ability to meet these targets, other tasks such as training, safety and hygiene in practice being regarded as peripheral to, or even in conflict with, the primary task. The emphasis was such that after a machine breakdown, for example, the production supervisor would increase the rate of working to a level where excessive scrap was produced. With little control over their work the operators abrogated more responsibility, a typical reaction being 'Sod it!'. Their feelings of cynicism and helplessness constituted a frame of mind which led to even less concern with careful recording and reduced efforts when things went wrong. The cycle became self-perpetuating.

The Job Redesign Project

The original objective of this project was to explore the reasons for low morale in the department. At the outset all agreed that problems existed, although the diagnoses varied.

After prolonged discussions with all the interested parties the department was reorganized. The partition separating the two rooms was removed and the machinery rearranged to promote team work. Two semiautonomous work groups were instituted. Each team has been made responsible for the complete production and packing of sweets and contains both men and women. They organize their own work, setting their own pace (i.e. cooker speeds), allocating and reallocating jobs amongst themselves, deciding who shall work overtime, organizing their own meal and tea breaks, etc. Since the groups effectively have become self-supervising, the need for separate supervisory roles has disappeared. Over a period of time the structure has evolved such that the department is now managed by a single manager without any supervisory support.

Targets agreed as 'fair' and based on work study standards are set for each team on a daily basis, planning now making efforts to even out production requirements over the year for this department (though not elsewhere in the factory). Because of their increased responsibilities and skill levels, most of the operators have received a small pay increase. The new method of working is probably best seen as underpinned by a new informal contract whereby the teams endeavour to meet the targets sought by management in return for the freedoms and benefits described above. The effect has been to give the operators control over their own performance, and to give the manager the chance to plan ahead and anticipate problems rather than act in a purely 'fire-fighting' role.

The Problem

Only very minor changes were proposed to the management information systems when the job redesign exercise was first implemented. This was partly because no one appreciated the pervasive impact of such systems on the working of the department, and partly because there was a naive expectation that any necessary changes would become self-evident. However, the inadequacies of the old systems, as described above, soon became apparent. The old information systems, as well as being poorly administered and poorly understood, were quite inappropriate for dealing with the new method of working: quite simply they were *management* systems designed by managers to enable them to plan and evaluate the production process. Now that the staff controlled their own working day, these old systems became even more unsuitable. For example, the staff set their own pace of work and chose to work faster in the morning to 'break the back' of their target by lunchtime. But to adjust their rate of work they needed regular information on exactly what their target was, and on how much had been produced, packed and scrapped. Without such feedback they could not regulate their own behaviour.

This of course involved fundamental changes in the uses to which information was put. The old style of management by exception, with superiors directly increasing their controls when performance slipped, was quite incompatible with the concept of responsibility being devolved to teams. Certainly management maintained overall control, but had to learn to let the teams make their own decisions and mistakes. When in difficulty, the teams were encouraged to use the manager and any other experts as skilled resources. The rest of this case study focuses on the ways in which the information systems needed changing to meet the needs of the people *within the department* as well as of those outside it.

Making changes in this direction proved more difficult than was imagined. Some examples illustrate the difficulties faced when designing the new information and control system. In the first place, the production operators (traditionally men) count and judge their progress in terms of the batches of material they produce. Most of the operators hold clear views on the number of batches they regard as 'fair' for each product line, which as it happens would give a performance of approximately 100%. In practice then there is little discrepancy between the performance which management seeks and the batch targets which the operators perceive as fair. Management for their part work and think in terms of kilograms packed, production efficiency and plant utilization. Their concerns are that the required amounts of goods are produced at an efficient level of performance and that the plant is operating for as much of the working week as possible. Logically of course batch targets, weight packed and efficiency should correspond very closely since targets are based on standard times and batches are of fixed weights. For example, work study standards may require that 1500 kilograms of sweets are produced for a particular line in a day. In practice this may correspond to 50 batches. If a team produces and packs 50 good batches, with no scrap, then it will, by definition, achieve a performance of 100% efficiency.

However, there are very real complications. For example, considerable scrap may result – especially when machinery is malfunctioning. Thus a team could meet its batch target and yet not produce the weight of packed sweets required. In addition, if a team works a large amount of overtime (i.e. extra hours available), then production efficiency will be reduced unless the target is exceeded. In both cases efficiency will be too low. On the other hand machine breakdowns and other allowable losses, by reducing the hours available to production, have the opposite effect of increasing efficiency above 100% if the planned target is achieved. Thus, it is quite feasible for a team to reach its target and yet be inefficient, or to fall below its target and yet exceed 100% efficiency. In the first instance machine utilization will have been fairly good, and in the latter fairly poor.

There is also the added complication that the packers (traditionally women) do not think in terms of batches. If anything they monitor their work by the cages they have packed (a cage is broadly equivalent to four batches). Many, however, claim they keep no tally of their workload at all: they simply pack what comes through to them. Unfortunately the historical division between producers (men) and packers (women) is deeply ingrained throughout the firm. Although the creation of teams has gone some way towards integrating the two groups within the teams, this has only been partially successful.

There is the added problem that the departmental manager, with no supervisor to help, is not always available to record the necessary production information. He is concerned that the operators on the shop floor are not sufficiently 'information conscious' to record the data diligently. As such he has proposed that a new post, that of clerical assistant, is created to collect and process the necessary information as well as to organize and manage whatever system is eventually designed. The factory manager is nervous about this proposal since he believes it would ensure that the operators will continue to see themselves as 'doers' and have little regard for the information aspects of their job since it will remain someone else's responsibility.

Case Study Tasks

Your basic task is to design an appropriate departmental information and control system which caters for the needs of the operators as well as of management, and at the same time is consistent with the aims of the new work organization. Questions 1–5 below are appropriate for teaching sessions of one or two hours. Questions 6–10 may require longer periods of time. It will help if students work in pairs or small groups to solve these problems.

1   What are the main problems with the information system prior to the job redesign exercise?
2   What do you think of the departmental manager's way of running the department before the changes?
3   What do you think of the departmental manager's proposal that he is given the support of a clerical assistant?
4   What criteria would you specify to guide the design of the new information and control system?
5   Would you have different systems for production and for packing? Give reasons for your choice.
6   What would your system(s) be? Include in your specification the content of the feedback and the method and frequency of its presentation.
7   What will be the impact of your system(s) on the operators and on the departmental manager?
8   What will be the effects of your system(s) elsewhere in the factory, in particular for production planning, work study, and maintenance engineering?
9   What are the advantages and disadvantages of introducing a computer-based system?
10   What general lessons can be learned from this case that are applicable to other sorts of information and control systems?

Essential Reading

Emery F E (1980) Designing socio-technical systems for greenfield sites, Journal of Occupational Behaviour 1: 19–27

Oldham G R Hackman J R (1980) Work design in the organizational context, in Research in Organizational Behavior, Vol 2, edited by B M Staw and L L Cummings, JAI Press

Additional Reading

Galbraith J R (1973) Designing Complex Organizations, Addison-Wesley

Miller E J Rice A K (1967) Systems of Organization, Tavistock

Sime M E Coombs M J (eds) (1983) Designing for Human–Computer Communication, Academic Press

Taylor J C (1978) The socio-technical approach to work design, in Designing Organizations for Satisfaction and Efficiency, edited by K Legge and E Mumford, Gower

Trist E L (1959) On socio-technical systems, reprinted in W A Pasmore and J J Sherwood (eds) (1978) Socio-technical Systems: A Source Book, University Associates

CASE 7

Decision Making: British Rail

Riccardo Peccei and David Guest

Organizational Setting

This case is about the management of innovation and technological change in British Rail. British Rail is a public corporation whose central duty is to provide a service to transport passengers and freight. In 1984, in the midst of a variety of major reorganizations, the main railway business (excluding subsidiaries) employed about 160 000 people. The case described here was initiated in 1966, at which time around 300 000 were employed.

In 1966, the organizational structure was complex. A geographical structure consisted of a headquarters and five regions, within each region except Scotland there were a number of divisions and within each division a number of areas. An area manager might be responsible for up to 1000 men. Alongside the geographical structure, a functional structure existed, which was largely paralleled at head-quarters, within regions and within divisions. This included conventional functions such as finance and personnel; in addition, and central to this case, there was an operating department, and separate technical departments known as the chief mechanical and electrical engineering (CMEE) and chief signal and telecommunications (CS&TE) departments. There was also an important research and development activity with a research centre at Derby. In many respects, therefore, British Rail is a large and highly complex organization and this is a case about decision making in a bureaucratic environment.

Background to the Case
Description of the Remote Control of Trains (RCT) Project

In early 1966 British Rail (BR) decided to explore the possibility of developing and introducing a system for remotely controlling the movement of coal trains through discharge terminals at three Central Electricity Generating Board (CEGB) power stations in Yorkshire.

The standard procedure when a train arrives at a power station is for the driver to stop the locomotive just outside the hopper house where the coal is to be discharged. When the way is clear the driver engages an automatic slow speed control on the locomotive and then proceeds through the hopper house at a speed of a half a mile an hour. The unloading operation normally takes about 45 minutes to complete. The common practice is to use relief drivers for the discharge operation, thus enabling the regular drivers to take a 'physical needs' break at the power station where messing facilities are available.

The remote control system enables the CEGB operator at the power station to control the movement of coal trains during discharge operations directly from his panel in the hopper house by means of high frequency electric impulses transmitted through a trackside conductor loop to a receiver unit fitted to the locomotive. This would in fact enable the driver to leave the locomotive on arrival at the power station and take his break while the train is moved under remote control. The main benefit of the scheme for BR derives from the saving of about a dozen relief drivers at the three power stations. The total cost of developing and introducing the scheme was estimated at approximately £80 000 in 1967, with direct staff savings of around £20 000 per annum.

The Initial Decision to Authorize Development of Remote Control of Trains (1966–8)

The RCT scheme originated with the Operating Department of BR's Eastern Region at York. It must be seen against the background of the 1965 nationally negotiated single-manning agreement allowing trains to new CEGB power stations to be single- rather than double-manned, with drivers being entitled to a 30 minute break between the third and fifth hours of duty. This presented local management with the problem of integrating the new break requirement into the existing pattern of working at power stations. Two alternatives were initially considered by the Eastern Region. One was to allow the coal trains to stand idle for half an hour either before or after discharge to allow drivers to take their break. The other was to use relief drivers at the power stations. In the event management rejected the first alternative on both operational and efficiency grounds and opted for the use of relief drivers. But this solution was expensive and was therefore considered to be far from ideal. Instead, the Operating Department of the Eastern Region proposed the idea of remote control of discharge operations as an alternative.

In early 1967, after trying unsuccessfully to interest Headquarters management in the RCT scheme, the Eastern Region asked BR's Electrical Research Department at Derby to prepare an initial costing for the scheme. The Research Department was approached because it was already working on a safety system for controlling train speed automatically from a ground installation, and was interested in the more advanced application of the driverless train concept involved in the RCT system.

The Research Department concluded that the proposed scheme would be economically justified, estimating that it would pay for itself in approximately four years. On this basis the Eastern Region's Operating Department, in consultation with the Research Division and BR's other main Eastern Region technical departments, the CMEE and the CS&TE departments, decided to prepare a more detailed feasibility study for the RCT scheme. This study was completed by mid-1967.

Each power station was costed for two schemes, a short and a long version of the remote control system. In the short version, remote control was to be introduced only on the half mile an hour section of track going through the hopper house. In the long version, remote control was to cover the whole power station loop, including a 15 mile an hour section of track leading into and out of the power station. The Research Department was particularly interested in the 15 mile an hour system because of the technical challenge involved and the potential payoffs for the further development of automatic train control technology in BR. However, the long system would be more complex and expensive to develop and its full economic benefits could not be properly quantified and evaluated. As a result Eastern Region management, with the agreement of the Research Division, decided to proceed with the less ambitious half mile an hour scheme which would give the maximum return on investment in the short term – the financial break-even point for this system, it was estimated, would be reached after three years.

A number of other important decisions relating to the project were also made at this stage. On the technical side the most important choice that had to be made was whether BR should design and develop its own remote control equipment or use technology already developed and operating on railways abroad and adapt it accordingly. In the event the Eastern Region's Operating Department, in consultation with the Research Division and the other technical departments, decided to develop the technology in-house, taking advantage of the work already done in this area by the BR research team at Derby. However, this decision appears to have been made without carrying out a systematic evaluation of the possible costs and benefits involved in adopting this solution instead of going for existing technology. At the same time they decided that the next step in the programme should be to develop and install prototype RCT trackside and locomotive equipment at Eggborough power station in preparation for a trial demonstration of the system under actual working conditions. The Research Department agreed to take responsibility for the initial design and specification of the RCT system, in consultation with the CMEE and the CS&TE departments. However, the actual construction of the equipment was to be put out to contract since the Research Department did not have the spare capacity to undertake the work. The Operating Department retained responsibility for the overall coordination of the project through one of its staff based at York.

Before work could begin on the project, the scheme first had to be cleared with the CEGB, with BR's Headquarters Operating Department in London and with the unions in BR. The CEGB readily agreed to the project and in November 1967 gave its formal approval for development work to be carried out at Eggborough. BR's Headquarters management was more difficult to convince. In particular, the HQ Operating Department was of the opinion that alternative ways of arranging breaks for drivers could be found which would neither cause delays nor require the use of relief drivers at power stations. It therefore questioned the need for the RCT scheme. It also felt that the Eastern Region's projected manpower savings from the scheme were based on over-optimistic estimates of future traffic requirements at power stations. Most importantly, however, HQ management felt that, in view of the major industrial relations implications of the RCT project, it would be extremely difficult to sell the concept to the unions and that, for a variety of reasons, it would be best not to raise the issue with them at that stage. Management in the Eastern Region, however, strongly pushed for the project and in February 1968 was eventually given verbal approval from Headquarters to proceed with the RCT scheme at Eggborough. No physical work on the system was to be undertaken at the power station, however, until the initiative had been cleared with the unions (ASLEF and the NUR).

Following a prolonged debate between regional and Headquarters management about how best to approach the unions on the matter, a national level consultative meeting was set up with ASLEF and the NUR in June 1968, specifically to discuss this issue. Management at this stage only referred to BR's intention to carry out remote control experiments at Eggborough. It made no mention of its longer term plan to introduce RCT elsewhere. The unions agreed to the Eggborough experiment but stated that they would wish to observe the operation in practice before committing themselves to the principle of remote control working at power stations. On this basis it was agreed that management would proceed with the wiring of one track and the fitting of one Class 47 locomotive with experimental remote control gear. Management estimated that this work would take between nine and 12 months and agreed to hold a demonstration for the unions at Eggborough when the system was ready.

The Problem

First Phase of Development of the RCT Scheme (1968–72)

Once the Eggborough experiment was cleared with the unions the technical departments were given the go-ahead to proceed with the necessary development work on the scheme. Management, as we have seen, estimated that it would take approximately a year to design and install a prototype RCT system at Eggborough and, consequently, told the unions that they could expect to see a demonstration of the system by the late spring of 1969. In the event, however, progress on the project was far slower than expected. Trial tests did not commence until April 1970 and it was not until October 1970 that management was able to arrange a demonstration for the unions.

There were a number of reasons for this slippage in target dates. From the start a number of unforeseen technical problems were encountered, including difficulty in maintaining a sufficiently high signal strength over the hopper grids to activate the locomotive remote control equipment resulting in train run-back problems, and problems of wheel spin on wet or greasy rails. Progress on the project was further delayed by the late delivery of equipment by suppliers, by scheduling problems in getting a Class 47 locomotive released from traffic in order to fit it with the necessary RCT equipment, and by the need to suspend all work on the installation of ground equipment at Eggborough for a period of about three months in early 1970 due to a complete shut-down of the power station by the CEGB.

By the spring of 1970 the Eastern Region came under increasing pressure from the HQ Operating and Industrial Relations departments to set up a demonstration of the RCT system for the unions as promised back in 1968. In August 1970 the Eastern Region's Operating Department called a meeting of all the regional departments involved in the RCT project to review the situation and decide on the next steps to be taken to progress the initiative. At this meeting it was decided to hold a demonstration for the unions by October since it was felt that any remaining technical problems could be ironed out by that time. It was also decided to fit remote control equipment to a second locomotive and to install ground equipment on the second line going through the Eggborough hopper house to enable the technical departments to gain experience of remote control operations with two locomotives working at the same time. Provided BR got clearance from the CEGB and the unions on these matters, management expected to be able to start conducting final evaluation trials of the RCT system at Eggborough by mid-1971.

The CEGB formally approved the installation of ground equipment on the second line at Eggborough in October 1970. In the same month a demonstration of the RCT operation was held for national officials of the NUR and ASLEF. However, this demonstration was not wholly successful due to a run-back of the train during the RCT operation requiring the driver to take over manual control and apply the brakes to the locomotive. Despite some mixed reactions to the demonstration, the unions agreed to BR's request for a further locomotive and section of line to be fitted for remote control, and in February 1971 informed management accordingly.

By this time, however, the HQ Operating Department had openly begun to question the value of the Eggborough experiment and whether the initiative should be pursued further. From the very beginning, as we have seen, Headquarters management had had strong reservations about the RCT initiative and had only agreed to it under pressure from the Eastern Region. The delays experienced in developing the system, the malfunction which occurred during the trade union demonstration, and the fact that after two years of development work the experimental equipment was still not in working order all served to confirm Headquarters' initial doubts about the viability of the scheme. At the same time, following the reorganization of the BR board in 1970, there was a general move towards greater centralization in BR aimed at establishing tighter Headquarters control over regional policy and expenditure, and also over regional initiatives such as the RCT project. As a result, in the spring of 1971 HQ management requested that all development work be suspended at Eggborough until BR had clarified its policy in relation to the scheme and the expenditure involved.

This decision was strongly contested by the Research Department and by management in the Eastern Region, particularly since they felt that Headquarters lacked a clear understanding of the basic nature and aims of the project. Headquarters' decision to suspend work on the scheme appears, in fact, to have been based in part on the mistaken belief that the project was only intended to cover Eggborough, that it had not yet been costed, and that its main aim was to save second men rather than relief drivers. HQ management failed to be convinced by the arguments put forth by the Research Department and the Eastern Region in favour of the scheme, and in mid-1971 the RCT project effectively came to a standstill. Suspension of work on the scheme coincided with a major reorganization of the Research Department at Derby, as a result of which key personnel were transferred to other work within BR's new Research and Development Division.

Second Phase of Development (1972–5)

In September 1972, following the reorganization of the Research Department, HQ operating management, acting on a request from the R&D Division and the Eastern Region, called a meeting of all the relevant departments to review the position on the RCT project and outline a policy for the further development of the scheme. After reviewing the cost estimates for the scheme it was agreed that, in view of BR's recent wage awards and rising operating costs, the financial case for the project was even stronger than originally estimated in 1967. From a technical point of view it was recognized that wheel slip and low signal strength still posed potential problems. However, the technical departments were of the opinion that these problems could be overcome in the near future. At the same time the R&D Division reintroduced the idea of using the long 15 mile an hour version of the RCT system and proposed that the Eggborough tests be resumed on this basis. This proposal was accepted at the meeting despite reservations from the Eastern Region's Operating Department which felt that this proposal was too complex and difficult to implement. The Eggborough experiment was therefore intended to proceed to a two-track, two-locomotive stage, including full loop return at higher speed, with a view to providing a full demonstration of the system to the unions by June 1973. After this, a trouble-free trial period of between six and 12 months was envisaged before the system would become fully operational. The decision to proceed with the project received the full backing of the HQ Operating Department which, henceforth, became more directly involved in the RCT initiative – in effect taking over responsibility for the project from the Eastern Region.

Progress on the scheme was once again much slower than expected. Contrary to plan, the RCT system was not ready for testing by mid-1973. As a result the June demonstration to the unions was first rescheduled for August and then postponed indefinitely. In the event, it was not until late 1975 that management was able to hold a demonstration for the unions. A number of factors contributed to this new delay in the development of the project, including the late delivery by suppliers of the additional 15 mile an hour locomotive equipment necessary for the long system RCT operation at Eggborough, and problems created by movement of staff within the organization. More importantly, by this stage a basic disagreement had emerged between the Research Division and the CMEE Department over the nature and design of the RCT equipment.

The CMEE Department was at the time developing a multiple unit control

(MUC) system for transmitting control signals between two locomotives attached at either end of a freight train. In contrast to the remote control system which used tone modulation for transmitting signals, the MUC system used a more modern and versatile digital code to convey commands. The CMEE Department therefore proposed that the RCT system be redesigned on a digital basis to make it compatible with the MUC system. The Research Division, which had been responsible for designing the RCT equipment, agreed that the tone system was outdated, but argued that it would be premature to consider any alternatives to the RCT system before all the implications of the changes proposed by the CMEE were examined in detail.

In late 1973 top management in BR, concerned by the lack of progress on the project and by the inability of the technical departments to agree on the type of equipment to be used, called for a general review of the RCT scheme. The financial case for the project was reconfirmed as part of the review. At the same time, however, acknowledging the complexity of the long RCT system, the review team decided to adopt the short system at Eggborough, thereby reversing the decision which had been made in 1972 when the project was resumed. No decision was made as to whether to adopt a tone or a digital system. Instead, a joint CMEE, R&D, and CS&TE working party was set up to look into the matter.

The issue of whether to adopt a tone or digital system was not resolved until October 1974 when the working party eventually agreed to adopt a tone system on the grounds that (1) there was a need to progress the project as quickly as possible; (2) the tone system was already developed; (3) the area of operation at Eggborough was self-contained.

While this debate was in progress the Research Division was experimenting with different track loop layouts at Eggborough to resolve the problem of signal strength in the hopper house. Different layouts were tried out. In early 1975 tests with the loop fixed in a vertical plane to the central walk-way of the hopper house eventually gave satisfactory results. On this basis the technical departments proceeded to fit the second line at Eggborough in June 1975. Soon after this, work on the fitting of the second Class 47 locomotive was also completed. Once the technical departments were satisfied that the system was in working order, arrangements were made to hold a demonstration of the updated RCT system to the unions with two locomotives running in parallel through the hopper house under remote control. The demonstration, held in October 1975, was technically successful.

Third Phase of Development (1975–8)

Following the October demonstration the technical departments started work on preproduction lineside and locomotive equipment to replace the existing experimental equipment, with a view to holding formal evaluation trials of the RCT system as soon as the scheme was cleared with the unions. At this point, however, the project ran into major problems on the industrial relations front.

Management contacted the unions to seek their agreement in principle to the introduction of remote control operations at power stations in November 1975. The unions responded by asking for clarification on a large number of points relating to the scheme (e.g. whether BR intended to adopt the short or the long version of the RCT system; whether the equipment was designed to be fail safe; whether the wheel-slip problem had been resolved; whether the time it took the driver to prepare the locomotive for operation by remote control would be taken out of his break). The first national level consultative meeting with the NUR and ASLEF to discuss these issues took place in February 1976. Then, following a second round of discussions in September 1976, ASLEF formally rejected the RCT scheme but gave management no specific reasons for its decision. In contrast, the NUR agreed to a 12 month trial at Eggborough. However, in agreeing to formal evaluation trials the NUR did not commit itself to accepting the principle of remote control – the union agreed to the trials only on condition that the issue be reviewed afterwards. Management accepted the NUR's conditions and, on this basis, urged ASLEF to reconsider its position on the matter so as to allow extended trials to be conducted at Eggborough in the near future.

While these discussions were in progress, management, under sponsorship from the HQ Operating Department, finalized a £110 000 investment submission for the RCT project, covering the fitting of 12 locomotives with remote control and the outlay for the lineside equipment at the three power stations. The target date for the operational commissioning of the scheme at the three power stations was set for December 1978. The locomotives to be used in the scheme were the new Class 56s due to come into service in BR in 1977–8 to replace the existing Class 47 locomotives. BR's Investment Committee approved the outlay for the scheme in January 1977 and soon thereafter the technical departments undertook to transfer the remote control equipment from the two Class 47 to two Class 56 locomotives, in preparation for evaluation trials of the RCT system at Eggborough, lasting between six and 12 months. The technical departments expected to have the two Class 56 locomotives fitted and ready for trials by July 1977. At this stage, therefore, management was keen to clear the trials with ASLEF as soon as possible so as to be able to keep to the proposed new timescale for the project.

Management, however, was unable to make any breakthrough on the industrial relations front. Thus, in March and again in June and September 1977, ASLEF, in response to further approaches by management, reconfirmed its opposition to the RCT scheme and rejected the idea of trials, arguing that, in view of the current unemployment situation, the union could not agree to allow jobs to be cut from the railway industry. ASLEF's refusal to agree to the trials, however, was also closely linked to the issue of the manning of the new Class 56 locomotives, a question that had been under discussion with management since late 1975. Management wanted the new locomotives to be manned in accordance with the existing manning agreements providing for single-manning under normal circumstances. ASLEF instead insisted that the new locomotives be double-manned in all circumstances. The union never formally linked its acceptance of RCT trials to BR's acceptance of double-manning of Class 56 locomotives. However, in practice, ASLEF let it be known that it was unlikely to cooperate on any scheme involving the new locomotives until management agreed to its request for double-manning.

Given ASLEF's position, management, at this point, was uncertain about how best to proceed with the RCT issue. The HQ Operating Department and the technical departments were in favour of taking up the matter again with ASLEF and, in the case of a negative reply, of informing the unions of management's intention to go ahead with the trials anyway as soon as the two Class 56 locomotives were ready. The Personnel Department, on the other hand, was of the opinion that it would be best not to press ASLEF on the RCT issue until such time as the bigger question of the manning of Class 56 locomotives was resolved. Given the delicate situation with ASLEF, the Personnel Department also argued against taking any unilateral action on the RCT issue, suggesting instead that management leave the matter in abeyance until the manning issue was resolved. In the light of this advice the BR Board and the HQ Operating Department decided not to take any further action on the RCT matter for the time being and to call a halt to all development work on the project. Accordingly, in June 1978, HQ management instructed the technical departments to stop all conversion work on the two Class 56 locomotives until further notice. The adapting and fitting of the remote control equipment to the new locomotives, in fact, had taken the technical departments much longer than originally expected. As a result, the RCT system was not yet in working order by the time HQ management decided to suspend work on the project.

By mid-1978, therefore, 10 years after development work on the project had started, the RCT system was still not fully operational and ready for trials. At the same time the project had not yet been successfully cleared with the unions. Even if ASLEF eventually agreed to the trials, there was no assurance that they would be successful from a technical point of view, or that once they were completed the unions would necessarily agree to the principle of remote control and to the full implementation of the scheme at the three power stations. At this stage therefore, management has to decide what to do about the project. Three broad choices were open to BR, to press ahead with the scheme despite the uncertainties involved, to abandon it, or to start afresh with a new approach.

Case Study Tasks

You have been hired by BR as an external consultant to advise them on improving their decision-making processes with particular reference to the introduction of remotely controlled trains. In particular you have been asked to undertake the tasks listed below. Questions 1–3 are suitable for between one and two hours' work; Questions 4–7 may take longer.

1   What should British Rail do now? Should it:
    a   abandon the scheme
    b   press ahead and introduce it as soon as possible
    c   try an alternative approach?
2   With hindsight, did British Rail take the correct decisions in the early stages (1966–7) of the project, and what do you think was the key decision?

3 What, in your view, were the major causes of the delays in implementing this scheme?
4 How do you feel BR management handled the trade unions? What specific criticisms do you have and what lessons can you suggest for the future?
5 How would you conduct an evaluation of the quality of decision making in this case?
6 How rational do you feel the decision-making process was in this case?
7 What are the lessons from this case for large bureaucratic organizations such as British Rail?

Essential Reading

Lindblom C E (1959) The science of 'muddling through', Public Administration Review 19: 79–88
Mintzberg H Raisingham D Theoret A (1976) The structure of 'unstructured' decision processes, Administrative Science Quarterly 21: 246–275
Wright G (1984) Behavioural Decision Theory: An Introduction, Penguin

Additional Reading

Bonavia M R (1981) British Rail – The First 25 Years, David and Charles
Child J (1984) Organization: A Guide to Problems and Practice, 2nd edition Harper & Row
Cooke S Slack N (1984) Making Management Decisions, Prentice-Hall
Crozier M (1964) The Bureaucratic Phenomenon, University of Chicago Press
Peccei R Guest D (1984) Evaluating the introduction of new technology: the case of word processors in British Rail, in Microprocessors, Manpower and Society, edited by M Warner, Gower
Simon H A (1957) Administrative Behaviour, Macmillan

CASE 8

Power and Politics: TVN

Iain Mangham

Organizational Setting and Background to the Problem

TVN is an independent television company holding the franchise for broadcasting to a large section of the population in the north of England. It was awarded its franchise in 1981, after the previous holders had been deemed by the Independent Broadcasting Authority not to have supplied an adequate service. In particular the previous franchise holder – Instant Appeal Entertainment Corporation – had failed to provide the required number of programmes with local interest and had, with the exception of the period immediately prior to the award of the franchise, resolutely filled the screens at both local and national level with chat shows and entertainment spectaculars. Under the terms of the franchise TVN were mandated to rectify these failings; they were required to create programmes of local interest and supply to the network a balanced diet for viewers. Their franchise comes up for renewal in five years' time.

The senior management group – with whom we shall be particularly concerned in this case study – consists of a number of people from the old franchise holder, Instant Appeal, and a number brought in from other companies (including one from the BBC). The new managing director, Neville Cottingham, a thrusting executive in his mid thirties, has no experience in television, having been recruited by the chairman of TVN to 'give the company some commercial flair'. The chairman also has little experience in television. Cottingham has brought with him as confidant and industrial relations director one of his colleagues, Tom Beverley, from his days at Snowdon Double Glazing. They have been in position for a couple of years, the previous managing director having left to rejoin Instant Appeal in its film division. The sales director, Tom Skidby, in his late fifties, man and boy with Instant Appeal, was one of the original bidders for the franchise and is on the board of TVN, as is Eric Walkington, a man of similar age, again an original signatory for the franchise and currently finance director. Walkington is also an Instant Appeal man, as is the director of programmes, Tony Dancer, who was acting managing director for a period immediately prior to the advent of Neville Cottingham. Dancer is a tall, spare individual with over 20 years' experience as a maker of distinctive television films and a considerable reputation as a scheduler and commissioner of productions. He too has a seat on the board and, as director of programmes, a considerable number of links both formal and informal with the watchdog of the industry – the Independent Broadcasting Authority.

The Problem

The Basic Situation

TVN under its previous managment which, of course, included Dancer, had a reputation for producing international packages – blockbusting megastar programmes full of glitter and showbusiness bazzaz, costing scores of thousands of pounds and selling around the world. Its turnover, although large by industry standards, was but a small part of the business of Instant Appeal and its profits, which were proportionately large, accrued to the parent company. Little of it was returned to TVN in the form of investment, but, on the other hand, little was demanded of TVN in terms of cost control or efficient management. The new company stands alone and both the chairman and Neville Cottingham are determined to render it efficient and effective. To them this means controlling costs and ensuring that TVN enjoys a 'good reputation' with its audiences, with its advertisers, with its employees, with the City and not least with the IBA. This year it is on line to make substantial profits, partly as a result of Dancer's shrewd selection of programmes (which brings in the advertising) and partly as a result of the efforts of the chairman and the managing director to control costs.

The industry as a whole, and particularly the independent sector of it, has a reputation for high spending. Since the government takes a slice of the profits by way of levy, many employees have come to regard money spent on programmes (and upon their own contributions to them) as in some sense not real – money which otherwise would go to the Exchequer. TVN's association with Instant Appeal – the glamorous world of showbusiness – has reinforced this tendency to treat funds with relatively little concern. Throughout TVN, at all levels, the culture of Instant Appeal still prevails. This is particularly true of the Programme Department (controlled by Tony Dancer) which spends millions of pounds annually. Productions regularly run over budget – sometimes by as much as 200 or 300% – and there is a suspicion that very little control is exercised over any programme maker by Dancer or any of his staff, although the overall budget is more often met than not. The culture of the department is such that any attempt at control would be labelled 'interference with creative freedom' and much resented. Dancer himself epitomizes this approach and resolutely refuses to discuss the affairs of what he takes to be his area of responsibility with Cottingham or with anyone else. He bases his refusal on the nature of his appointment (ratified by the IBA and requiring the incumbent of such a position to be a suitable person and not subject to direction by others) and upon the fact that Neville Cottingham, having little experience of television, is not in a position to say what should or should not be done.

Cottingham regards the cavalier approach to expenditure as little short of 'immoral'. In areas that he can control – largely those of direct operations such as engineering or publicity – he has succeeded in reducing costs and in streamlining the operations of the company. Together with his industrial relations director, Tom Beverley, he has confronted the unions over the question of manning and special payments and, after a strike which closed the studios for some weeks (and caused considerable annoyance to the programme makers), he succeeded in imposing some industrial relations discipline on the floor. He has also instituted regular communication meetings with staff at all levels and is, with the notable exceptions of the unions and the programme makers, regarded as 'good news' by a considerable number of those employed at TVN. It is, however, clear to many that his dictat does not extend to the programme department. It is equally clear that he and Dancer are personally antagonistic.

Detailed Information on Problems

The head of engineering, Frank Selby, recruited from another independent TV company and sympathetic towards Cottingham's aims, is not alone in seeing the complexity of issues facing the managing director: 'He is faced with the problem of getting things right fast. Very fast. And he doesn't know the industry well. Lots of neat management techniques, but essentially he is a stranger to what goes on. A breath of fresh air, highly energetic but, no doubt about it, on a collision course with Dancer and those of his men who indulge their fantasies at the company's expense. Trouble is, they have bloody good fantasies. They turn out good programmes, but at a cost. Tony Dancer is a smart operator. I've a very healthy regard for him. He's probably the most able programme director I've worked with, and when I say able I mean in all sorts of ways. He's got a very good head on him. He is able to negotiate on behalf of the company on all sorts of complex matters to do with networking and so on and he's got tons of courage, and if he feels he must do something, he'll pursue it and pursue it and pursue it. Very much his own man, though, and when you put him alongside Neville, a chap with a hell of a track record elsewhere, tremendous rate of achievement, then there is going to be argument, conflict at a level which is higher than the healthy one which ought to exist. Because they both want to do their own bloody thing. A trial of strength.'

Tom Beverley, the industrial relations director, sees things in a similar fashion: 'We've got a number of characters around here who really do have their own individual styles, classically Tony Dancer, very powerful personality, like Neville Cottingham in many senses, got a tremendous ego, very selfish, power conscious, but a completely different way of operating from Neville which he freely acknowledges – boasts about it. He likes to accumulate as much information as he can possibly get and give away as little as he possibly can. Information is power to him. He'll tell people what they need to know and then tell them what to do. That's Tony's style. The creative bit, based on instinct and feel – if it's right, do it and pick up the pieces afterwards or ignore them. Neville would be mortified to hear it and would deny it, but he and Tony are similar in some characteristics, both driven by an urge to have their ideas accepted, but Tony's way of operating is anathema to Neville who is much more open. There are continual clashes between the pair of them and will continue to be and I fear for the result of that because sooner or later there's bound to be a parting of the ways. Who goes and where and when is another matter. The tragedy is that we need both of them to stay.'

Dancer recognizes the issue and reacts to it characteristically: 'It's not up to me to hold people's hands. Neville's a big boy now. If he does not like what I am doing it's up to him to do something about it, not down to me to be running in and out of his office telling him every little thing that's going on. If I am employed as the bloody programme controller, that's what I will do – control the bloody programmes. I'm given an overall budget, I'm told I have to get it right by the company and if they don't think I've got it right they can get rid of me. Don't play games. Either they want me to do the bloody job or they want Neville to do it for me. Can't both do it, particularly when one of us knows less than bugger all about it.'

Matters are brought to a head during a meeting of the Programme Committee. This group has been brought together at the instigation of Neville to bring about better coordination between the programme makers and those who supply the services. It has met on two previous occasions and has a reputation for being the arena in which Tony and Neville offer mock combat to each other. Neville, as perceived by Tony, seeking to 'pry' into programme matters and Tony, as perceived by Neville, determined to exclude all from contact with what he takes to be 'his patch'. The company is offering to the network a new late night programme which is reputed to be 'adult', 'frank' or 'downright offensive' according to one's sensitivities. No one other than the lawyers and the programme makers have seen any of the recorded episodes, but rumour is rife and has been picked up by the newspapers. Neville quotes from one of them:

'I gather from this that, quote "Slamm makes the News of the World and the Sun look tame", unquote; that it quote "is taking on everyone, the Queen, the Royal Family, the Prime Minister, the Opposition, the Judges, the Churches, the Unions . . .", unquote.'

Tony twirling his pencil and lying back in his chair smiles and then begins to laugh quietly.

'I don't know what it is that you find amusing in all of this, Tony. I was asked about Slamm the other day by the Chairman and I had to tell him I knew nothing about it other than it was over budget.'

It's not down to him to know about it. Nor you for that matter.'

'Oh, so I have to learn about what TVN is doing from reading the newspaper, do I? Do I? How the hell am I expected to cope with questions when I don't know the first thing about what is going on? It sounds as though we are in for a rough ride on this one if the leaks are anything to go on: "It is understood that the IBA has censored material which it took to be antisemitic." '

'Untrue. Nothing antisemitic about it.'

'No censorship then?'

'Didn't say that. They took it to be antisemitic. It wasn't. Just a joke about pencil sharpeners: They insisted it come out.'

'What else had to come out, Tony?'

'Look, where is this leading us, Neville? It's my job to deal with the IBA and I'm doing it. Why don't we discuss something important like why it is when I hire freelance producers they can't find a bloody desk to sit down at? Why it is that getting a typewriter around here is like extracting a bloody tooth?'

'I want to talk about programmes, Tony. As managing director I am responsible for this company . . .'

'And I am responsible for its programmes. If you want to talk about them, how about talking about the awards we picked up last month? Two, better than any other independent. Or the ratings, let's talk about the ratings. Three in the top seven last month, that brings in the advertisers, doesn't it? Let's talk about that . . .'

'What about Slamm, Tony, will that get an award? Will that be in the ratings?'

'Don't know. Like all programmes it's a risk and I'm paid to take them.'

'And I'm paid to know about them.'

'All you need to know you can get from The Sunday Times.'

Case Study Tasks

Imagine that you are the managing director, Neville Cottingham. How would you define the situation with which you are confronted? What action(s) would you take and in what sequence? It is as well to remember that the position of TVN on the Stock Market is, as with all such companies, a matter of confidence in those responsible for its direction and that the programme director is a key person to the maintenance of this confidence. Locate your definition and your action(s) within an appropriate theoretical framework. The questions and references below will help you in locating a framework, defining the problem and resolving the issue. Questions 1–3 are appropriate to teaching sessions of one or two hours. Question 4 requires a longer period of study, reading and discussion.

1 What kinds of question does Neville have to ask himself in order to define the situation carefully?
2 Who else should he address his questions to? Why? And what kind of questions should he be asking?
3 What are the options open to Neville after this meeting and what are the likely consequences of each?
4 Assuming something can be done about the Neville–Tony issue, what steps can be taken to ensure that similar issues do not recur?

Essential Reading

Bacharach S B Lawler E J (1980) Power and Politics in Organizations, Jossey Bass
Korda M (1975) Power, Ballantine Books
Pfeffer J (1981) Power in Organizations, Pitman

Additional Reading

Bailey F G (1977) Morality and Expediency, Blackwell
Mangham I L (1985) Power and Performance in Organizations, Blackwell
Mintzberg H (1983) Power in and around Organizations, Prentice-Hall
Salancik G R Pfeffer J (1977) Who gets the power – and how they hold on to it: a
strategic-contingency model of power, Organizational Dynamics 5: 3–21

CASE 9

Organizational Consulting and Development: John Player & Sons

Roy Payne and Bill Reddin

Organizational Setting

This case is about John Player & Sons who make, market and distribute cigarette and pipe tobaccos. They have been doing so since their foundation in the middle of the 19th century. The case describes their situation in the 1970s when a number of things in their internal and external environments were changing, or perceived to be about to change. The case relates parts of their attempts to deal with these changes by describing their retention of a well-known behavioural science consultant to guide his organizational change programme in the company.

Background to the Problem

A Brief History of John Player & Sons

John Player & Sons (JP&S) was originally a family business, engaged primarily in the manufacturing of pipe tobaccos, which together with a number of similar companies combined to form the Imperial Tobacco Company in the early 1900s and now renamed the Imperial Tobacco Group. JP&S is one of the largest two units of the Tobacco Division of the group and is mainly concerned with the manufacture of cigarettes. The company has three cigarette factories in Nottingham and a pipe tobacco factory in Stirling.

At the time of the case study JP&S employed some 6000 factory employees, 2000 staff, 400 supervisors and 250 in management grades.

Company Structure

The Imperial Tobacco Group (ITG) owns other cigarette manufacturers in the UK and these are competitors of JP&S itself. The Board of ITG has its headquarters in Bristol and keeps tight control over policies at all its subcompanies, particularly policies relating to marketing, new product developments, manufacturing techniques and research and development activities. Funds for all these activities and the approval to pursue them were all controlled by ITG. This often meant that managers at JP&S put considerable time into projects for approval by ITG only to have them turned down. Many senior managers at JP&S found this a very frustrating relationship, particularly as they were often not made aware of the wider situation which might have caused ITG to abandon a project.

JP&S had its own board of directors and the chairman was also on the board at ITG, even so he might not be allowed to tell JP&S managers why decisions had been taken by ITG if policies were involved that the board of ITG wished to remain secret. The directors of JP&S were also heads of functions and the organizational structure was typical of a large manufacturing company. The directors were responsible for the departments of production, finance, research and development, marketing and sales, technical engineering, personnel and the 'leaf' department which was responsible for selecting and buying the tobacco leaf itself. With the chairman this meant a group of six directors, one of the functional directors also being vice-chairman. Within each department there were the usual specialist groups found in large manufacturing companies (e.g. training, work study, systems, maintenance, R&D, engineering) and these were hierarchically arranged with first line supervisors in the manufacturing and other large departments such as engineering. Apart from the fact that strategic decision making (as opposed to strategic thinking) was based at ITG (referred to as 'The Centre'), JP&S was a very good example of what Mintzberg (1979) describes as a 'machine bureaucracy'. As he points out, there are problems of both vertical and horizontal integration for large companies with high levels of specialization (Lawrence and Lorsch 1967), and this was true of JP&S. In a document about the organization development (OD) programme the company expressed it this way: 'In the human skeleton articulation occurs at the joints between the bones – for that is where the action is, not in the bones themselves, but between them. So in an organization we should pay more attention than hitherto to the development of effective interfunctional operations'.

While not strictly speaking making it a part of the structure, JP&S had adopted 'management by objectives' in the mid 1960s; to some extent this determined the roles and relationships in the company.

Management by Objectives at JP&S

The mid 1960s saw increased interest in the use of behavioural science by large organizations. JP&S not only availed itself of current ideas about leadership styles and organizational change, but also about management by objectives (MBO), which was then much in vogue. Indeed, this style of approach to changing behaviour fitted comfortably with the production orientation which had prevailed in the company for many years, and since it was still successful in many areas of the company several years after its introduction, it may well have had an influence on the directors of JP&S which led them to seek wider use of behavioural science techniques. For example, they used consultants in ergonomics and social sciences on the design of a new factory (see Clark 1972 for a description). Seventy managers had completed stage 1 of the Blake managerial grid (Blake and Mouton 1964) for training senior management in behavioural science concepts.

By 1970 MBO was working successfully in the marketing and sales, traffic and despatch, purchasing and stores, engineering, 'leaf' and production divisions and was scheduled to be installed in R&D, personnel, and accounts. There was a permanent MBO team to facilitate its installation and development, though the members of the team changed roles regularly to spread the experience throughout the company.

Organizational Climate and Culture

The headquarters of JP&S was located in Nottingham and housed in a group of buildings which were oldish, multistoried and separated by a main road. There were three different production buildings on the site as well as many offices. Despite the elderliness of the buildings the visitor would be quickly impressed by the standard of upkeep, the quality of the furnishings and fabric, and the well dressed, polite staff who greeted visitors. At the time of the organizational change project we are about to describe, the managing director of the company described JP&S as 'benevolently autocractic'. Relationships were noticeably polite and somewhat formal. Staff took trouble to ensure that correct titles were used ('Are you Dr or Mr?'). There were several restaurants where staff could obtain food and each was open only to designated groups of people, the designations being hierarachically determined. If a person was to be promoted from one level to another and this entitled them to eat in the next restaurant up, then they were allowed to take coffee in that restaurant during the weeks before the promotion actually took place. If groups of people from several layers of management wanted to have a working lunch, then they would have to go out of the company to do it.

There was a slightly militaristic air about the company. Even quite senior managers would call the directors 'sir'. The restaurant where the senior managers ate was called 'The Mess'. The directors had their own dining room. The food was of good quality in all restaurants, but it got better the higher you went up the hierarchy, and it also became free at the highest levels.

There were positive attitudes to work at all levels of the company. Work was taken seriously and a failure to adopt this attitude had been known to result in disadvantageous consequences. Since the company paid its employees well, by both local and national standards, it was not easy for most people to find better employment, even in the days of low unemployment that existed in the early 1970s. The company, therefore, had many good quality employees at all levels, a large number of whom had grown up with the company and received most of their training and experience in it. The hierarchical and status conscious values in the company were partly responsible for lowish levels of trust between different levels in the company, though this was exacerbated by a concern for secrecy and confidentiality of information. This secrecy stemmed from a real need to protect the company's innovations in products, but this real concern had broadened into a system of classified

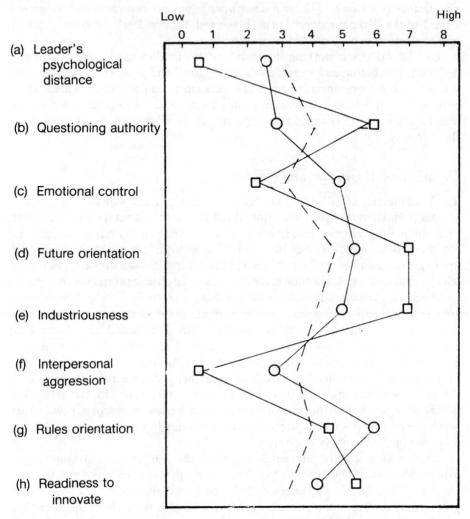

Figure 4 The actual organizational climate in December 1971 (O——O, *n* = 160) as compared with the projected ideal organizational climate (□——□, *n* = 10) and norms from 14 other organizations (– – –, *n* = 357).

information similar to that found in military organizations: managers were graded by their security levels. Salary information was closely guarded in the company and the organization chart was kept only by a handful of directors and senior managers, partly because it showed the nature of the grades in the company and who belonged to them. All correspondence addressed to the consultant was labelled 'confidential', 'strictly confidential', etc. All this combined to create a culture where 'doing things the Player way' was important, not only for day to day relationships, but also for personal success within the company.

While the change programme was being carried out, a survey of the organizational climate as seen by managers was done three times, by the London Business School. The results of the first survey are shown in Figure 4.

Figure 4 shows average scores for eight dimensions of organizational climate taken from the business organization climate index (Payne and Pheysey 1971). The data from JP&S were collected at the end of 1971 when the OD programme had been in existence for over a year, so many managers had had experience of it. Figure 4 shows the climate as seen by 160 managers and supervisors and the JP&S climate is compared to the average scores of 357 individuals from 14 other companies. These were all manufacturing companies, all employed more than 250 people, and some were even larger than JP&S. As the figure shows, JP&S has a climate similar to most other companies though it is higher on emotional control and rules orientation and lower on questioning authority. This picture is consistent with the description already offered. What are perhaps of greater interest are the 'ideal climate' scores. All the directors of JP&S and others who were part of a steering committee for the OD programme were asked to describe the climate they would see as ideal for JP&S. As the figure shows, there is a large discrepancy on all dimensions except rules orientation and readiness to innovate. The senior people at JP&S wanted to reduce the psychological distance of senior people from other staff, to increase the questioning of authority, to decrease the suppression of feelings, to increase planning and industrious behaviour and to decrease interpersonal aggression.

The Problem

Duty

In 1970 the duty on tobacco accounted for over 80% of the ex-factory costs of cigarettes (over £1000 per ton). Because of the huge proportion of the costs taken out by the duty it was possible to make limited adjustments in day to day profits by making minor changes in the amount of moisture in the tobacco in each cigarette. The difference in each cigarette would be negligible and not noticeable by the customer, nor would it spoil enjoyment of the product. For this reason the real criterion of success in the tobacco industry was not so much profit as 'market share'. Holding on to one's market share, or even better increasing it, was vital to sustaining long-term profits, and this was one of the major criteria used by the company to judge itself. Changes in the tax structure in 1978 mean this is not true of the industry today.

Manufacturing and Production

During and after the Second World War the company was able to sell all the cigarettes it could make as the raw material was in short supply. As the availability of tobacco altered during the 1950s the market began to become more competitive and the company was forced by a declining market share to change its marketing strategy. Until the early 1960s, however, the company had been dominated by a production orientation. It had three main factories and its high concern for production is demonstrated by the fact that one of these was used to assess new developments in production technology. In the mid 1960s the idea of building a brand new, technologically advanced production facility was promoted and by 1967 planning was under way. The factory was to be built some miles from the existing sites. During this period of technological transition the autonomy of the individual production factories had been considerably eroded and they were now largely under the control of senior production management. The new factory was intended to take this process even further.

The Market and Marketing

The 1960s had seen a considerable change in the market of JP&S. They had been slow to respond to changes in consumer preferences such as a desire for smaller cigarettes and for filter tips and at one time their market share had dropped to around 25%. This had prompted them to recruit a marketing director and brand managers from industries other than tobacco. This was a great success in that their market share moved back to over 33%, which had been maintained for several years by the time they approached W J Reddin to assist them with changing their organization. The success of the new marketing function and the power it developed threatened the primacy of the production function, though as Clark (1972) points out the two functions were physically separated and, although they involved two groups of people with very different backgrounds, values, training and habits, this physical separation enabled each to ignore the other to some extent. Nevertheless, relationships between the two functions were beginning to cause concern. The market of JP&S was also about to change as a result of Britain's entry into the EEC. This would not only lead to increased competition but would involve changes in the laws affecting additives and thus the blending of cigarette tobaccos, as well as the duty structure. One important implication of the latter was that JP&S needed to add to its products a cigarette to compete at the top end of the price range. The John Player Special was launched to fill this gap in their product range while the Reddin programme was being carried out.

Other Environmental Changes

Apart from the above influences on the market there were other changes which were beginning to influence the tobacco industry. The most obvious was the government legislation about placing health warnings on packaging and limiting advertising in other ways. This also created pressure from various consumer groups and other lobbies, making the whole tobacco industry sensitive to its public relations image. Many resources were being put into public relations and into research on new smoking materials which would not have the negative health consequences associated with tobacco. All this was also occurring at a time when ITG was diversifying into food and other industries. This meant that resources for developments within JP&S itself were carefully scrutinized by 'The Centre'. A more general environmental change recognized by JP&S was the increasing acceptance in British industry, commerce and government that employees desired and deserved more say in decisions about company practices, procedures and plans. This was combined with increasing trade union demands for information and participation which JP&S realized might be enforced by entry into the EEC. JP&S had a well-defined relationship with the Tobacco Workers Union on the production side and with the craft unions on the engineering side of the business; but there was growing pressure for unionization on the staff side which was agreed some years later, but was at the time an additional source of instability. The company also had a 'no redundancy' policy, but both they and the trade unions, which were trying to gain entry into the company, could see the implications of a situation where the market was likely to decline due to the health issue. The market has indeed declined, as is well known. In summary JP&S was facing turbulence from market, political, technological and internal organizational forces.

Choosing an OD Programme

As previously mentioned, the senior management at JP&S had considerable interest in, and exposure to, behavioural science by 1970, including the Blake managerial grid. The first stage of this six-stage OD programme makes managers focus on their managerial style. The central tenet of the Blake managerial grid is that there is one best style of managing. This ideal style is one in which the manager simultaneously has a high concern for getting the job done, and doing it well, and a high concern for developing and using the people he is managing. Managers who concentrate on the task at the expense of people are less effective, and managers who concentrate on the people at the expense of the task are equally ineffective.

Although most managers felt they had enjoyed the Blake course and profited from it, the senior management were not totally convinced and stopped sending managers. They also decided not to do other stages of the Blake programme concerned with team development and interfunction relationships. Instead, they continued to explore other approaches to OD, both in the United States and the UK. After this exploratory period they decided to retain W J Reddin to develop and implement a major OD programme to be called the 'organizational effectiveness programme'.

The Reddin Organizational Effectiveness Programme

Reddin's OD programme has many similarities to that of Blake and other OD consultants who adopt an organization-wide approach to planned change. The majority of OD consultants with this approach start by changing and/or socializing individual managers so that all managers share a common conceptual framework, language and values about what makes organizations effective. Next the focus is on changing relationships within teams of managers, and then between teams and across functions, etc. All these activities are carried out using processes consistent with the philosophy taught to individual managers so that a new culture is created.

Table 3 Three-dimensional organizational effectiveness programme

Stage	Designed to improve	Primary results	Duration	Who attends
1 Managerial effectiveness seminar	Managerial effectiveness	Managerial effectiveness improved Flexibility increased Preliminary objectives established	Five days	Each manager from top man down in groups of 12–36. Teams of four managers who work together. Focus is on examining style, learning the Reddin concepts and language, and improving working in teams by sharing feedback on style and performance. Intensive experience involving long hours and for many managers is first experience of being informed about the effects of their behaviour.
2 Team role laboratory	Team role structure	Team objectives established Team reorganized if necessary Teamwork methods introduced	Three days	A manager and his subordinates focus on their styles and working relationships and make plans to change them. As people know each other well and have to work together this can be a very powerful change experience for both individuals and teams. The manager has normally been through this as a subordinate of his superior.
3 Managerial effectiveness conference	Managerial objective setting	Managerial objectives confirmed Superior–subordinate blockages removed Coaching relationships established	Half day	Each manager and a single subordinate discuss progress and work on blocks in their relationships which might be inhibiting their effectiveness. It is designed to be a two-way exchange.

4	Corporate strategy laboratory	Organization policies and design	Organization diagnosis made Organization policies reconsidered Organization structure reconsidered	Three days	The executive committee or top team works together to consider objectives, strategy, etc. Team-working process also examined to ensure they are effective and to continue learning about team processes.
5	Team effectiveness conference	Team objective setting	Progress toward team objectives reviewed Additional team objectives set Blockages inhibiting team cleared	One day	Same as team role laboratory. They see if they have achieved changes planned at TRL and discuss blocks, design ways to remove them, etc.
6	Interteam effectiveness conference	Horizontal team effectiveness	Interteam blockages removed Interteam effectiveness standards established Interteam optimum operating arrangements agreed	One day	Members of two departments or functions. They share images of each other, remove blocks and make action plans to change working relationships.
7	Divisional effectiveness conference	Vertical team effectiveness	Multiple levels agree on objectives Vertical information flow increased Resistance to change decreased	One day	Vertical slice of managerial levels who work in small teams to brainstorm company problems and suggestions for improvements which top team respond to, giving reasons for acceptance or rejection.
8	Work-unit idea conference	Worker commitment	Foreman–worker relationship strengthened Work flows modified Unit output increased	Half day	Foreman and workers generate ideas for improvements which manager has to respond to.
9	Corporate effectiveness conference	Organization-wide commitment	Corporate objectives and policies clarified Objectives and policies accepted	Half day	Top man meets all managers and some workers in group meetings to present policy and get feedback.

Finally, all parts of the organization agree objectives and plans for the future development of the company. Reddin has designed nine stages in his programme and they can be used in varying combinations and at varying intervals to suit the particular company. These stages are described elsewhere (Reddin 1970).

Table 3 describes the main stages, their objectives and briefly what and who they involve. In practice most companies send their managers to Stage 1, the 'managerial effectiveness seminar'. As the first stage in the programme it teaches the basic concepts and ideas around which much of the rest of the programme is built. Reddin's model of managerial effectiveness differs from Blake's in that it proposes that there are several styles of management which can be effective because different situations demand different managerial behaviours. Getting a task completed effectively might best be done by a task-centred style, but developing a person's interpersonal skills might best be done by a people-centred style. In Reddin's model there are four effective styles of managing, and four less effective styles of managing. Both sets of styles are derived from the same two dimensions used by Blake and other theorists of leadership: these are concern for task and concern for people, or in Reddin's terminology, task-oriented and relationship-oriented styles. If each of these two dimensions is dichotomized into high and low, this produces four basic styles: high on both task and relationships, low on both task and relationships, high on task and low on relationships, and low on task but high on relationships. According to Reddin any one of these four basic styles will be effective if it is used in a situation which demands that style of behaviour. Any of the styles will be ineffective if they are used in situations which demand some other style. Reddin has developed a quite comprehensive set of concepts and methods for assessing both managerial styles and situational demands.

Much time is spent at the managerial effectiveness seminar learning these concepts, analysing style and situational demands, and planning how to make the two more compatible and thus increase managerial and organizational effectiveness. The same conceptual frameworks are used in other stages of the organizational effectiveness programme, particularly the 'team role laboratory', but the fundamental aim is to give people throughout the company a common language and framework for designing and running the organization.

Most of these stages are held away from the work site to ensure that participants are not interrupted and to intensify the learning experience. In JP&S Stage 3 was not performed because this sort of activity was carried out within the MBO scheme. Stage 8 was not done either because the programme did not include supervisors, though it was expected it might extend to that level eventually.

By June 1970 the directors of JP&S had all attended the managerial effectiveness seminar and they had had two team role laboratories both led by Bill Reddin. At this point, and after consultation with senior managers, they decided to implement a full-scale organizational effectiveness programme. At the end of two years 324 managers had taken part in the managerial effectiveness seminars, there had been 30 team role laboratories, four inter-team effectiveness conferences, two divisional effectiveness conferences, 15 follow-ups of the team role laboratories (called team effectiveness conferences) and 30 other meetings directly concerned with the organizational effectiveness programme. At a conference two years later a team from JP&S reported on the programme. The formal programme had just finished though there was to be a general continuation of the OD expertise acquired by the company. Their report reads, 'A very conservative estimate of the time involvement so far in the formal stages of the organizational effectiveness programme by level of management is:

chairman	40 person days
directors (6)	260
senior managers (40)	800
middle managers (60)	900
junior managers (210)	1500
total	3500 or 15 person manager years.'

Case Study Tasks

The questions below relate to the design of organization development in a company anticipating change. They should be worked through in the order given.

1 *Formal agreement* The consultant drafted a formal agreement which he wanted the company to sign. Several elements in it were to test their commitment to the programme and to take change seriously. If you were the OD consultant would you get a written agreement? Give reasons for your answer.

   Assume you did decide to get a written agreement, what sorts of things would you put into it and why?

2 *Designing the Organizational Effectiveness Committee* At the start of the programme an Organizational Effectiveness Committee was established. This was a steering committee for the programme. Who do you think ought to be on such a committee? What would you set as its main tasks or roles and to whom would you have the committee report? Explain your decisions.

3 *Selection of internal consultants* It was agreed with JP&S that there would be three internal consultants selected from the existing workforce to organize and facilitate the programme for two or three years. Their main work would be to conduct the managerial effectiveness seminars and the team role laboratories and to generally administer the programme internally: choose hotels, arrange schedules, assemble course material, decide who would attend in consultation with line and staff managers, etc. They would be trained by Reddin and his consultant colleagues.

   Given what you know about JP&S and the OD programme, what criteria would you use to select these internal consultants? Why?

4 *Team building design* A large number of team role laboratories were held. The first was for the senior management team and was conducted by Reddin alone. Then, an outside consultant assisted him with the six team role laboratories for the next two levels down and the internal consultants took the process further down the organization. The team role laboratories were held in hotels away from the work site and started at 5.30 pm on the first day and finished at 12.30 pm on

the fourth day. There was no formal teaching in the usual sense. Team members were all from real working groups and were asked to complete some pre-laboratory work before starting the actual laboratory. This work was used to raise issues in the laboratory and the team had to reach consensus about what they wanted to change: how, when, who, etc.

What sorts of issues and/or activities would you get members to think about as pre-laboratory work to such a team-building exercise? What issues, if any, would you try to avoid? Give reasons.

5 *Objectives for the organizational effectiveness programme*   The directors agreed an initial set of objectives for the programme. If you were a director of this company what sorts of objectives would you set for this sort of programme? Why?

6 *Likelihood of achieving objectives*   Given what you know about JP&S and the organizational effectiveness programme, how likely do you think it is that the programme will have achieved the objectives you have set for it? Justify your views.

You may find it useful to rate each objective on the following scale:

Likely to have achieved this objective	Likely to have made some progress	Unlikely to have achieved this objective

7 *Changing the climate in JP&S*   Given the size, scope and nature of the OD programme, to what extent do you think the climate at JP&S might have moved towards, or away from, the 'ideal climate' described by the directors and members of the Organizational Effectiveness Committee as it is shown in Figure 4?

Essential Reading

Beckhard R (1969) Organization Development Strategies and Models, Addison-Wesley

Golembiewski R T (1979) Approaches to Planned Change, Part II: Macro-level Interventions and Change Agent Strategies, University of Georgia Press

Additional Reading

Argyris C (1970) Intervention Theory and Method, Addison-Wesley

Argyris C Schön D A (1974) Improving Professional Practice, Jossey-Bass

Blake R Mouton J S (1964) The Managerial Grid, Gulf Publishing

Bowers D W (1973) OD techniques and their results in 23 organizations, Journal of Applied Behavioral Science 9: 21–43

Clark P A (1972) Organizational Design: Theory and Practice, Tavistock

Lawrence P R Lorsch J W (1967) Organization and Environment, Harvard University Press

Legge K (1984) Evaluating Planned Organizational Change, Academic Press

Mintzberg H (1979) The Structuring of Organizations, Prentice-Hall

Mirvis P Berg D (1977) Failures in Organization Development and Change, John Wiley

Payne R L Pheysey D C (1971) G Stern's organizational climate index: a reconceptualization and application to business organizations, Organizational Behaviour and Human Performance 6: 77–98

Porras J L Berg P O (1978) The impact of organization development, The Academy of Management Review 3: 249–266

Reddin W J (1970) Managerial Effectiveness, McGraw-Hill

Reddin W J (1971) Effective Management by Objectives, Business Publications

Reddin W J (1975) Every manager's clear responsibility, Management in Action January

Reddin W J (1978) A consultant confesses, Management Today, January

Spooner P (1973) Players assesses the value of its OD shake-up, Business Administration 1973: 362–365

Watzlawick P Weakland J Fisch R (1974) Change: Principles of Problem Formation and Problem Resolution, W W Norton

CASE 10

Small Businesses: Family Firms and Management – J. & S. Nicholson Ltd.

Robert Goffee and Richard Scase

Organizational Setting

J and S Nicholson Ltd is a family-owned construction company with 150 employees in the south of England. Its trading activities include house construction, small-scale repair and renovation, interior fitting and industrial development. This case focuses on a set of key managerial and organizational issues confronting the founder and managing director, Jim Nicholson, at a critical point in the development of the business.

Background to the Problem

Jim Nicholson established his business in 1960 at the age of thirty. Previously, he had always worked in the construction industry, first as a labourer and later as an apprenticed carpenter. For 10 years he worked in the joinery department of a large national construction company where he was promoted from supervisor to manager. He then left to start his own business partly because he wanted more independence and partly because he felt that, in the long run, he would earn more money. He began as a self-employed individual, concentrating on small-scale repair and renovation. However, the business rapidly expanded and within two years he employed 20 men. This success was largely based upon his technical skills – the firm quickly gained a reputation for high quality work – and his ability to weld together a team of tradesmen into a highly productive working group. In common with many owners of small businesses, Nicholson led 'by example'. He spent much of his time engaged in manual work alongside his employees. He regularly worked the same hours as them and shared their general physical day to day working conditions. He paid himself the same rate of pay as them and while he benefited from the profits, his employees received annual bonuses for their high productivity. He kept his office administration to a minimum and he personally undertook the 'paper work' and 'book-keeping' in the evenings and at weekends so as not to interfere with his day to day productive activity.

However, as the business expanded, Nicholson's direct involvement in operative work diminished and he became increasingly concerned with the negotiation of new contracts and office administration. He was able to withdraw by carefully selecting highly skilled employees who were able to work independently and responsibly. Indeed, the opportunity to take decisions 'on the job' both increased work satisfaction and allowed the necessary flexibility for coping with the unpredictable circumstances of building work. His workforce, then, was both highly motivated and productive. This earned them high wages and good bonuses and reinforced their commitment to the business.

Four years after start-up, Jim Nicholson asked his brother Steven, who had been working as an assistant contracts manager in a local building firm, to join the business. He had four major motives. First, there was a need for additional managerial skills because of the growing administrative workload in the business. Second, his brother was able to inject the additional funds necessary to pay for new business premises. In addition, Steven had many good business contacts in the local building industry. The most important consideration, however, was the family tie. Jim felt that only a family member could be entrusted with a share in the ownership and control of the business.

By relinquishing operative work and delegating various administrative responsibilities to his brother, Jim had more time for initiating and developing new projects. By the mid-1970s the business had grown and diversified, first into house construction and industrial development, and then into interior fittings. This brought about organizational changes and the need for a management structure. But an extensive functional hierarchy did not develop. Instead, Jim created a holding company (owning 100% of the shares in its subsidiaries) which was 50 : 50 owned by himself and his brother. Beneath this, three separate subsidiary companies were established, first for small works and for construction, and later for interior fitting. According to Jim, such a structure had several advantages. He felt that it reduced the overhead costs of an extensive managerial hierarchy and encouraged flexible decision making which is necessary for operating efficiently in the building industry. Furthermore, it enabled day to day decision making to be delegated to the senior managers of each subsidiary company. Yet, at the same time, this structure allowed Nicholson to retain tight overall control since each of the subsidiary companies was a separate cost centre for which budgets could be drawn and operating performances could be clearly and regularly assessed.

Each of the three subsidiaries had separate boards with Jim Nicholson acting as chairman for the small works and construction subsidiaries and Steven Nicholson as chairman of the interior fitting subsidiary. Managing director of the small works subsidiary was Reg Walker, aged 56, who had joined the firm as a carpenter in its early days and subsequently worked his way up to achieve his current position in 1975. Alan Pearson, aged 43, was managing director of the construction subsidiary and had joined the firm in 1974 after a successful career with a large national contractor. At the interior fitting subsidiary the managing director was Graham

Jackson, aged 39, who had joined the company in 1970 and played an important role in the establishment of the third subsidiary in 1978. On the main board of the holding company Jim Nicholson, always the more dominant and active of the brothers, was both chairman and managing director, Steven Nicholson was a second director and an experienced accountant, Graham Sharpe, sat as financial director.

By the early 1980s, then, Nicholsons was a well established business which had successfully grown and diversified while, at the same time, retaining the 'feel' of a family firm. Essentially, the Nicholson brothers still owned the business, played a key part in its management, and were able to retain close, face to face contact with all of their employees. But they had also recruited and developed a management team which enabled them partially to relinquish their personal involvement in many day to day business matters. By early 1982, however, Jim Nicholson faced a series of problems which threatened the long-term viability of the business.

The Problem

To understand the problems it is necessary to describe in more detail the ethos of the company and the attitudes of several key senior managers. Although expansion had required the introduction of more formalized control procedures, there was still a remarkable absence of rigid rules and working practices. Work continued to be organized largely through personal and informal systems of consultation within which Jim, as founder, owner and managing director, played a key role. This helped to maintain the culture of a family firm where 'personalities' mattered more than 'plans', 'structures' or 'hierarchies'. Nicholson's employees valued the informal atmosphere of the business and the fact that, as one commented 'you did not feel like a small cog in a great big wheel'. The senior managers also felt that an absence of rigid job definitions gave them the autonomy and scope for initiative which they would not enjoy in a larger firm. Indeed, many explained, with considerable pleasure, that their jobs were quite unlike those which they saw described in management text-books.

Although Jim Nicholson regarded the maintenance of cost-effective, informal, personal and flexible work practices as an important part of his job, he was also concerned to promote 'professionalism' within the business. As he remarked, 'We got the business to where it is largely on the basis of gifted amateurs. But it's got beyond that stage now. It's got to be run by professional managers, to a degree. However, the moment we lose the entrepreneurial flair we start to go downhill.'

Graham Sharpe, the financial director, was a strong supporter of the need to professionalize: 'Increasingly, we have got to recruit people of higher technical standards. We cannot rely on the guy that's drawn himself up by his bootlaces . . . . We have got to pick up men who are of a higher technical standard, with, of course, first class experience in the industry.'

Despite this perceived need to professionalize, Jim Nicholson continued to place overriding emphasis upon first-hand industrial experience as a prerequisite for effective management. As he said, 'One of our strengths as a company is that right at the top we all have technical experience, in detail, of what our business is all about. I can do the job of any one of my contracts managers. I've done surveying. I've done estimating. We've come up from the bottom. So no one can pull the wool over my eyes. I've kept a feel for what's going on . . . I've never got too remote.'

Generally, Jim Nicholson's eye for detail and personal involvement in the business helped to motivate employees at all levels. He had a particularly good relationship with the skilled craftsmen in the small works subsidiary, which he often visited 'to see how things were going' and have 'a chat with the men'. Contact with Reg Walker, the managing director of the small works subsidiary, was especially close; both had backgrounds in carpentry and they had a deep mutual respect for each other's skills and technical abilities. According to Reg, he and Jim Nicholson were able to reach decisions 'almost by a process of telepathy'.

Jim's relationship with Alan Pearson was rather different. Pearson had progressed from a management traineeship with a large national contractor to become a senior contracts manager before joining Nicholsons as managing director of the construction subsidiary. He had been attracted by Jim Nicholson's personality and the opportunity to work in a smaller firm where, in his words 'manuals, procedures and technical specifications weren't everything'. Nevertheless, from Jim Nicholson's point of view, Pearson was valuable precisely because he possessed the technical competence to undertake the more standardized large-scale industrial projects which became increasingly important within the business in the late 1960s and early 1970s.

The relationship of the two men had not always been easy. Jim was sometimes disappointed with Pearson's inability to take initiatives and develop new projects in construction. For his part, Alan Pearson felt 'limited by the fact that too often I'm not the master of my own destiny. While I've been gradually developing new ideas Jim has suddenly come in with a project that requires everything else to be dropped.' Nevertheless, the two men recognized each others' talents and were frequently able to sort out their differences in a personal and amicable fashion.

The most pressing and immediate problem facing Jim Nicholson related to the situation with the interior fittings subsidiary. The managing director, Graham Jackson, was widely regarded as a 'high flier'. After joining as a foreman in the small works subsidiary he rapidly established a close relationship with Jim Nicholson, who was impressed by his technical abilities, application and imaginative flair. It was Jackson who first alerted Jim Nicholson to the potential market in interior fitting for retail outlets, restaurants, pubs and hotels. The first fitting contracts which were undertaken had been initiated and managed by Jackson almost single-handedly. This success quickly led to the establishment of the interior fitting subsidiary in 1978 with Jackson, still only 33, its managing director. With the severe contraction in new house construction and industrial development work after 1979, the interior fittings subsidiary represented over 50% of the total trading turnover of the subsidiaries by 1982; construction had contracted to 30% and small works accounted for 20%.

Steven Nicholson had been chairman of the interior fittings subsidiary from its inception. In the early days he and Graham Jackson had worked well together. Steven, a more cautious and less dominant personality than his brother, had complemented Graham Jackson's forceful entrepreneurial style. In addition, his local contacts had proved useful in establishing trade. But as the subsidiary became more successful, Jackson felt increasingly constrained by Steven. Indeed, the relationship was the cause of considerable dissatisfaction for Graham Jackson. He was becoming frustrated by what he saw as Steven Nicholson's 'interference'. Like his brother, Steven tried to keep closely involved with developments but, in Graham Jackson's view, he lacked the business sense of Jim Nicholson. As Graham remarked, 'Without a shadow of doubt Steven would like to know everything that's going on. But to be quite honest, he hasn't got the positive business mind of Jim. I break things down into simple elements and build on them and so does Jim. But Steven's mind works differently. He makes it more complicated and we end up going around in circles. I'm positive. I find out what the problem is, talk about it, resolve how to get on with it, then do it. With Steven we just do an awful lot of talking and never get anywhere. As chairman he should be looking more at the business *over all* and he should have more confidence in the people he's got.'

Further, Jackson felt that too much time was being wasted in debating key managerial decisions: 'The essence of this game, unlike manufacturing, is making decisions on the spot. This is a risk business and the only way I can be effective and profitable and successful is to make decisions based on instinct. You can't go back to the board on every decision because no decisions would be made. You'd be floundering!'

The way Jackson now coped was to 'just get on with it, so that by the time Steven finds out, it's hopefully too late!' As he said, 'I've learnt to keep things quiet – especially on the big jobs. Otherwise I know I'm going to be bombarded with questions that'll disrupt my life for at least three days – and I can't afford that time. Quite often now the contracts are all tied up before Steven even knows about them. It's led to a few rows, but what else can I do?'

Jackson was also dissatisfied by what he saw as a serious communication block within the company as a whole. In his view, Steven impeded rather than facilitated communication with Jim Nicholson. As he expressed it, 'I think that Jim, with all his business commitments, wants to talk to fewer people now. He'd rather talk to me through Steven. But the problem is this. Jim will make a suggestion to Steven, Steven will then make it to me and I may say it's not possible. But Steve, because Jim has said it to him, will try and force the view on me. Then we get to a situation, like last week, where I have to refuse point blank to go along with something. It was an impossible situation. As a result, Jim came down direct to see me. We went out to lunch together and within 10 minutes we'd sorted it out. Communicating through Steven to Jim it's too rigid – there's no flexibility. But sitting down with Jim, it was all resolved in 10 minutes!'

There were problems, according to Jackson, in communicating with the other subsidiaries. There were no formal meetings between the senior management of each subsidiary and the information which was passed on by Steven to him often seemed designed only to create competition and justify criticism. As he explained, 'I'm always being hit over the head by Steven on our cash forecasting. He says it's not accurate enough. But it's very difficult in this business. There are so many different types of cash flow on each contract. Sometimes you've got an advanced payment, other times a hire purchase agreement. Sometimes a standard agreement, other times, special terms. But according to Steven we're not as good as Construction. Well, a month ago I thought I'd talk to Construction. I had a big conversation with their financial director and found out that his cash forecast was no better than mine!'

Finally, Graham Jackson was also unhappy about his future prospects in the business. In his view, the potential for expansion in the interior fittings subsidiary, particularly given the renewed interest in 'design' amongst major national retail chains, was enormous. But he wondered whether a substantial personal commitment to the company would be appropriately rewarded in the long term. One of the reasons for this were the strong rumours that Steven Nicholson intended to employ his son in the interior fittings subsidiary in order to 'groom' him for an eventual managerial position. (Jim Nicholson was married but had no children.) In this context Jackson had begun to reassess his career prospects and his future in Nicholsons. He summed up his feelings as follows: 'Essentially, I suppose, I've always wanted to work for myself. In fact, I almost took a chance a few years ago but I felt I wasn't ready. Working here has certainly enabled me to head up a business but its not the same as being your own boss. I'm still answerable to someone else. I'm disillusioned because I thought this was the next best thing. But I'm beginning to wonder now. It's a shame because Jim Nicholson has marvellous, almost inspirational qualities and, as a person, I still have a lot of time for Steven. But what's my future here? When it comes down to it, this is the Nicholsons' business and I suppose the family's interests will always come first. Maybe I've got no alternative but to go and set something up on my own.'

Jim Nicholson was aware of the problems at the interior fittings subsidiary, and concerned about their immediate and longer term implications. Relations with Steven had always been amicable but Jim had long been disappointed with his brother's reticence to take business initiatives and his concern with 'the wrong sort of detail – the administrative niceties rather than getting the job done and the bottom line!' Nevertheless, Steven *did* have administrative skills and he had always used his local contacts to facilitate business deals and promote the good name of Nicholson's within the community. In the long term, however, it was clear to Jim that Steven, despite being five years his junior, had neither the capacity nor the desire to take on overall charge of the business.

Who, then, would eventually succeed him? Certainly Graham Jackson looked as if he had the right combination of technical skills and entrepreneurial flair – and his links with Jim had always been close. But Jim Nicholson had been disturbed by reports from his brother that Jackson had deliberately deceived him over two recent contracts and Graham Sharpe, the financial director, had recently complained about Jackson's 'uncooperative attitude' towards him in the calculation of actual and budgeted expenditure (the main method of financial control over the subsidiaries). There was even some talk that he was thinking of leaving Nicholson's. In Jim's eyes this signalled a lack of commitment in Jackson which would make promotion in the near future impossible. However, Jim Nicholson did not seriously consider Reg Walker and Alan Pearson as potential successors. Reg Walker's strengths derived from his loyalty rather than independence, his technical skills rather than market awareness. Alan Pearson was more a 'manager than an entrepreneur' and his approach was appropriate primarily for the type of large-scale construction project which now formed a diminishing part of Nicholson's overall business.

The succession issue, then, was Jim's biggest worry. Now in his mid-fifties he was increasingly attracted by the idea of passing on the managing directorship and withdrawing to a less onerous role as chairman. In fact, a recent heart complaint and a severe warning from his doctor about 'overworking' had made him determined to resign as managing director within two years. But without recruiting from outside the firm this now looked impossible. More immediately, however, there was the problem of reconciling the interests of his brother and Graham Jackson. The interior fittings subsidiary was now too important to be jeopardized by what he saw as a series of increasingly bitter personal squabbles. But what could he do to keep Graham Jackson without, at the same time, damaging relations with his brother?

Case Study Tasks

Review the development of Nicholson's and identify the background factors which help to explain Jim's difficulties in withdrawing as managing director and the conflict between Steven Nicholson and Graham Jackson. The more specific questions listed below relate to some of the factors involved.

1 List the major problems facing Jim Nicholson.
2 How would you describe Jim Nicholson's managerial and leadership style? How did it affect others?
3 Was Jim Nicholson right to bring his brother Steven into the business?
4 What were the managerial consequences of the decision to establish a holding company with subsidiaries?

  Now imagine that you are Jim Nicholson.

5 How would you attempt to deal with the problems of the interior fittings subsidiary?
6 Assuming you intend to resign as managing director within two years, who would you appoint as your successor?
7 Would you restructure the companies? If so, how? How would you see the organization developing in the long run?

Essential Reading

Goffee R Scase R (1982) Fraternalism and paternalism as employer strategies in small firms, in Diversity and Decomposition in the Labour Market, edited by G Day, Gower
Goffee R Scase R (1985) Proprietal control in family firms: some functions of quasi-organic management systems, Journal of Management Studies 22: 53–68
Scase R Goffee R (1980) The Real World of the Small Business Owner, Croom Helm, Chapter 5

Additional Reading

Child J (1984) Organization: a Guide to Problems and Practice, 2nd edition, Harper & Row, Chapter 4

Mintzberg H (1979) The Structuring of Organizations, Prentice-Hall

Salaman G (1977) An historical discontinuity: from charisma to routinisation, Human Relations 30: 373–388

Scase R Goffee R (1982) The Entrepreneurial Middle Class, Croom Helm

Tavistock Institute of Human Relations (1976) Interdependence and Uncertainty: A Study of the Building Industry, Tavistock

CASE 11

Organizational Structure: Gamma Appliances

Andrew Kakabadse

Background and Problem

'Well, that has been most fruitful', said Timothy Edwards, senior consultant with Human Resource International Inc. 'It's imperative that we meet again, but this time with Bert Fischer and at your head office. You have my CV to give him?' continued Timothy. Felix Benjamin, Director of Operations Control (DOC) of Gamma Appliances nodded, shook hands with Timothy and left. Timothy sat down, reflected on the meeting and flipped through his notes.

The meeting had been arranged at the request of Felix Benjamin. He had said that he wished to talk with a consultant who could help key personnel in his organization manage imminent changes. At the meeting, he had stated that his organization had already implemented substantial changes. Timothy had paid special attention to the history of the company.

In the topsy-turvy world of electronic office equipment, Gamma Appliances, a subsidiary of a large multi-national American corporation, had shown a healthy profit in the 1960s and early 1970s, but its performance was beginning to slip. Gamma, with its head office in the north-east of England, had recently begun to show a dip in profits, and latterly a loss, exemplified by the following figures:

1974	£3.75 million profit
1975	£3.10 million profit
1976	£3.10 million profit
1977	£2.30 million profit
1978	£1.60 million profit
1979	£½ million profit
1980	£50 000 loss.

The American parent company had decided to appoint an American as chief executive officer (CEO) on the departure of the previous incumbent in early 1980.

On his arrival, this new CEO stated that he would not tolerate any further losses. He acknowledged that Gamma faced certain problems that might take some time to put right. However, he expected that by late 1981 the company would break even. He did not expect the situation to change in 1982, but by 1983/4 the company should be showing a healthy profit.

Gamma Appliances currently manufactures a range of office reprographic equipment, varying from small portable photocopiers to the latest, large, sophisticated electronic photocopiers. On certain product lines, the company had wasted time, money and effort in updating them. On other lines, despite minor design changes, the company had manufactured the same product line for the past seven years.

Hank White, the new CEO appointed to Gamma, was aware of the problems he confronted. Although no one had stated it, he knew that, as far as the parent company was concerned, he had only a limited period of time (unspecified) to turn the company around. Hank had worked in the field of electronic engineering most of his life. He recognized that the parent company had only a limited interest in reprographic equipment, as it had diversified substantially into other fields. He saw the parent company really as a finance house, managing a number of separate businesses, and really not too sympathetic if any of those businesses did not perform to expectation.

It was recognized in the USA that other key positions needed to be filled. A few months later, Bert Fischer had been appointed as director of business services (DBS). The only other new appointment was that of Felix Benjamin, as director of operations control (DOC), in January 1981, when the post became vacant. The board was completed by four other directors in the areas of personnel, product manufacture, product design and financial control together with the company secretary. These last five directors were British and had all been in the company for at least five years.

White had almost immediately introduced a policy of cost cutting. In 1980, the company had three manufacturing plants. The smallest and least profitable plant, at Kenworth, was sold in April 1980. The labour force was made redundant or remained with the new owner. The remaining two plants at Texford and Followfield experienced cuts. By December 1980 an organization of 5320 employees had been cut to 3478.

According to Benjamin he was appointed to continue with this uncompromising policy. He considers his track record to be the reason he was offered the job. One of his previous positions was as director of production with a British medical equipment manufacturer. He had found their key plants to be badly mismanaged. The problems he had identified were as follows: poor product quality, inability to meet project completion dates, supervisors who had lost control of the workforce, and high labour turnover.

After substantial negotiation and opposition from his colleagues (in that previous job), Benjamin had won the backing of a majority on the board in the company to implement a policy of forcing the unions to maintain existing agreements concerning product quality, levels of supervision, overtime payments, bonus payments and timekeeping on the shop floor. As expected, this led to a series of strikes.

The strikes eventually petered out because the management did not back down. Benjamin states that he used this period of disruption as an opportunity to force some of his senior management colleagues in the company to resign. He considered them to be the real reason why the key plant had become unproductive. According to Benjamin, he manufactured a situation of strikes and confrontation in order to break the power of the unions over shopfloor operators and to force certain key managers in the organization to resign. After the strikes, this plant became one of the most productive in the company.

Benjamin continued to mastermind White's redundancy programme at Gamma, with the cooperation of the personnel department, concerning the managerial, professional and administrative staff. Up to today (November 1982) he has made 372 staff redundant. Further, Benjamin has attempted to examine the operating expenses of the business services division. This division is the revenue-earning part of the organization – it sells the photocopying equipment. Despite substantial opposition from Fischer and other senior managers, Benjamin has forced the following changes:

1   The company car policy has been revised. Previously, all sales and senior marketing personnel had been given a large, status car for their own use. Currently sales and marketing executives are offered a car in the medium-sized saloon range.
2   High performing sales persons were rewarded by money bonuses or free annual holidays to Europe, the Bahamas, etc. These have now been cut.
3   Additional administrative cuts and cost-saving exercises have been introduced.

The relationship between Fischer and Benjamin seems tense. Benjamin reports that Fischer resents his attempts to tighten up the business services division, as Fischer was appointed to do just that. Benjamin states that Fischer is incompetent and was only appointed as he is a long-established manager in the parent company and a personal friend of the CEO.

It was no surprise that Benjamin reported that morale within both management and workforce was low. He also considered management to be ineffectual and ineffective. The reason Benjamin had approached Timothy Edwards was that the company needed to concentrate on ways of increasing revenue. The cost-cutting exercise is virtually complete. No one in the company has considered ways of increasing revenue.

Timothy sat back and reflected on this information. Within a week, Benjamin contacted Edwards to come to the head office and meet Fischer.

Meeting with Fischer (DBS) and Benjamin (DOC)

'I'm well aware of my responsibilities, Felix', stated Fischer acidly. 'I know this is the revenue-earning part of the organization, but have you been listening to what I've been saying for this past hour? Selling photocopiers is not easy. You don't seem to understand that!'

The meeting between Edwards, Fischer and Benjamin had started at 9.30 am; it was now 11.30 am. The tension between the two men was obvious. Timothy, in his usual style, listened, commented little and made numerous notes. As the two men argued, he glanced through his notes. They read as follows:

1 Benjamin states Business Services is overmanned.
2 Fischer disagrees because he feels the process of selling office equipment is not understood or appreciated within Gamma.
3 Fischer considers the problem that Business Services is facing to be that of poor staff motivation. He perceives that (a) certain managers find the structure confusing in terms of not fully understanding their job, not knowing who to report to and over what issues; (b) relationships between managers seem to be poor – Fischer stresses that the success of Business Services depends on people's willingness to collaborate with each other; (c) certain managers seem to be duplicating services; (d) although present system allows for certain flexibility, control and coordination have become impossible.

'I wonder if I could interrupt', said Timothy cutting across Benjamin and Fischer's heated argument. 'For me to make sense of what you are saying, I need to see and understand your organizational structure.'

Fisher responded immediately, and took out of his top drawer a sheet of paper which had been folded several times, unfolded it and spread it over his desk (Figure 5). 'Now, Business Services is split into five major parts and these are. . .', began Fischer.

Twenty-seven minutes later: 'Mm . . . an interesting structure. Oh! What do the asterisks mean?' Timothy asked.

'Hhm, those are fairly recent appointments that I, with Hank White's approval, have made', replied Fischer quietly.

'I see', said Timothy. 'Now, can you tell me something about your business, as I know little about it. For instance, how do you sell?'

'Basically it's simple. We have large customers who purchase equipment in bulk and also retailers who may order some of our larger equipment, but would basically stock the smaller equipment', responded Fischer.

'I see! Then what? From the organization structure, I see you provide support services.'

'Yes, these are our engineers. Their job is to provide support, if and when needed. Really, it is up to the customer to contact the engineering support service. Our response is quick – we say and mean within a day', replied Fischer.

'Fine. Thank you. I think I have an overall picture. Hmm . . . in order to understand some of the problems you are facing, I think I need to interview some of your managers. Is that possible?' asked Edwards.

'Yes of course. I think that is very necessary,' responded Benjamin. 'Now, it's probably right that you see some of the other directors, more to get a general picture, but you need to see most of the key guys in Business Services. I think you should see . . .', continued Benjamin, 'and I'll arrange for all these interviews.'

The Interviews

'Come in. You must be Tim Edwards. Felix Benjamin told me you'd call', said the General Manager (GM) Sales. This was Edwards' fourth interview. He began his standard introduction, explaining what he was doing, and that he wanted to know

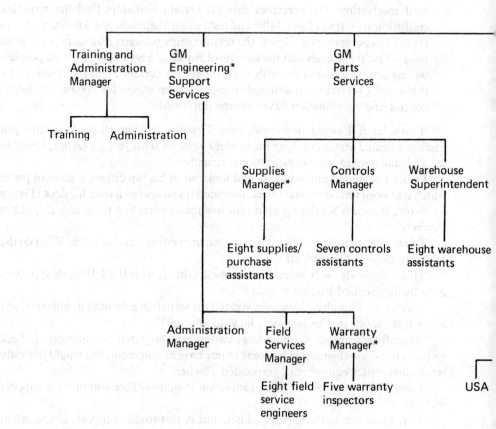

Figure 5 The organizational structure of the business services division.

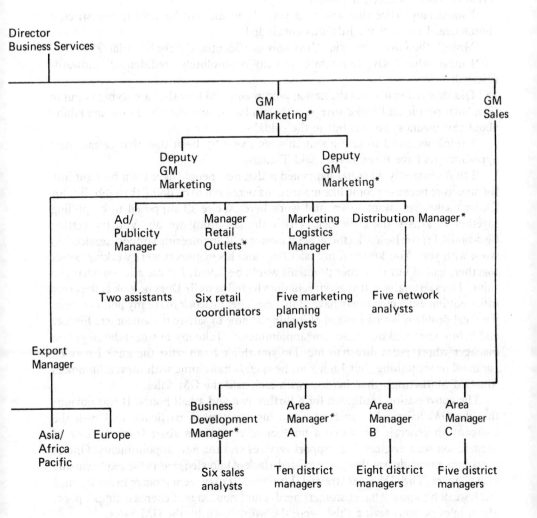

how each manager spent his time, his range of duties, the perceived support, constraints and opportunities in each manager's job, and whether improvement of any sort was considered necessary.

'I must emphasize that anything you say to me will be kept in the strictest confidence. I mean that', Edwards concluded.

'Mmm', the GM Sales said, 'Just how confidential is "confidential"?'

'I mean what I say. Everything you say is absolutely confidential!' Edwards asserted.

'Did they tell you about the new appointments and how they are trying to put in their own people and make sure that the old hands like me who know something about this business are left out in the cold?'

'I think we need to talk about this, as I've only been told that certain new appointments have taken place', said Timothy.

'I think basically what has happened is that new people have been brought into the structure because people like me are considered not to be doing their job. But for Christ's sake, you want to try and work here. We're all supposed to be pulling together to satisfy the customer. That's the last thing we do. You try getting bird-brain Trevor Peacock (the general manager of engineering support services) to work with you. You know, if my sales boys and his engineers were working better together, half of our customer problems would be licked. Let me ask you what you think. Does an engineer just service, or does he sell as well? Does he look at the other office equipment a client may have? I just can't get Peacock to see my point of view. The real problem is that instead of looking at how to satisfy the customer, Fischer and White start making these new appointments. Take my business development manager who reports direct to me. Do you think I can trust the guy? I may be paranoid or something, but I tell you, he spends more time with Steven Summers (the GM Marketing), than he does with me', said the GM Sales.

The conversation continued for a further two and a half hours. It was obvious that the GM Sales felt aggrieved about his situation in particular and with the company in general. He stated a number of complaints apart from the lack of cooperation with engineering support services and the new appointments. One of the comments made was that there existed a lack of knowledge as to the requirements of customers. The GM Sales stressed this point. 'It may seem strange to say it, but I think we don't know what customers need. Our knowledge of clients is simply poor. Me, a sales person, saying this', were the words used by the GM Sales.

Edwards' next important appointment was with the GM Marketing.

'From the way you've been talking and asking questions, it seems to me you've been influenced by the sales group. Look, let's go through what marketing does', said GM Marketing. The conversation was now 50 minutes old.

'You must realize the competitive nature of our business. We have our rivals and they are household names. Half of our problem is picking up the crumbs the big boys leave us. Does that mean that customers go for brand loyalty or product loyalty or just purchase what they know about? You know, if it's the last of these three, we've got a problem, according to Hank White, because we aren't getting to potential customers', said the GM Marketing.

'I hope it's not the first two, because then you really have got a problem', responded Edwards.

'Touché', smiled the GM Marketing. He continued. 'Anyhow, let me continue. Where was I? . . . So, in my opinion, the customer is a bit flighty; it is difficult to obtain information about customer needs; we are in a very competitive business, but also customer loyalty is so unpredictable. Yeah. . . .' Pause. 'OK. That's the outside, now what about us inside. Do you really want to know my true opinion? You're going to think we're terrible. I think bloody engineers and sales are the real problem. Those two don't get on. They need to provide a full service to the customer. On top of that, that bloody Sales GM just won't play the game. We are trying to set up a unified policy and he's got so many different contacts and contracts with clients that if some guy wants some sort of deal, he may contact me. He may then also contact the sales guy and negotiate a separate deal. Problem is that Sales is run by a chap from the past, when selling was a bit of a cowboy activity. He's a one man band', continued the GM Marketing.

'You understand the problem? You know, this question of information on customer trends and needs. Where do we get our information from? I think this whole organization is too technology driven. If I'm honest, I'm not sure what questions to ask from whom. Yet, we conduct surveys, examine sales returns, try to talk to sales, if that were possible, talk to retailers, hold conferences and promotions. We try our best', finished GM Marketing.

The conversation continued for some time.

Timothy interviewed most of the key managers in Business Services. The picture that was emerging was one of gloom, despondency, lack of trust and cooperation amongst managers, especially between the marketing, sales and engineering support groups. In addition, particular issues did emerge, such as that the forecasts made by the marketing group concerning expected demand for photocopiers per period were inaccurate, with the result that the company faced a critical problem of overstocking.

It also became clear that the engineering support service department was overspending on the budget, as most of the warranty claims, in terms of mechanical faults occurring on reprographic units under two years of age, were not being challenged and compensation was paid to the customer. The parts department was making a profit, according to the director of parts, by analysing the pattern of demand on all spares. Part of the process of analysis involved accumulating requests for spares from the field engineers, in order to judge the pattern of real need for particular spare parts in the various parts of the country. In this way, the director of parts could then estimate his likely expected annual stockholding capacity. By not overstocking, he was able to show profit. Timothy recalled the comments of the general manager of engineering support services.

'The GM parts services doesn't realize the spares my engineers want on time. He wants to see what is real as opposed to possible demand, so that he does not become overstocked. That drives me crazy. It drives me crazy because half my warranty claims arise because our customers need spares, can't get them on time, and eventually the bloody things get f . . . ed! Well, all that means is that my guys have to collect the machine, bring it here to our workshops, repair it, take it back to the customer. All this is bad business. Inconvenience for the customers, inconvenience for us, and as a result we lose some potentially good clients. This place needs sorting out. These damn Yanks are doing f . . k all about it!'

The one person Edwards had not interviewed was Felix Benjamin.

'So you feel you've seen enough', commented Benjamin. He continued, 'and the irony is, you want to interview me. OK. Go ahead'.

Benjamin's view of the organization was similar to that held by others. Then a comment by Benjamin caught Edwards by surprise.

'Have any of the others told you that Business Services serves as much as an outlet for some American products and as far as half of those bastards are concerned, my production side may as well be closed down?'

'No one said a thing to me. Please go on', responded Edwards.

The story that emerged added a new dimension to the picture that had been formed. Essentially, three plants in the USA were manufacturing similar product ranges, but of a greater variety and sophistication. Benjamin thought, but was not sure, that the Americans, long term, wished to close down the manufacturing plants of Gamma and simply use the UK as a marketing and sales outlet for American manufactured products. The reason he came to this conclusion was that the third and newest plant in the USA was operating under capacity. He felt that to increase the manufacturing output of the third USA plant, it was necessary to reduce the output of the UK plants. As a result of this additional undercurrent, the manufacturing and product design directors did not trust White and especially Fischer. In fact, the lack of performance of Business Services was seen as Fischer not trying, as well as more fundamental organizational problems.

Edwards had agreed with Fischer and Benjamin to prepare a report by an agreed date. One Wednesday evening, two weeks before the report was due, Benjamin rang Time Edwards: 'Hi, Tim!. . . Look, we've got a crisis. Can you make a meeting on Friday at 6.30 pm, and can you have something of your report written down? The CEO, DBS and I need to meet you!' Tim Edwards agreed to the meeting. He jotted down the key points arising from the interviews.

The Crisis Meeting

Edwards was introduced to the CEO, Hank White, for the first time.

'I wonder if we could start the meeting by your presenting to us a summary of your findings to date. We can then tell you the reason for this sudden meeting.'

Edwards presented each of the board members with the following notes:

1   All the managers interviewed indicate that the present structure is not working. In addition, there seems to be overmanning and duplication of activities.

2   There exist few effective coordination and control activities.

3   The lack of control and coordination means that managers are not inform-

ing each other as to whom they visit, how many times and with what outcome.

4   Most managers have developed contacts with numerous clients and retailers which often overlap, but have not informed each other as to who are their contacts. So, any one client may be relating to two or three separate employees of the company.

5   The more assertive clients use the current situation to advantage. If a client is unable to negotiate something in his favour with one manager, he merely contacts another person he knows in the company and sees if he can negotiate a more favourable outcome with him, thereby revising the original decision.

6   The majority of those interviewed feel demotivated. Many openly stated that if they could find another job and leave, they would do so.

7   Little attention has been given to increasing sales through some sort of reorganization.

8   Far greater attention needs to be given to the sales process, i.e. how sales are conducted and the skills sales people require in the organization.

9   Overstocking of manufactured equipment is a serious problem. Too many units are manufactured in anticipation of demand.

10   Overstocking is largely due to poor marketing data concerning customer needs and demands. The business services division does not seem to understand or be capable of generating sufficient data indicating customer needs and demands.

11   It is considered that lack of cooperation amongst senior management is a serious problem which requires attention.

Silence!

'I think you have confirmed and clarified everything we suspected', White stated. Silence! He continued, 'Let me tell you why we have a crisis and what we would like you to do.'

'First, the president of the group, of which Gamma is only one subsidiary, paid us an unexpected visit last week. He looked round the plants, examined the marketing forecasts and after some discussion made it clear that we need to be more profitable, probably by reorganizing, otherwise senior management of Gamma may be removed.'

He continued, 'Second part of the discussion involved the new ZB35. The ZB35 is the latest in reprographic technology, designed and manufactured in the USA, and has just been awarded a top design prize by the Science Society. The president has stated that we are to market the ZB35 from October 1983 onwards and manufacture it as early as 1985. This is just terrible! We know nothing about the product, its perfomance, or what spares to stock.' He paused.

'Perhaps I should state the third reason', said Benjamin quietly. 'Last weekend the board members of Gamma Appliances went to a quiet hotel in Wales to discuss these problems. To the utter astonishment of everyone, Hank White and Bert quarrelled bitterly. Unpleasant things were said. Hank made it clear that Bert's future is in question unless he reorganizes Business Services. You see, we must increase our revenue. We need to do something, and quickly, to reunite the top management team', Benjamin concluded.

Silence.

Substantial discussion ensued for the next two hours.

'Please! Please! Please! We have talked enough! Tim, you have seen what we are like. You now understand our crisis. We need to move quickly. To give us some idea of what to do, could you work over the weekend to prepare a plan that will help us move forward? If agreeable with you, we can meet at 8.00 am on Monday', said White.

'Tim, we need a blueprint. If you like, a master plan of the reorganized business services division, or if you consider it necessary, Gamma Appliances overall. We need a new organization structure. Can you sketch out what the new structure should look like?' asked a worried-looking Benjamin.

Tim looked at the group. 'OK, I'll have a go. We meet Monday, 8.00 am.'

Case Study Tasks

You are to take the role of Tim Edwards (helped by a group of advisers if preferred) and prepare answers to the following questions:

1 What are the major problems facing Gamma Appliances, and why have they arisen?
2 Is there a need to reorganize Gamma Appliances in general, or the business services division in particular, and if so, what should the new organization structure be?
3 What are the advantages and disadvantages of the new organizational structure?
4 Are redundancies inevitable? How should they be managed?
5 What needs to be done to ensure that your organization is implemented and operates successfully?
6 What sort of strategy would you adopt in terms of Gamma's working relationship with the USA?

Essential Reading

Child J (1984) Organization: A Guide to Problems and Practice, 2nd edition, Harper & Row

Handy C B (1976) Understanding Organizations, Penguin

Additional Reading

Ansoff H I (1982) Managing discontinuous strategies change: the learning action approach, in Understanding and Managing Strategic Change, edited by H I Ansoff A Bosman and P M Sturm, North Holland

Kingdon D R (1973) Matrix Organization: Managing Information Technologies, Tavistock

Perrow C (1967) A framework for the comparative analysis of organizations, American Sociological Review 32: 194–208

Pugh D S Hickson D J (1976) Organization Structure in its Context: The Aston Programme, Saxon House

SECTION 2: Personnel Management

There are various ways of defining what personnel management is all about. It can be seen as an all pervasive activity, that is the responsibility of every manager or supervisor, or as a specialist activity demanding the professional expertise of a distinct, separate department. But, leaving aside organizational location, it may be conceptualized analytically, from 'systems', 'Marxist' or 'symbolic order' positions.

From a 'systems' position it may be seen as concerned with acquiring appropriate human inputs from the environment and 'transforming' them (or 'motivating', 'training' and 'developing' them) to achieve optimum effectiveness so that the organization may survive and grow in that same, often turbulent and changing, environment. In which case, the personnel manager may aspire to be the 'organizational diagnostician', concerned with contingent problem-solving. Or it may be viewed as mediating the contradictions of capitalism; that is, responsible for accommodating the dilemma that, although the 'labour commodity' is a major means to further the interests of dominant groups in capitalist society, it is liable to subvert those interests. The personnel manager is then enmeshed in issues of control, using rational techniques to counter the problems created by other rational techniques – he (or she) is the 'man in the middle'. But such ambiguities and paradoxes are not always seen as constraints. They may equally be opportunities for the personnel manager to trade and negotiate meanings, within loosely coupled relationships, in order to generate commitment – that most subtle form of control – through the manipulation of the symbolic order. When the image of organization is displaced by that of community, the personnel manager emerges as a cross between rhetorician and political leader.

We hope that these cases address all these issues but, in particular, emphasize that personnel management impinges on all management jobs. The problems that surround 'personnel' issues – whether pay, or health and safety, or absenteeism – are multifaceted and interrelated. A change in one policy or part of the system, by whatever manager, is likely to have ramifications throughout. Thus, in providing answers to the problems posed in the case study questions, this complex web of interrelationships and consequences must be considered. One criterion for the success of a case is the extent to which it highlights this interconnectedness in its narrative. Readers may therefore find it useful to refer back to the matrix in the Introduction (Table 2) as a pointer to the relevant issues.

Taking the 'conceptual' issues, the cases in Section 2 may be viewed from 'systems', 'Marxist' or 'symbolic order' perspectives.

First, the selection of topics covered reflects a 'systems' view with cases on the acquisition of human 'inputs' (selection and recruitment, payment systems), their 'transformation' (training and skills, health and safety at work, management appraisal and development, and again payment systems) and their 'outputs' or, more accurately, 'outputting' into the environment (absence and turnover, redundancy). Issues concerning those other organizational outputs, such as performance and satisfaction, as well as the broader socioeconomic environment, permeate all the cases, while the legal environment is of particular concern in the case on equal opportunities at work, and those, already mentioned, on health and safety and on redundancy.

Second, all the cases can be seen as reflecting management's attempts at exercising control ('Marxist' perspective) or seeking to gain commitment ('symbolic order' perspective) through a range of human resource management strategies. It may be interesting to consider which side of that coin is most in evidence in the cases – and whether both the emphasis and rhetoric employed varies with the level in the hierarchy at which they are directed. It should be noted too that many of the concepts that underlie the cases in Section 1 – for example uncertainty, power, motivation and satisfaction, are useful in considering such issues of control and commitment.

Broader questions about the nature of our capitalist industrial society are implicit in most of the cases in this section. But if the case on absenteeism provides illustration of the subversive nature of the labour commodity, those on health and safety, redundancy and equal opportunities would seem to point to its vulnerability and relative powerlessness.

Turning from these general issues, we will briefly summarize the content of the cases. In Case 12 Nigel Nicholson illustrates how absence is at the centre of a web of interconnected influences, linking the individual level of analysis with group and organizational levels. The sum total of these factors can be conceived as the unique 'absence culture' of the organization, but the relationship between absence, recruitment strategy and payment system has very general relevance to a range of organizations.

In Case 13 Chris Brotherton examines some of the procedural and technical problems associated with recruiting and selecting graduates. The case highlights the common problems with, and ineffectiveness of, systems that have arisen in an ad hoc manner, rather than being consciously designed. The relationship of selection strategies with the closely allied ones concerning salaries and training is brought out in this case.

In Case 14 Don Wallis is concerned to identify what benefits the organization is seeking, which of them it values most highly, and what it would accept as evidence of success, following the installation of an ostensibly improved training course. Hence the focus of this case is largely on the choice of training as an alternative strategy to a 'selection' or 'equipment' solution, and its subsequent evaluation.

While appropriate training is clearly one way of enhancing the probability of maintaining safety at work, Sandra Dawson in Case 15 tackles a wider range of issues involved in the development and maintenance of health and safety at work. The case illustrates the organizational and market constraints – not to mention issues of power and politics – which undermine the implementation of an effective health and safety policy, even when good intentions exist. The appointment of specialists and the construction of procedures is clearly not enough when firms are subject to economic recession.

The effects of economic recession are the focus of Case 16, in which Stephen Wood presents a description of the development of a situation in which a number of staff must be made redundant. The issues surrounding redundancy, such as the social and psychological costs to those likely to be involved, employer and union strategies and the legal context, are raised. The case deals with the development of a redundancy policy, in the firm's context, while maintaining production levels at the time and after redundancies are made.

Case 17 by John Burgoyne concerns the strategic planning of management development in a large public corporation, facing a changing mission and an uncertain future. The case does not focus on a particular decision or incident, but on the general question of what priorities and issues should be attended to, and how the problems – including those associated with developing an evaluation strategy – can be addressed.

In Case 18 Dan Gowler and Karen Legge consider some issues involved in wage payment system design. Designing a payment system at the individual level is centrally concerned with questions about work motivation, performance and satisfaction. But from a management and organizational point of view, it is equally concerned with questions of control – of effort levels, quality, unit costs. For a payment system to act as both motivator and controller it must have the potential to satisfy individuals' needs but also reinforce managerially desired behaviours. But to do this the motivational principles it embodies must not be undermined by the organizational situation in which the payment system has to operate. This case examines a situation where the payment system does not match the context in which it operates, adverse side effects are emerging and questions of its redesign are being raised.

Finally, in Case 19, Sylvia Shimmin and Joyce McNally illustrate some of the factors which operate against the legal requirements for equality between the sexes in employment – from assumptions of men and women concerning job opportunities and pay differentials, to unwritten policies and procedures and trade union reactions.

CASE 12

Absence and Turnover: The Absentee Bus Crews

Nigel Nicholson

Background to the Case

You are placed in the role of the researcher, employed by a government agency in the early 1970s to investigate absence in a number of industries and geographical regions. Part of your informal contract with the participating organizations is to give them feedback on your findings. Well into your study, you come to the Coal Valley Bus Company, where the absence seems to be a more acute problem than in any other organization you have visited. Absence and lateness are the regular cause of disrupted bus services and are rated as the chief concern of local management. The following case study presents what your investigation reveals. Your task, after studying the case material is to frame recommendations for action.

The Local Culture

The Coal Valley Bus Company is a privately owned enterprise, running local services in a relatively isolated conurbation in mainland Britain. The area has a strong, traditional, working-class identity as a community, founded in the late Victorian era on locally mined coal and associated industries. The postwar period has seen a major decline in the region's employment as the area's coal deposits have been worked out, and all but one of its pits have closed. The future of this one remaining pit is in doubt; it is classed as uneconomic and nearing the end of its exploitable coal reserves. Other traditional industries in the area – foundries and workshops – have been hit hard by the recession, and several have closed. There has been some growth in light industry – many, such as two clothing factories, employing more women than men – but this growth has not compensated for the decline in traditional local industries. The result has been unemployment levels well above the national average, and some migration out of the area of the younger, better educated and more ambitious inhabitants. If anything, these trends have reinforced the cohesive and insular character of the community, where extended family ties thread a network of connections between people in different organizations, and between people at different levels of the same organization. As a visitor to the area you get the feeling that everyone knows everyone else. The atmosphere of the locality is also one of a warm, open-natured friendliness. The people have a deserved reputation for their love of life, sociability, a passion for sport, hard drinking and poor diet – you observe the last of these at first hand when you accept an invitation by a local to the traditional 'tea' of sandwiches and sugary cakes. The people in the region also have a reputation – mainly communicated to you by local managers who have come from other parts of the country – for being work-shy and lazy. From your conversations with people it is certainly apparent to you that there is a traditional mistrust of employers. In its politics the area is solidly socialist.

The Organization

The Coal Valley Bus Company was founded between the wars, but it was the period immediately following the Second World War that was the heyday for the company and other bus firms like it. They were a mainstay of local community life in those days of low car ownership. They were also a respected source of employment for the sudden influx of men coming from the armed services on to the labour market. The occupation was held in high esteem, compared to the dirty and dangerous work of mining, and men were proud to exchange one uniformed service for another. Pay and conditions were competitive with other local employment. The postwar decline of the area, however, saw a change in the climate of the industry. The status and demand for bus transportation fell with the growth of private car ownership, and rising overhead costs severely limited the profitability of public transport enterprises. The result in recent years has been some contraction of services and depressed wage levels relative to other local industries. The axing of local railway services in the mid-1950s helped the company to achieve sufficient equilibrium to survive, for it now has a monopoly of local public transport in an area where private car usage is still below the national average.

Three years ago the company was taken over by a large private transport consortium, giving them ownership and control over almost all the bus companies within the wider region. This change had more impact on the management of the enterprise than its services, which continued more or less unchanged. Top management for the company moved to the consortium headquarters at the regional capital, Coalport, some 50 miles away, with day to day operations continuing to be run from the old local company office. Since the takeover the local company has had a succession of top management changes – these roles being used as a training ground for young upwardly mobile managers from Head Office. The total number of people employed by the organization at the time of your investigation is 780, including 600 drivers and conductors. The remainder are maintenance staff, cleaners and ancillary personnel (e.g. canteen staff), route inspectors (to check running times, fares and other routine operations) and management. All crew personnel and inspectors are members of a national trade union with strong local leadership and 'closed shop' organization. Workshop and other personnel are also unionized.

The bus crews work a weekly rota system – this means that drivers and conductors are paired on a particular route on one shift for the whole week. The following week each is paired with a different driver or conductor for a different route on the opposite shift. Shifts are early or late. Start and finish times vary according to routes, the earliest starting at 5.00 am and the last finishing at 11.30 pm. There are a small number of 'split' shifts – an early start and late finish with a break of several hours in the middle of the day. These are required to provide additional cover for peak time services. Weekend overtime working is paid at time and a half, and overtime is offered to workers on a strict rotational basis, by union agreement. The duty rota system in force some 10 years ago had crews allocated to particular routes, but, again by union agreement, this had been abandoned in favour of the present rotational system, considered to be fairer because of the unequal workload on different routes. A float of 30 drivers per shift is maintained to cover for absences on the 130 duties per shift. One-man bus operation has just been introduced on a small number of routes, but in the teeth of strenuous union opposition. There was a short strike over this issue last year. The current climate of union–management relations is thus one of muted conflict. Although the company pays lip service to equal opportunities legislation, only a handful of women are currently employed in bus crews, all of them as conductors.

Conductors are recruited direct from the local labour market. Drivers are recruited exclusively from conductors, and, after training, are paid 15% more. Inspectors are recruited exclusively from drivers. Pay is a flat hourly rate with no bonus system. All company employees have free transport on all the consortium's transport services. The sick pay scheme, under a national agreement, provides scaled benefits up to 18 weeks' full pay for employees with 10 years' service (i.e. it tops up state health benefits to full pay). Only absences of longer than three days, certified by medical notes, are eligible for benefits. Thus busmen lose pay for short absences. Many of the busmen are ex-miners, and a number are registered disabled with upper respiratory ailments. Many others who are not registered disabled also suffer chronic bronchial and chest disorders as a result of their previous employment in mining. Labour turnover is approximately 10% per annum, mainly due to the retirement of older drivers and inspectors, and the migration out of the area of young short-service conductors.

The Problem

Your first contact with the company is with the area operations manager at the Coalport regional headquarters of the bus consortium. He talks to you long enough to authorize your investigation and to give you a letter of introduction to the (latest) Coal Valley district manager, but it is apparent from the numerous telephone interruptions, the piles of paper on his desk, and his rather harried air, that he hasn't really time to give you any insights into the problems of the Coal Valley Bus Company. Indeed, you form the impression that he doesn't really know much about the area or the company, though he is clearly well in touch with the balance sheet of its operations. However, he does offer the opinion, just before you leave, that 'absence is endemic up there' and that the people of the region are 'work-shy by nature'. He says he'll be interested in what you discover, but doesn't think that you'll be able to solve any of their problems.

A similar opinion is voiced by the young district manager when you first visit the Coal Valley main depot and offices. He is new to the area and this is his first post in operational management. He was formerly in the head office as a route-planner, and is keen to make his mark in his new post. He says absence is a major problem, running at 'at least 13%'. He thinks this is probably about average for the region but reckons, allowing for the chronic sickness of a minority of the workforce, that it could be reduced to around 5%. He says that on many mornings they have insufficient spare manning to cover services, due to both absence and lateness. He says he has been horrified to discover that this has led to a long-established practice of sending out inspectors in cars, normally reserved for route inspectors' duties, to collect men from their homes in the mornings when they don't show up for scheduled duties. He claims that the employees have come to expect this, and await the arrival of the cars as a free taxi service to work, quite happy to take the day off if the car doesn't come.

He says discipline doesn't seem to work. Sick notes are easily obtained from family doctors; suspension is often welcomed as an enforced absence; and dismissal doesn't deter the many who get almost as much money from social security and unemployment benefits. He says he recently sacked three men whose photograph he happened to see in a local paper's crowd shot at an away fixture of the local football team, when the three had all been sending in sick notes for absence. He says he's tried sick visits from the personnel office to check up on absentees, but he says this doesn't deter people, and anyway, he hasn't sufficient staff to do this comprehensively. He bitterly cites the case of one man who has been off for three weeks with a cut thumb, and says he is powerless to do anything so long as the man keeps sending in sick notes. He also tells you that people can often recover lost earnings from casual absence through working overtime. He says that he finally managed to persuade the union to back him in withholding Sunday overtime for persistent offenders, but he says this has not had much of a deterrent effect. 'They'd still rather have the time off', he says, and adds that in any case he suspects men are getting round this by banking their overtime and sharing it out. He says he believes several men are 'moonlighting'. He sees the absence problem as centering on a 'core of offenders', but gloomily concludes that sacking them would do no good, since the new intake would be no better. 'Most folk round here don't want to work shifts', he says, 'and we're scraping the bottom of the barrel with our recruitment intake'. He says this is not like the old days, and there are now two 'classes' of busmen: the 'old guard' of long service men, who are reliable workers, but less so as they have become disillusioned with the decline of their once honoured occupation, and the 'young Turks' who have drifted into bus work as a temporary expedient, and found it a free and easy yet secure job. The former, he says, are mainly to be found among the drivers and inspectors, the latter mainly among the conductors. Armed with this information, you commence your investigation.

The Results of the Investigation

Your first step is to look at the personnel absence records. For each employee there is an index card recording the start and finish of each absence they have had, and whether it was certified as a 'sickness' absence, 'accident', 'permitted' (i.e. prior permission given) or 'unauthorized'. You are told by the personnel records clerk that the only use made of these records is for disciplinary purposes. Periodically, a single record will be scrutinized when an inspector or manager forms the impression that an individual's absence may be excessive, and 'from time to time management have a blitz on absence' by going through all the records and trying to discipline the worst offenders. Since no summary records are compiled to show overall absence levels or running totals over time, you undertake this task with the last full year's records. You note that almost all absences are classified as 'sickness', apart from odd single days off, so you elect to ignore the company's classification system and generate a more reliable and objective record by summarizing the total volume of absence (*time lost* per man, standardized by the total amount of possible working time) and the total incidence rate (*frequency* of absence spells per man).

You generate two summary records. First you derive a running total of all crew members' time lost and frequency over the last full year. This shows that absence time lost has seasonal peaks (early autumn and late winter) and troughs (summer and early winter), and that for most of the year it exceeds 17% of possible working time. Not only have management greatly underestimated the total volume of absence, but you note that absence is running at a significantly higher level than in any of the other regional bus companies you have surveyed. Absence frequency is uniformly high throughout the year at around 16 spells per 100 men per week, though you note that there are peaks of up to 20 spells per 100 men on weeks when there were important local sporting fixtures. It is clear that frequency is also much higher than in other companies you have visited.

The second set of summaries you produce are time lost and frequency population profiles of conductors and drivers. These reveal a wide spread in absence rates, but with distributions skewed towards the high end, i.e. very few people have little or no absence. There is also a highly significant difference in rates for drivers and conductors. Drivers' time lost average is 27 days per man per year; conductors' is 40 days. Drivers' frequency average is 3.6 spells per man per year; conductors' is 11.8. From your analysis of personnel data you also note the two groups differ greatly in their ages and lengths of service. Drivers' average age is 44; conductors' is 25 years. Drivers' average length of service is 19 years; conductors' is two years.

From your questionnaire survey of busmen you also observe that conductors report higher satisfaction than drivers with all aspects of their jobs, especially on the 'work itself' subscale of your instrument. Indeed, conductors' satisfaction levels are higher than in any other company you have visited; drivers are on a par with others.

The next step of your analysis is to relate crew members' absence to their satisfaction scores and biographical data. This reveals the following data: (1) drivers' absence is unrelated to their job satisfaction, but dissatisfied conductors tend to have a higher absence frequency than satisfied conductors; (2) younger, shorter service drivers have a higher absence frequency than older, long service drivers, and short service conductors have a higher absence time lost than long service conductors.

At the same time as you are coding and analysing these data, you embark on the final phase of your data gathering – a series of interviews with drivers, conductors and inspectors.

It is immediately apparent from your conversations with crewmen that most like the job itself a great deal. There are frequent expressions of appreciation of the job variety provided by the route rosta, and of the freedom of 'being your own boss' on the job. 'Comradeship' and contact with the public are also widely appreciated, and some note with pride what an excellent community service they provide – making unscheduled stops for passengers, helping travellers with prams and luggage, etc. Several also say they like the job security and the 'open air' of outdoor work. An almost universally voiced dislike is early rising for the morning shift. Busmen, especially conductors, often report disliking particular duties where contact with the travelling public can be less than rewarding, e.g. late night buses and school buses. A couple of busmen complain about the 'petty officialdom' of inspectors.

On the whole conductors seem more satisfied with their jobs than drivers, an impression that is subsequently confirmed by your questionnaire analysis. Some evidence for the existence of two cultures is provided by drivers' critical comments about conductors. A number refer to the 'deliberately sloppy way they wear the company uniform'. You ask the busmen how they would feel about a 'regular man system', where there would be permanent pairings of drivers and conductors. Every interviewee says they prefer the present system, commenting that you could 'get bored' or 'might not get on' with your partner on a regular man system. Almost all are also opposed to the one-man operation system, on the grounds that it is 'too much work' for one person to do, though some accept that its spread across more duties is inevitable.

In your interviews you also ask them about absence and its causes. Most admit that it is high, but don't see themselves as the chief offenders – even when their own actual absence records contradict this, as you note later when correlating their records with other data. In interview they give a variety of reasons for their own absence. Illness is the most common reason, but many also mention 'sleeping late' and difficulties in rising at 3.30 am for the first buses. Others give such diverse reasons as 'family outings', 'feeling fed-up', 'hangovers', and 'the job getting on top of you'. Some say that they'll go absent rather than come in late, because if there are spare men at the depot they would be sent home without pay anyway. If they were undecided about whether to go absent for any reason, many say their wives and colleagues would encourage them to stay off work. Your interviews also reveal some evidence of 'moonlighting' – busmen with second, part-time jobs.

When you ask about how justifiable is casual absence, a number say that 'it's up to you, if you can afford it'. One man says, 'they don't check up on your absence and ask your reasons'. Most believe it is quite easy to obtain advance permission for absence from management, but few say they have tried to. One says: 'I asked permission once and was refused – I learned my lesson from that, and have never asked again since'. Finally, your interviews with inspectors confirm that they see two 'cultures' of young versus older busmen, and that the former 'don't care about the job'. Inspectors complain that 'management is too soft', and that inspectors only have the power to observe and report. 'We report and they [the management] don't act' says one. Most of them blame the sick pay scheme for encouraging absence. They express respect for the busmen's union, which they say is 'good but tough'.

Case Study Tasks

Individually, or in groups, students should consider some of the questions listed below. An alternative approach is for students to take the role of the researcher, and write a report for the company which, in clear and simple language (a) gives a general account of the company's situation and the causes of absence, and (b) contains recommendations for a plan of management action.

Key questions and issues for consideration are as follows:

1   What are the current costs of absence to the company and other parties?
2   How does the regional 'culture' affect absence? Could this be changed in any way by a company initiative?
3   How does the local organizational culture affect absence? How could this be changed?
4   What is the relationship between work attitudes and absence? How does this accord with the literature on this subject?
5   What is the relationship between biographical variables and absence? What does this signify?
6   What is the relationship between absence and the so-called 'withdrawal' behaviours of lateness and turnover? Does the concept of 'withdrawal' help or hinder our understanding of these behaviours?
7   How do job design, work organization and social relationships affect absence? What changes in these would alter the 'absence culture'?
8   What is the relationship of absence to work conditions, pay and 'hygiene' factors? What scope is there for remedial action via these variables?
9   What should be management's strategy in relation to absence? In particular consider the use of recruitment strategies, sanctions, incentives, supervisory control, information systems, medical certification and the role of the personnel function.
10 Is there other information or data that would be helpful in more precisely defining the company's absence problem and the scope for action?

Essential Reading

Johns G Nicholson N (1982) The meaning of absence: new strategies for theory and research, in Research in Organizational Behaviour, Vol. 4, edited by B Staw and L L Cummings, JAI Press, pp. 127–172
Muchinsky P M (1977) Employee absenteeism: a review of the literature, Journal of Vocational Behaviour, 10: 316–340
Nicholson N Johns G (1985) The absence culture and the psychological contract: who's in control of absence? Academy of Management Review (in press)

Additional Reading

Allen P T (1982) Size of workforce, morale and absenteeism: a re-examination, British Journal of Industrial Relations, 20: 83–100

Chadwick-Jones J K Brown C A Nicholson N (1973) Absence from work: its meaning, measurement and control, International Review of Applied Psychology, 22: 137–156

Chadwick-Jones J K Nicholson N Brown C A (1982) The Social Psychology of Absenteeism, Praeger

Clegg C W (1983) The psychology of employee lateness, absence and turnover: a methodological critique and empirical study, Journal of Applied Psychology, 68: 88–101

Gibson J O (1966) Toward a conceptualization of absence behavior of personnel in organizations, Administrative Science Quarterly, 12: 107–133

Goodman P S Atkin R S (eds) (1984) Absenteeism: Issues in Theory, Measurement and Practice, Jossey-Bass

Lyons T R (1972) Turnover and absenteeism: a review of the relationships and shared correlates, Personnel Psychology, 25: 271–281

Morgan L G Herman J B (1976) Perceived consequences of absenteeism. Journal of Applied Psychology, 61: 738–742

Nicholson N (1976) Management sanctions and absence control, Human Relations, 29: 139–152

Nicholson N (1977) Absence behaviour and attendance motivation: a conceptual synthesis, Journal of Management Studies, 41: 231–252

Nicholson N Jackson P R Howes G (1978) Shiftwork and absence: an analysis of temporal trends, Journal of Occupational Psychology, 51: 127–137

Steers R M Rhodes S R (1978) Major influences on employee attendance: a process model, Journal of Applied Psychology, 63: 391–407

CASE 13

Selection and Recruitment: HAL

Chris Brotherton

Organizational Setting

HAL is a multisite corporation, with its head office in Milton Keynes. HAL is involved in the manufacture and distribution of data transmission devices (for example, minicomputers and work stations). It has developed from its origins in the 1920s as a small family firm which manufactured telephone handsets, to a major conglomerate employing over 10 000 people. Data transmission is a rapidly changing market with many competitors, two of which control over 65% of the present market.

Background to the Case

The selection procedure was originally designed by a consultant with broad experience in computing requirements, but who has long since left the company. Various elements of personnel policy have developed as the company has grown.

For some years now, the company has found difficulty both in recruiting and retaining graduates. In common with many companies recruiting graduates, HAL's policy is to attract bright, flexible young people who exhibit qualities of leadership and who have a high level of motivation. The selection procedure has grown with the company. HAL advertise in the national press, and take part in the university recruitment round each year. About 3000 applications are received each year for between 20 and 150 posts in management, technical support or sales. Candidates for all posts are asked to complete a standard application form which is used for initial screening. After two junior personnel staff have read the application forms, between 600 and 700 candidates are invited to first interview. HAL asks its more experienced personnel and line managers to conduct the first interviews. Inevitably managers have to fit this in to a busy schedule, and they may be poorly prepared and therefore likely to fall back on 'stock' questions to get them through the interview. The interviews take place either at the head office, or at one of the 20 universities visited by HAL during the spring. Based on first interview performance as rated by the interviewers, about 300 candidates are invited to a second interview at which a line manager and a personnel manager see the potential recruits individually for half an hour. A graduate employee, recruited in the previous year, shows candidates around the plant and answers questions. Candidates are then asked to take two psychological tests: the Computer Programmer Aptitude Battery (CPAB), developed as a measure of programming aptitude; and the Raven's Advanced Progressive Matrices, first developed in 1941, but revised in 1962, which provides a measure of general intelligence. Candidates also complete a group leadership exercise based on providing the best solution to an army field manoeuvre. The assessments of the first and second round interviewers and the graduate host, the total test scores and group leadership score are taken to a panel drawn from a sample of line and personnel managers who have taken part in the process. The panel produce a rating ranging from 'must employ at all costs' and 'acceptable', through 'would employ if no alternative available' to 'do not employ under any circumstances'. The ratings are then put to the personnel director who consults the finance director about salary, and then issues a letter of appointment or of rejection. In the last two years, about 40% of offers of employment were rejected, and over the past eight years more than 45% of those recruited have left HAL within two years. Experience of the market for graduate recruits at the time of the study suggests that these figures are high, but not unusual.

The Problem

Analysing the Selection and Recruitment System

You are the newly appointed personnel director in HAL, and have become concerned that recruitment costs are running at around £0.5 million a year, and that basic training costs for newcomers amount to a further £0.75 million. In particular, you have been horrified to learn of the refusal and turnover rates among graduate recruits, and you have decided this is one area you must improve immediately.

You have therefore asked a university research group to examine the existing procedure. You have stipulated that the group use existing records (however imperfect) and you have stressed that time is short – you are determined to take action quickly.

The university group found that all of the application forms for those invited to first interview had been carefully filed for each of the past five years, as were the test record sheets for CPAB and Raven's matrices, line manager and personnel manager ratings, the group leadership scores and the panel ratings. Copies of the original offer of employment complete with initial salary were all on file. Assessments on initial training courses and ratings of appraising staff, conducted by the recruit's superior of the day, were available, as were data on salary progression. Unusually, the researchers had access to an almost complete set of data!

Because the pattern of recruitment varied year by year, the group decided to

select two separate intakes at which a minimum of 50 graduates joined HAL. This
was done, although the intakes were four years apart.

Data Analysis and Results

For the data analysis, the researchers relied on the usual method of product–moment
correlations between the predictors (the psychometric test, the interview rating, the
group exercise, etc.) and the specified criteria (salary, training assessment, etc.) This
was because the selection decision ought to enable prediction of how the graduate
recruit progresses through the company. Product–moment correlations (r) have the
following characteristics: Two sets of measurements are obtained on the same
individuals or on pairs of individuals who are matched on the same basis. The
correlation coefficients are then computed. The values of the coefficients vary
between $+1.00$ and -1.00. Both of these extremes represent perfect linear relationships between the variables, and 0.00 represents the absence of a linear relationship.
A positive relationship means that individuals obtaining high scores on one variable
tend to obtain high scores on a second variable (e.g. people scoring high on a measure
of intelligence also do well in training assessments). The converse is also true. A
negative relationship means that individuals scoring low on one variable tend to
score high on a second.

The Criteria

Superior Ratings   Here, a seven-point scale ranging from excellent to poor was
used to help superiors make the assessment. These assessments would normally be
expected to provide a good indicator of job performance. However, examination of
the distribution of the ratings indicated that more than 92% were confined to the
second and third points in the scale. Taking the assessments for each year's intake,
the team found the following pattern of correlations between superior ratings:

Year A:	12-monthly and 24-monthly assessment	$r = 0.31$
Year B:	12-monthly and 24-monthly assessment	$r = 0.23$.

These figures are lower than might have been expected. It is also possible, since some
graduate recruits seem to have been rated by the same manager on different
occasions, that an element of bias inflated the correlations. Further examination of
the pattern revealed *negative* correlations $(-0.10$ and $-0.16)$ between assessments
for both intakes when the new recruit was moved between sites and put under
different managers.

Salary   The previous personnel director always maintained that he gave extra
increments to those rated most highly by selectors, to ensure that good applicants
took up offers of employment with HAL. This procedure suggested that salary
might provide a good criterion against which to judge selection. Certainly, there was
a good spread of salary differential and salary did correlate positively and fairly
strongly with the ratings of the final selection panel (0.51). However, by the time the

appointee had reached the second year of employment, the association between salary and initial level was minimal.

Quite obviously, the finance department was beginning to claw back increments once the initially high salary was set. Presumably, the finance department was concerned to maintain what it saw as an equitable overall salary policy. Examining the general position of salary for years not included in this exercise, it was found to be affected also by external factors such as government pay policy. So the extent to which salary truly reflected merit and progress was limited.

Success in Training   The researchers had been informed that graduate recruits to all HAL divisions attend courses in programming and in management during the first year of their employment. Performance on these courses is rated on a five-point scale by the training officer. Unfortunately investigation revealed that information was available only for the intake in year A. The distribution of ratings indicated that 80% of all candidates were rated either 3 or 4. Only 16% were rated 1 (high). Furthermore, the HAL training scores correlated between 0.13 and 0.19 with superior ratings. Again, these figures are low.

Promotion   It is the stated aim of the HAL recruitment programme that entrants should be able to be appointed to grade 4 within two years. In fact for year A, 19 had attained the grade below (grade 3) and 28 had attained grade 4, while for year B, one had attained grade 3, and 63 grade 4.

These figures are misleading, however, because the year A intake reached their two-year point at a time when the company was contracting.

The university group concluded that the promotion criterion at HAL is insufficiently variable to aid in selection validation, making the point that this could indicate inflexible promotion opportunities.

Turnover   Clearly turnover is an important criterion, in selection policy terms, against which to judge effectiveness. The turnover rates for both intakes were very high:

	Year A intake	Year B intake
Percentage leaving in first year	47.0%	41.2%
Percentage leaving in second year	40.1%	26.4%

(In year A, 20% of the graduate entrants had been made redundant in the course of a general reduction in the workforce.)

The university team also sought to analyse the reasons for leaving, using HAL's own classification system. Unfortunately, for the purposes of selection validation, the system had been changed between year A and year B. The broad reasons for leaving were recorded as follows: 11.5% unsatisfactory performance; 65.6% dissatisfaction or better opportunities elsewhere; while 22.9% left for domestic or personal reasons. Of course there is no way of knowing if the reason given for leaving is the 'real' one, or whether it is given as an 'acceptable' response at the time.

The Predictors

Interviews   Record sheets were available from the interviews of all original applicants. These provided ratings by the personnel manager of the candidates' maturity, stability, drive and interview performance; and ratings by the line manager of their intelligence, common-sense, imagination, technological outlook and interview performance. The records also included an overall assessment, agreed by the interviewers. Analysis of the records demonstrated very high agreement, both between raters and between the separate scales.

The Psychometric Tests   Analysing the results from the CPAB, Raven's matrices and the group leadership exercise, and correlating them with the salary and training criteria, revealed the following pattern:

	Year A (salary)	Year A (training criteria)	Year B (salary)
CPAB	0.41	0.29	0.32
Raven's matrices	0.21	0.37	0.19
Leadership exercise	0.17	0.12	0.14

Further analysis revealed that the CPAB correlated 0.69 with the Raven's matrices, raising the possibility that both are tapping some general intelligence factor. Also the graduate host ratings, taking years A and B together, correlated 0.79 with the overall assessments of the personnel and line managers.

These are the preliminary findings given to you by the university research group – they will be presenting you with a full report shortly. However, you have decided to make an issue of graduate recruitments at the next board meeting of HAL.

Case Study Tasks

As part of your preparation for this meeting you have asked yourself seven questions. These are given below. To answer them you can work alone, or in a small group consisting of members of line management and the personnel and finance functions.

1   What are the major problems with current selection and recruitment procedures?
2   What is wrong with the criterion measures?
3   What is wrong with the predictors?

4 How can you find out if the current systems operate to the disadvantage of women and ethnic minority groups?
5 How should you change the system? What will be the strengths and weaknesses of the new system?
6 What changes should you make to the psychological testing procedures?
7 How will you monitor the new system?

Essential Reading

Cronbach L J (1970) Essentials of Psychological Testing, 3rd edition, Harper & Row, Chapter 5
Landy F J Trumbo D A (1980) Psychology and Work Behavior, Dorsey Press, Chapters 3–8

Additional Reading

Dunnette M D (ed.) (1976) The Handbook of Industrial and Organizational Psychology, Rand-McNally, Chapters 18–20
Guion R M (1965) Personnel Testing, McGraw-Hill.
Howell W C (1975) Essentials of Industrial and Occupational Psychology, Irwin, Chapter 6
Buros O K (ed.) (1978) The Eighth Mental Measurements Yearbook, University of Nebraska, Buros Institute of Mental Measurement

CASE 14

Training and Skills: Royal Navy

Don Wallis

Organizational Setting

This study takes place in the Royal Navy. Although the events on which it is based took place in the 1960s, the issues are just as relevant today. Like other military organizations in peacetime, the Navy is preoccupied with training its personnel to a high level of operational and technical readiness for events which, it is hoped, will not materialize. There is a conspicuous involvement with advanced technology, often ahead of its development and usage in civilian practice. In this particular case we are concerned with the requirement to train men who service and maintain electrical and electronic equipment.

Background to the Case

Shore-based Naval training establishments ('stone-frigates' as they are known colloquially) have some special problems to overcome. They have to instil and constantly update the knowledge and skills of a large labour force whose annual turnover may be measured in thousands and whose period of service within the Royal Navy is unlikely to exceed a decade. At the same time, the 'management' (officers and petty officers) have to help the young trainee recruits (ratings) to adjust their expectations and motivations to the orderly routine of a disciplined, non-unionized, working environment. Not only are these trainees there to acquire technical skills; they are learning a whole new way of life.

Local Circumstances of the Training

At the time two separate establishments, some 20 miles apart, took part in the training of young male school-leavers who had enlisted to serve as electrical and radio mechanics. Every five weeks about 80 recruits joined the first establishment. Here they received basic induction courses to the Navy, accompanied by revisionary instruction in English and mathematics (including nine hours on elementary trigonometry) designed to bring them all to a suitable standard before embarking upon their specialized technical training. After five or six weeks they moved on to the second establishment, where training continued for a further 12 or 17 weeks depending on whether they were to specialize in electrical or radio and other electronic equipment. Training was therefore organized in a 'block entry' fashion, as is common in major civilian training organizations and exemplified by courses held at the British Manpower Services Commission's skill centres. Classes of 10–20 trainees were formed at the start and remained intact throughout the courses, unless sickness or failure at a main examination led to an individual being 'back-classed'. Since pay, status and seniority were all enhanced when a mechanic became qualified, there were strong incentives to succeed.

Though naval mechanics were not expected to become high-grade diagnosticians and fault-finders, their training was designed to equip them with a general background of theoretical and practical knowledge supplemented by specific abilities to maintain a ship's electrical and electronic systems. This entailed competent handling of test apparatus, soldering-irons and electrical fitting tools. Their training courses therefore included conventional classroom instruction through lectures, texts and demonstrations, integrated with laboratory exercises and practical work. In the case study you are following, the primary concern is with classroom instruction, from which about 40 hours were allocated to Common Electrical Training, nine hours to Motors and Generators, and 65 hours to Electronics Course I.

The Problem

The Problems from an Organizational Viewpoint

When this study took place the Navy was encountering serious, seemingly intractable problems. On the one hand, equipment was being transformed by pervasive innovations in electronic equipment of all kinds. Yet the enhancement of operational efficiency which new technology permitted could only be assumed if the equipment was reliably maintained at peak efficiency. This problem was widely construed as a demand for additional and more highly trained technical personnel. On the other hand, in the prevailing climate at that time of 'full employment' and a generally muted enthusiasm for military careers, there was little to encourage the view that an expanded recruitment drive would suffice. On the contrary, there were influential voices arguing that standards would have to be relaxed in the next decade. Recruits for the electrical mechanic trades had to be volunteers. And they had to achieve a prescribed minimum score (RT) on the Navy's battery of selection tests of intellectual and educational standards. (The average RT for these recruits was equivalent to an IQ of 112, on a scale where the mean IQ is 100 and the standard deviation 16.66.)

Situations like this are common enough in any 'high-tech' organization, not only in the military services. There are several different strategies which can be followed; and three of them which the Navy took very seriously are summarized here.

The Equipment Solution Press for better designed, more reliable, and more easily maintained equipment. A complementary approach, often adopted in computing and transport systems where continuous operation and safety are first priorities, is to build in duplicated ('redundant') circuits and deal with breakdowns simply through disposal and replacement rather than repair, e.g. faulty circuit boards in a computer which can simply be replaced. Limitations of the equipment solution are its costs, and its inability to guarantee that systems which happen to be installed correctly now will always be working optimally.

The Personnel Selection Solution This is the solution often favoured by organizations that do not want to train their own staff. Even those organizations which do, like the Navy, are disposed to look first for the highest quality personnel they can attract, on the dubious assumption that the 'brightest' and best qualified persons will always be the most suitable to work at any job. The premise is that, if your existing staff do not seem able to keep your electronic systems running optimally, despite your admirable training courses, then try to select potentially more competent ones. A limitation of this approach is that you encounter the 'degrees of freedom of action' problem. If, as in the Navy, you cannot simply recruit (say) all the most intelligent and highly educated applicants as electrical mechanics – because other naval branches want their share of them, and you also want your mechanics to be young, healthy, emotionally stable and well motivated – you may soon run out of eligible and suitable candidates.

The Training Solution This is the strategy on which our case study concentrates. Here you examine your training system and judge whether improvements are possible through more relevant training, better instructional methods, modifications to examination procedure. Two circumstances influenced the inclination of naval training authorities towards this strategy; though not necessarily to the exclusion of others. First was their anxiety about whether recruits to the electrical branch would continue to reach the entry standards hitherto found necessary to cope with the training as given. Secondly, they were worried about a shortage of experienced instructional staff, particularly among graduate teachers specializing in electronics.

In thinking about this strategy, you should take account of the underlying philosophy which is still prevalent in industry, and was then implicit in naval training too. It is that other things (like costs) being equal, successful vocational training is contingent upon five constituents: (a) quality of trainees; (b) quality of instructional staff; (c) relevance of training course content with respect to the jobs which trainees will do *eventually* as well as immediately; (d) quality of instructional methods; (e) continuous evaluation of how effective is the training itself, in addition to objective assessment of trainees' performance. While the naval organization was attentive to all these factors, their interest so far as we are concerned was focused upon (d).

A Psychological Perspective on the Problems

Each of the five training constituents represents a potentially fruitful area of intervention to an applied psychologist. You may think of others too. Just what the psychologist chooses to investigate in a situation like this, and assuming that the organization concedes his/her choice, will be strongly influenced by an appreciation of whatever seems most promisingly relevant among current advances in the state of the art.

Before our case study started there had been significant psychological initiatives in a number of areas affecting vocational training theory and practice. At a theoretical level there were rival claims for operant conditioning ('shaping' of learning through small incremental steps in instruction, with reinforcement of explicit, correct, responses), and for cybernetic models of skill and its acquisition (guided and error-actuated learning, promoted by systematic feedback of information about the accuracy of responses). At a corresponding practical level, there were various kinds of so-called 'teaching machine' and other modes of presenting 'programmed instruction' (PI). Both theory and empirical research appeared to support the notion that if the content and presentation of the training course were redesigned along the systematic lines advocated by 'programmed learning' enthusiasts, two substantial benefits would follow. First, learning could proceed more quickly and attain higher levels than with conventional teaching and training approaches. Secondly, the instruction could be self-administered and monitored, allowing much reduced costs from instructional staff; it was also expected to encourage stronger positive motivations towards learning.

Description of the Case

This is necessarily brief. Try to read the full account in Wallis and Wicks (1963) and Wallis (1964) or the extended summary in Wallis et al. (1966). Two field experiments were conducted, one in each of the naval training establishments mentioned earlier.

The first was really a 'feasibility' or pilot study of whether the new training method (PI) was at all *likely* to prove more effective and efficient than conventional teaching methods. PI can be self-administered by a trainee, under the control of a teaching machine. (Interactive forms of computer-aided learning are the current analogue.) Or it can be provided through less sophisticated, but cheaper, programmed textbooks. Trigonometry was chosen as the subject matter, since a suitable PI course equivalent to what was normally taught during nine hours of lessons was already available.

Three groups of 23 naval technician recruits were taught either by the conventional classroom methods or by one of the two equivalent forms of programmed instruction. They were closely matched with respect to previous mathematical knowledge, reading comprehension, general intelligence and educational background. This experiment produced encouraging results. 'Automatic' instruction, i.e. self-administered PI, seemed to be quite as effective as conventional human teaching, at least when the teaching machines were used. Not only was just as much trigonometry learned, but it was retained equally well after an interval of two weeks. There was also evidence of a faster rate of learning with PI. Recruits were favourably disposed towards the teaching machines, though less so towards the programmed textbooks; yet a preference for teaching in the customary manner was also expressed by many.

The second study was altogether more ambitious in scope and more closely embedded in the realities of practical training. Promising, but far from conclusive, evidence had emerged from the first experiment to suggest that the new training method *might* repay application in the Navy on a wide scale. But doubts would have to be removed about the likelihood of success when long periods of technical training were converted to PI, and when the course materials had to be programmed 'in-house'.

Programmed instruction with teaching machines was prepared for each of the electrical and radio courses referred to previously. Equivalent classes of up to 20 trainees were taught either by this method, or by the usual classroom methods. Progress tests, written qualifying examinations, laboratory work, and expressed attitudes were all used as comparative measures. At first two conditions of PI were investigated. 'Full automation' was represented by complete withdrawal of human teaching and support. 'Partial automation', however, meant that normal instructional staff were on hand to supervise and give help, but only if help was sought. The teacher's role under this condition was passive and minimal.

Neither of these systems of training turned out quite so well as 'hard-line' PI enthusiasts predicted. Only the radio courses compared favourably with the existing method. Moreover, despite early keenness among the trainees, marked aversion to 'machine' tuition became widespread after the first few weeks of some of the courses.

A third training system, known as 'integrated PI', was therefore devised in order to combine the optimal features of both the new PI methods and conventional teaching. In essence this system capitalized on the economic benefits of self-instructional PI by allowing *one* instructor officer to handle *two* classes in parallel, thus doubling his 'productivity'. His teaching role was carefully redefined, so that while all the basic instruction and progress-testing was accomplished through PI, he was readily available for supplementary guidance and personalized tutoring whenever he or a trainee saw the need for this.

Results from the controlled introduction of this training method revealed striking improvements in the quality of training, as indicated by qualifying examinations and practical coursework. Moreover a questionnaire survey of attitudes, together with observations of general behaviour, showed that the former aversion to teaching machines and PI had been overcome. Training staff as well as trainees were enthusiastic. As a consequence the 'integrated PI' system was formally adopted and established itself as a standard for naval technical training.

A follow-up of technical personnel subsequently trained in this way showed that the initially high standard was maintained for at least 30 classes. The next six classes achieved slightly less good results, but still better than under the previous conventional (or indeed the experimental 'automated') systems.

Case Study Tasks

For your principal exercise tasks, assume that you have been made responsible for planning, conducting and evaluating the field trials of a new system of technical (electronic maintenance) training. The course content has been prepared already, following the same syllabus as the customary naval courses (still in operation . . .) do, but using radically different methods of instruction and presentation, i.e. programmed instruction and teaching machines. The machines are simply individually-operated devices for providing trainees with a moderately interactive instructional medium. (Free-standing microprocessors, programmed as computer-aided learning devices, are the current derivative.)

This new course of 'automated PI' has not been tried anywhere before. But if you are right in believing that basic research has demonstrated the validity of programmed learning principles, then you have reasonable grounds for going ahead with your trials. If, however, you *doubt* this established validity, then you will want to consider the advisability of a preliminary enquiry, perhaps using a less complex training objective than producing competent electrical mechanics. Here are some questions to address.

1   Would you launch straight away into a full-scale evaluation of the new technical training course and methods? If so, how long should the evaluation be continued? If not, what kind of preliminary investigation would you propose, and what questions or hypotheses would you expect it to examine?

2   What criteria of success and/or acceptability would you think are appropriate in a field evaluation of the new training? Consider these from the organization's standpoint as well as the applied researcher's. Distinguish what you regard as the minimum essential criteria from others which you think would provide additional relevant evidence.

3   What measurements or other forms of assessment would you use to operationalize these criteria? How would you collect the data?

4   How would you set up the research design for your training course evaluation? You should think about the *realities* of experimental studies in a real organization. Try to identify what constraints the naval training establishment may have to impose upon your handling of the situation, e.g. participants; control and comparison groups; stability of experimental conditions; possible 'Hawthorne' effects.

5   What outcomes from your evaluation will you anticipate as sufficient for you to recommend that:

   a   The Royal Navy should adopt the new training forthwith, replacing the existing conventional training?

   b   The Navy should *not* adopt it? In this event what else, if anything, will you recommend?

6   Comment on any weaknesses, serious or tolerable, which you have detected from your reading of the case study as it actually occurred.

7   As a supplementary exercise, you may like to refer back to the section where

three broad strategies of intervention were identified: equipment, personnel selection and training 'solutions'. Which of these strategies would you reckon should have priority, as offering the best promise of overcoming the organization's problems? You may assume that the financial outlay in following any strategy is about the same.

Can you think of adequate reasons why a fourth strategy, that of *job and organizational redesign*, was not seriously considered in this case? In a civilian industrial context, this strategy might be expected to encourage higher productivity or performance through the enhancement of the quality of working life, e.g. by reduced supervision, group autonomy, discretionary output targets, etc.

8   If the new training system *is* adopted within the particular naval training establishment, is this likely to produce consequent organizational 'disturbances' or ramifications elsewhere?

9   How does the 'vocational skills' training approach, as outlined in this case, differ from interpersonal and 'sensitivity' training, as applied in personal and management development?

Essential Reading

Landy F J Trumbo D A (1980) Psychology of Work Behaviour, Dorsey Press, Chapters 7 and 8
Stammers R Patrick J (1975) The Psychology of Training, Methuen
Wallis D Wicks R P (1963) The Royal Navy study. Occupational Psychology, 37: 44–84 (reprinted in Programmed Learning, 1: 31–47, 1964)

Additional Reading

Annett J (1978) Training in theory and practice, in Psychology at Work, 2nd edition, edited by P B Warr, Penguin, Chapter 3
Dunnette M D (1976) Aptitudes, abilities, and skills, in Handbook of Industrial and Organizational Psychology, edited by M D Dunnette, Rand-McNally, Chapter 11
Gagné R M Briggs L J (1974) Principles of Instructional Design, Holt, Rinehart and Winston
Goldstein I L (1974) Training: Program Development and Evaluation, Wadsworth Publishing Co. (especially Chapters 4, 5, 8)
Hinrichs J R (1976) Personnel training, in Handbook of Industrial and Organizational Psychology, edited by M D Dunnette, Rand-McNally, Chapter 19
Porter L W Lawler E E Hackman J R (1975) Behavior in Organizations, McGraw-hill
Skinner B F (1961) Teaching machines, Scientific American, 205: 90–102
Smith P B (1980) Group Processes and Personal Change, Harper & Row
Wallis D (1964) Experiments on use of programmed instruction to increase the productivity of training. Occupational Psychology, 3 and 4: 141–159
Wallis D Duncan K D and Knight M G (1966) Programmed Instruction in the British Armed Forces: A Report on Research and Development, HMSO

CASE 15

Health and Safety at Work: Texchem*

Sandra Dawson

Organizational Setting

Texchem is part of a large, UK-owned corporation which has extensive, textile, chemical and plastics manufacturing operations in the UK and overseas. This factory was built in the 1920s to produce artificial yarn. It has since been expanded and now comprises an ill-assorted collection of old and more modern buildings, plant and machinery. Its manual and craft payroll stands at about 1000, with 300 staff employees. The production of fibres, their spinning into yarns and their subsequent processing still form a large part of Texchem's work, although other products and processes have been introduced. Production is carried out on a 24-hour shift basis and is broadly divided between the production of chemicals, spinning and solvent recovery, and plastics production. A range of technologies is used, from continuous or semicontinuous computer-controlled process plant in the chemical complex to traditional labour-intensive batch production in other areas.

Background to the Case

The General Background

There are approximately 20 main chemical (solid and liquid) materials produced or used on site. A range of potential hazards arise from the use of these substances including risks of toxicity, corrosivity, fire and explosion. This is besides the dangers arising from routine mechanical and materials handling operations. From 1976 to 1980 the number of reportable accidents among payroll personnel (excluding staff) was in the region of 35 per annum – an accident frequency rate of between 40 and 60 per 100 000 hours worked. These statistics indicated a slight improvement over this period, but another measure, the duration rate, which gives the average number of

* This case draws on material collected in collaboration with Philip Poynter and David Stevens

hours lost per reportable accident, indicated otherwise. It had increased from 165 hours in 1979 to 229 hours lost in 1980.

Texchem is organized along functional lines. Overall control of all activities on the site rests with the general manager. Beneath him come the production, engineering, personnel and other functional heads, including the safety adviser. Each of the three main production areas is headed by a senior manager with day to day control in the hands of managers, to whom both day and shift foremen report. A works engineer is responsible for all the engineering staff regardless of the department in which they are working. The senior fire officer also reports to the works engineer.

The shopfloor workforce is predominantly male. Most of the employees have worked for Texchem for a long time and are very loyal to the company. Trade union membership is fairly widespread and trade union recognition and organization is well established. Process operators are represented by the Transport and General Workers Union (TGWU) while a range of other unions, mainly the Amalgamated Union of Engineering Workers (AUEW) and Engineering and Electrical Power Workers Trade Union (EEPTU), represent the craftsmen. Supervisory and management grades are represented by two smaller unions.

With the decline of the UK textile industry, particularly in the face of fierce overseas competition, Texchem in the last decade has reduced its operations and workforce – the latter by as much as 33%. The corporation as a whole has rationalized its production facilities, closed some manufacturing outlets completely and declared large numbers of redundancies. The pressure is on Texchem to cut costs and to secure efficient production.

The Policy and Organization for Safety and Health

Texchem fulfils the requirements of the Health and Safety at Work Act 1974. It has a formal safety policy which constitutes a special part of a recently revised corporate booklet. The preface to the booklet states that corporate management recognizes and accepts responsibility for providing safe working conditions and that it will provide resources to meet this commitment. It also includes a full statement of the 'organization and arrangements'. A main board director has special responsibility for health and safety, and below him all managers and supervisors have line responsibility for health and safety. Safety specialists are employed at three levels to advise and assist line managers. The corporate safety department is responsible to a nominated director for the provision of safety advice and training, for monitoring performance, and for coordinating safety services within the group. The divisional safety adviser covers a group of factories and is responsible for coordinating the efforts of the factory safety adviser, for ensuring uniform standards and for liaising with the Factory Inspectorate and other corporate functions. The role of site safety advisers is to check and advise on safe operations in each factory according to standards laid down by management. Procedures covering standard operations, permits to work, the use of material data sheets, safety training and inspections have all been developed and they are generally accepted as a routine part of working at Texchem.

There is a clear commitment to workforce involvement in health and safety. The safety booklet states that safety committees should be established in all units to include employee representatives appointed by recognized trade unions, working in consultation with management representatives and advising on all aspects of health and safety. In fact a site safety committee has existed in Texchem for many years. Its members are mainly trade union representatives from the various sections of the workforce. Only the chairman of the committee is necessarily a manager and he is usually a departmental head. The safety adviser and the fire officer are *ex officio* members. The committee has a membership of about 12 and usually meets monthly. In addition a process safety committee was set up in the mid 1970s, largely prompted by reactions to the Flixborough disaster. Its members are appointed by management with a view to ensuring that adequate technical skills are applied in considering hazards in existing, new or modified equipment. There are no trade union representatives per se on this committee, since it was thought that they would lack the necessary technical expertise.

The Problem: What Next for Health and Safety at Texchem?

In the six or seven years following the Health and Safety at Work Act 1974, Texchem had done all that was formally asked of an establishment to provide a self-regulatory system for health and safety at work. Beyond this formal level however, it was not possible to be so optimistic. Managers, specialists and safety representatives, in their different ways, all expressed fears that Texchem's self-regulatory system would not continue to maintain good standards of health and safety. At a substantive level there was much talk of compromise while at a procedural level there were signs of apathy and neglect.

There were two main reasons for disquiet. The first was the experience and fear of the massive economic recession which had hit the UK industry and had been particularly hard for this corporation. In many ways the impact of the recession overshadowed everything else. Workers had seen similar plants close down completely and their own workforce substantially reduced. The company newsletter regularly proclaimed the need to 'tighten belts', to 'cut costs', to 'increase productivity'. Everyone knew, or at least they were always being told, that despite 'being busy' productivity in their factory was 'dangerously low' and losses were substantial. The trade unions, notable for their cooperative attitudes towards management, were especially keen not to 'rock the boat'. Managers and technical specialists, equally aware of the threat to their own jobs, were vigilant to avoid expenditure which was not seen as absolutely essential.

The second problem was apathy and over-familiarity with well established procedures, particularly when other priorities were assuming overriding importance. Texchem's current organization and arrangements to deal with health and safety, established in the flurry of activity generated by legislation and Flixborough, had become part of the routine working environment. Without a dramatic increase in Texchem's accident statistics, and with increasing confidence that the Health and Safety Executive was not going to serve notices or prosecute for every infringement of statutory codes and regulations, no one now seemed to worry much about health and safety. Some procedures were moving into abeyance through neglect or else were subtly changing so that they became less significant. For example, inspections were having a diminishing impact. Those previously carried out by departmental managers and supervisors had now become the responsibility of the safety adviser. Monthly inspections by the safety committee were now sometimes cancelled because of poor attendance. Reports of inspections were no longer always followed up with recommendations, and those recommendations which were made were not always acted upon.

These signs of compromise and apathy would be cause for concern in any establishment, but they were particularly worrying for Texchem because, although employment in the factory was contracting, new processes and materials were still being introduced. Active participation in product and process innovation was vital for survival. From a health and safety point of view, it was not just a question of maintaining existing procedures, precautions and controls; active investigation and planning for health and safety was still required. Even with existing processes, questions about long term health problems associated with toxic and carcinogenic substances remained unanswered and called for further consideration. Although most people in the plant acknowledged that a lot more could be done to make the plant healthier and safer, no one was really pushing for action in this area. The time and resources necessary to identify hazards and to prescribe appropriate standards, safeguards and procedures were no longer being made as available as they had been. Nor were there many signs of determined efforts to gather and disseminate fresh knowledge both about existing hazards or those arising from the use of new materials or processes. Texchem's process safety committee had made a good start in analysing existing plant and materials, but the committee's level of activity was diminishing; attendance was erratic and the membership frequently changed, with a corresponding loss of continuity. In times of economic stringency, hazard identification was assuming less importance, partly because of a scarcity of resources and partly because people were reluctant to raise issues which they felt were unlikely to be taken up.

Moving from identifying hazards to prescribing and implementing controls, safeguards and procedures, everyone expressed concern that the overriding pressure to cut costs was already having profound effects. A decision had been made in one production area that a particular solvent was to be replaced by another, which had two virtues. It was cheaper, and likely to be technically superior. However, it was more hazardous and people were frightened that the carcinogenic risks posed by the new solvent were not fully known. 'No one really knows whether we'll all be dead in 20 years' time because of it', said one supervisor. But, even so, no one stood out against its introduction because it seemed to offer hope of greater efficiency, reduced costs and continuing employment – providing, of course, that one lived to take advantage of such benefits.

Even with fully identified and well understood hazards, there was now markedly less pressure from anyone to improve on – or even to maintain – existing standards. For example, there was a long-standing problem of fumes and dust in a chemical production area, where workers had complained of bronchial problems and nose bleeds. Investigations into this problem, as well as discussions about remedial actions, including additional ventilation or plant modifications, were dropped from consideration because of the costs involved. In another production area, where there was concern about the use of materials which may have been carcinogenic, random blood sampling of the workforce had been instituted with a view to identifying related physiological changes. These tests had now been discontinued because of a lack of resources either to continue doing the tests or to do anything about the problem should it be shown to be serious. In another area, the standards of safeguards provided for plastics moulding presses had fallen well behind those regarded as generally acceptable. Significant capital expenditure, necessary to update the machines, was requested by the departmental manager. It was noted by senior managers that the Factory Inspectorate was not apparently pressing for these changes and the manager's request was rejected.

In another area where the old and much modified plant produced toxic gases Texchem was unable to reach the prescribed threshold limit value (TLV) for one of the gases. No means of modifying the plant could be found which were economical. The informal and widely accepted departmental policy was to limit the amount of time people actually spent in this part of the factory. All the paperwork was done in another shed and the operators and foremen avoided spending 'too long' in the area at any one time. This ad hoc arrangement was typical of a general trend in which identified health or safety problems were now more likely to be 'solved' by administrative or informal arrangements than by acting on the hardware of plant or materials. Such a trend was justified in terms of relative costs. Hardware measures, which in the heyday of safety activities were regarded as the main weapon, were now only possible if they related to 'an acute risk' or 'were required by an enforcing authority'. Since many of the hazards at Texchem were associated with health problems which could take a long time to develop, neither of these criteria were likely to be particularly helpful. A greater dependence on personal measures was unlikely to be highly successful because of their dependence on vigilance, commitment and awareness which were in any case beginning to fade. Furthermore the safety adviser was not skilled or experienced in operating in this way. He had always relied mostly on hardware precautions and he was now somewhat at a loss to know what to recommend or how to implement any proposals that came forward.

Each of the main groups involved acknowledged and tolerated a noticeable rundown in resources and commitment to health and safety, but they spoke of it in different terms. The production and engineering managers coped most easily. Health and safety was now lower down their list of priorities and few of them were overconcerned by this change. They were all aware of their responsibilities under the safety policy, but they spoke of these more in terms of meeting statutory requirements than of exerting a major influence on their performance. Few of them recalled any discussion of health and safety in their annual appraisal, though they felt that it would be raised if a major health and safety problem occurred in their departments. Little attempt was made to monitor individual or departmental performance or to hold people accountable for health and safety. Managers, of course, said they always ᵗried to maintain standards and would neither openly flout safety rules themselves nor condone anyone else doing so. Nevertheless, their overriding priorities were cost reduction, increased efficiency and productivity, and these had become more central in recent times. This trend was even more marked amongst the departmental managers' immediate subordinates. Supervisors did not always even formally acknowledge their responsibility for health and safety and they always staunchly defended their own patch, regardless of criticism or comment.

In the midst of this declining concern for health and safety stood the safety advisor. Not a great technical expert himself, he was reliant on technologists and toxicologists for scientific advice and information. He believed that his job – like everyone else's – was in jeopardy. He felt his position to be particularly precarious because he knew that several of his counterparts in other companies had been made redundant. Such redundancies had been justified by saying that the company had adjusted to the demands of the 1974 Act and had established procedures, so that there was now insufficient work to justify the employment of a full-time safety adviser. Their duties had been merged with those of another person and 'health and safety' had become a part-time specialist occupation. From a personal point of view Texchem's safety adviser was torn between taking so low a profile that he could be made similarly redundant and undertaking his responsibilities so vigorously that he would incur the wrath of his superiors, and even contribute to the economic collapse of the company. He knew that aspects of the technical control of hazards were being neglected. He had the unenviable task of deciding on what he thought were feasible priorities, given extremely scarce resources. He also found himself placed under pressure by other people in the factory. For example, line managers had effectively cast some of their responsibilities on to him. Inspections and audits which had been part of their job had now 'devolved' on to him. He was also privately urged by the safety representatives 'to do more'. But safety representatives themselves were normally reluctant to push for major improvements because of fears of the consequences.

Individually safety representatives were not a major force for change and collectively they were also limited in their demands and impact. Many did not keep the position for long and several did not take up their rights to time off for inspection, information and training. They all felt themselves to be under great pressure to fight for the company's survival and within this to defend their own department. If they raised criticisms about health and safety, they came into direct confrontation with their supervisors and heightened their sense of insecurity. Although safety representatives formed a large majority of the safety committee, all participants identified the chairman (a manager) as having most influence over decisions and over the way they were carried out. The committee provided a forum of consultation but not for equal participation in decision making. Safety representatives had in general acquiesced in all the compromises mentioned earlier.

Notions of commitment and awareness were wearing thin at every level as compromise followed compromise. All the major parties to self-regulation condoned a clear 'make do and perhaps mend' approach to hazards. The diminishing concern for health and safety which management and workforce were unwilling or unable to counteract, gave an obvious role for external inspectors. However, they too, it seemed, were well aware of the constraints of economic recession. For them also the employer's duty to do all that is 'reasonably practical' to ensure the health and safety of employees allowed increasing leeway. They were reported as being 'understanding' of the management's dilemma. Although they were not happy about some conditions, they were, it seemed, unprepared to take significant action in the face of ad hoc, partial solutions to fairly serious problems.

Case Study Tasks

1 Supposing *either* that (i) you are a qualified graduate chemical engineer with 10 years' industrial experience, newly appointed to Texchem from another company to replace the safety officer, who has retired, *or* that (ii) you are a qualified graduate chemical engineer, who, having been 15 years in Texchem operational and technical departments, has just been appointed as departmental head of the chemical production area. Answer the two questions below.

  a What would you set out to do about health and safety in the plant in the short term (within one year)? What factors are likely to help or hinder you in your endeavours?

  b What would you set out to do about health and safety in the plant in the longer term (within five years)? What factors are likely to help or hinder you in your endeavours?

2 Suppose that you had worked as an operator for 10 years and were newly appointed as a TGWU safety representative for a production department; how would you set about fulfilling your role as safety representative? Consider, amongst other things: access to information and training, inspections, committee membership and activity, contact with the workers you represent, role in decision making and implementation.

3 What are the advantages and disadvantages of the two-committee structure? On balance would you advise retaining two committees? Give reasons for your answer and suggest alternatives, if appropriate.

4 Should responsibility for health and safety be given back to the line? How should this be done?

5 Do you think that consideration of a strategy for dealing with safety at work should be kept separate from a strategy for safeguarding health at work?

6 What advice would you give to national officials of trade unions who were concerned generally about the rate of progress in reducing the incidence of accidents at work and occupational ill health?

7 Is self-regulation of health and safety a viable concept in recession conditions?

Essential Reading

Dawson S Poynter P Stevens D (1983) How to secure an effective health and safety programme at work, OMEGA: The International Journal of Management Science 2: 443–446

Glendon A I Booth R T (1982) Worker participation in occupational health and safety in Britain, International Labour Review 121: 399–416

Additional Reading

Accident Prevention Advisory Unit (1980) Effective Policies for Health and Safety, HMSO

Beaumont P B (1983) Safety at Work and the Unions, Croom Helm

Broadhurst A (1978) The Health and Safety at Work Act in Practice, Heyden

Dawson S Poynter P Stevens D (1982) Activities and outcomes: monitoring safety performance, Chemistry and Industry 20: 790–796

Dawson S Poynter P Stevens D (1984) Safety specialists in industry: roles, constraints and opportunities, Journal of Occupational Behaviour 5: 253–270

Glendon A I (1979) Accident prevention and safety – whose responsibility? Occupational Health 31: 31–34

Nichols T Armstrong P J (1973) Safety or Profit: Industrial Accidents and the Conventional Wisdom, Falling Wall Press

Robens Lord (Chairman) (1972) Safety and Health at Work, Report of the Committee (1970–72), Cmnd 5034, HMSO

CASE 16

Redundancy: Office Engineering Company

Stephen Wood

Organizational Setting

Office Engineering Company (OEC) manufactures staples, staplers, paper clips and other office equipment. It is part of a larger group, National Office Company (NOC), which produces and markets stationery and other office-related products. NOC started after the Second World War simply as a marketing operation but began manufacturing staples and staplers in 1950. During the next 25 years it grew very rapidly, through both new product development and acquisition. OEC began production in a small works in South London with a handful of workers who helped the managing director, who was himself personally involved, to build up the manufacturing operations. In 1956 the company moved to a larger site in South London. At its peak production it employed over 450 workers, most of whom were either women on the machines, male setters of the machines or skilled apprentice-trained maintenance and tool-room men. Because of the importance of skilled jobs and recruitment of apprentice-trained labour, the AUEW is the sole union and primarily represents the male workers (union density was 60%).

By the 1970s, the demand for OEC's two main lines, types of staples and staplers, had reached such high levels that it could not be met with the plant's capacity. Production was achieved by locating as many machines as possible in the building, including gangways and corridors, and in what used to be the canteen, and producing in part of one of its other plants in North London. Eventually the firm was forced to subcontract some work, and began to look for a new site. A decision to build a brand new purpose-built plant was taken in 1977, and the building was completed in 1980. It was located in South Wales, partly because of the easy access to key markets in the south and because of government incentives.

Background to the Case

Prior to the opening of the plant in Wales, OEC could sell more than it produced; order books were consistently well ahead of production. In planning the new capacity, the management assumed that demand would continue to grow at the past rate of about 5% per year and that, in the short term, this production would not be met in the new plant. The long-term situation was more uncertain, and the main source of concern was the fear that a Japanese manufacturer, who had already started to sell with some success in the British and European market, would set up a manufacturing site in Britain. In planning the site in Wales, they had been constrained by available sites and their own capital funds; they had deliberately built the plant to give them flexibility and pitched its capacity at what they saw as the long-term demand, and assumed that they would continue production in South London for the foreseeable future, and if demand continued to rise they could increase production on one or other site either by recruitment or productivity gains. If the Japanese or another similar venture materialized, they could always retrench and seek to compete with them through increasing productivity, a possibility which the management thought they could achieve more readily in the new plant, as productivity had been relatively constant in the South London plant in the past few years. Whilst in the short term management anticipated encountering teething problems in the new plant as they recruited and built up a new workforce, they also expected to achieve some immediate productivity gains because of the newness of the plant and layout, although the basic technology of machine production was the same as in the London plant.

It was expected when the move was first planned that some personnel would move from London to South Wales, and that production would be phased into the new plant over a period of six months, with the workforce being recruited in stages, to reach a peak of 250 within nine months. Production at the North London plant would cease after three months when all the machines from there had been transferred to South Wales. It was planned to use this capacity for making a product from another part of the group and thus no redundancies were anticipated there.

In all, 35 personnel moved to Wales, all but one coming from the larger South London plant. The majority of these were managers or skilled workers. Several others were involved in setting up the plant and commuted down to work during the week, returning to London at weekends. There was a fixed number of workers whom the company could take to Wales according to the terms of the government assistance – not more than 10% of the workforce, and they had to be key workers. Nevertheless, through a general notice the firm had encouraged all workers to consider the move. The management did not anticipate that the women or many of the older workers would want to go. But they were keen for many of their highly skilled maintenance men and supervisors to take the option seriously. Many of the men with long service did not want to uproot and be separated from their children and in many cases grandchildren. Most of the skilled men, while not against moving, were not keen on Wales, where their labour market opportunities were seen to be very different from those in London, in which there remained a relative shortage of skilled labour. Some of the unskilled or semiskilled considered with varying degrees of seriousness moving to Wales. Some even went down with their wives on a trip organized by the company but came back feeling that it was too depressing and quiet. Some of those who worked at the plant during the start-up became increasingly keen, but felt the company did not want them to move. Furthermore, they felt that they were being discriminated against relative to the skilled men, and that those who had gone down to Wales to help the firm had been used and not thanked for their efforts, many of which they thought were exceptional. Workers talked of how they had been phoned up at six o'clock on a Sunday night and asked – or told, as it became known as the story line sharpened up – to go to Wales the next day.

In the end it took about a year to get settled production in the new plant; even then it was only at the targets set for six months after opening, and breakdowns were particularly frequent. During this period there were many rumours which fuelled considerable resentment against the management of OEC. Ever since it had become obvious that the South London plant was too small, rumours had circulated that the firm was planning to relocate and close it. When moving to Wales, the firm had discussed the situation with the union representatives and had sought to dispel rumours about the closure from an early date. They anticipated that they would require full cooperation from the workforce in the foreseeable future and were hoping that some of the key workers would move. Management did this mainly by reassuring them of the continuation of production at South London and by giving as much information as possible on the move and the situation at North London, although there was virtually no contact between the workforces in the various parts of NOC. They also encouraged their supervisors to keep the peace and 'play it cool', as the production manager told them. They would aim to deal with individual grievances sympathetically and as soon as they came up. They also continued to turn a blind eye to much of the custom and practice which they knew went on, such as the rather excessive overtime which the men in particular did. Furthermore no attempt was made to investigate some of the things management 'suspected', for example, the regular practice of some workers clocking each other on and off on a Saturday morning, so that they did not have to come into the factory.

Six months after the opening in South Wales, the men at South London discovered that the semiskilled and unskilled workers were earning more in Wales than they were – a fact which reflected the increasing use of work measurement and a different type of measured day work payment system. The union representatives put pressure on the firm to pay more, but management's initial reluctance to discuss the matter – as they claimed that they were paying similar rates but that the payment system and shift arrangements were slightly different – accentuated the resentment which the workforce felt towards the management. At the first Christmas after the move the workers did not receive their traditional bonus and Christmas turkey, a long-standing custom dating back to the chairman's personal involvement in the plant. The management of the South Wales plant did not want to encourage this and there was a desire to phase it out in London. Nevertheless, under pressure from the workforce, including a go-slow and a threat from the skilled men to take their tools home, the management at London acceded to the demand for this tradition, but did not guarantee that it would not be phased out in the future. As it was anticipated that production at South London would fall and that, with a reorganization of the plant, less labour would be required, management began, six months prior to the move to Wales, a policy of natural wastage, of not replacing leavers. None of those who moved to Wales were replaced, except a few senior managers who were replaced by managers from other parts of NOC, some of whom knew little or nothing about engineering.

After a few months breakdowns increased at the South London plant, and it became obvious that there were insufficient skilled men, as a handful had gone to Wales, and others had left (the annual turnover was usually about 20% for skilled workers). The evening shift, which had been predominantly women, was stopped because of the falling demand. But labour turnover, traditionally high (45%), continued to create problems on the day shift. Two key storemen left and the policy of not replacing them led to severe problems and bottlenecks in the system. Workers and supervisors began to put pressure on management for replacements, and the initial reluctance of management further aggravated some workers who felt they were being asked to do the jobs of two people. In the end several new workers were recruited to fill jobs which supervisors thought were necessary.

The Problem

In the spring of 1980, nine months after the Welsh plant had opened, almost overnight sales began to fall. The world recession was beginning and more significantly the Japanese had just made what appeared to be a very successful launch in Britain. Some future projections of the effect of a deep recession on the firm's sales looked very bleak. Furthermore, the building of a Japanese plant looked increasingly likely. The senior management of OEC and the chairman of NOC, faced with the projected decline in demand and imminent cash flow problems, decided they had a choice of four ways of dealing with the surplus: (a) assume that the fall in the demand for their product was temporary and/or could be made up by extending export orders, and run on short-time working while cutting all overtime; (b) close the South London plant; (c) reduce manpower in proportion to the immediate fall in demand; (d) control overtime in one or both plants and use short-time working or voluntary redundancy, while also attempting to improve medium-term performance through changes in working practices and associated manpower reductions.

The chairman, having been successful in building up the group and being bullish by temperament, was reluctant at first to accept that 'his firm', as he called it, would not continue to grow as it had, but eventually the first option was ruled out by the senior management as unrealistic, or at least too risky.

Having started the firm's manufacturing activities at the South London site, the chairman had a strong emotional attachment to it and to the men who had started it with him. He was, therefore, very uneasy about the second option, namely closing the plant and concentrating all production in South Wales. There had continued to be production problems in the new plant, although the younger production director stressed the irrationality of having an operation other than in Wales. He was convinced that productivity would increase substantially and that the full potential of the plant and possible economies of scale would not be realized until it was operating at much higher volume levels. In the short term demand was still beyond what could realistically be achieved in South Wales, and the second option was thought too risky, especially as they had found recruitment less easy than they had initially thought. A final concern about the second option was whether the firm could finance the redundancy payments; although the managment had given no guarantee of employment at the time of the move, the chairman argued that there was a kind of implicit commitment, which particularly extended to the older workers. He personally felt a great obligation to many of them. This feeling was not extended to the newer workers, whom he saw as coming from a less conscientious, younger generation. Because of these feelings he argued that if there were to be redundancies in the immediate future the firm had an obligation to pay above the statutory level and to attempt to find the older workers jobs within the rest of NOC. The finance director argued that the firm should retrench immediately and concentrate managerial efforts which he felt were getting dissipated between the two plants, and furthermore that no such obligation to the workforce existed and in any event jobs were easy to come by in South London. The sale of the site made the closure especially attractive to him, and he argued that if payments above the statutory minimum were to be made, the money should be found from within the group (NOC) and not the company (OEC) alone. The sales director was concerned about the ability of the Welsh plant to produce on its own the immediate volume at a time when it was important to achieve delivery and improve quality standards. The chairman was anxious to keep the London site and thought that even if OEC eventually ceased production there he might use it for something else, and eventually urged for a programme of limited retrenchment.

The problem with regard to the third option was also one of finance – and the chairman was very reluctant to spend money on severance payments because 'we don't get our pound of flesh for them', and was certainly reluctant to finance them from outside OEC. Because of the uncertainty of the future trend in demand, and the chairman's position, the personnel director became increasingly convinced that the final option was the answer and that a viable strategy would be to increase the productivity of the plant and use various methods to reduce the head count. He had been based at South London in the early part of his career and had an intimate knowledge of the plant, although not of the details of production.

The chairman decided that the personnel director should, in consultation with his colleagues, develop a strategy in keeping with the fourth option, but was also interested in his views on the other options.

Case Study Tasks

You are to adopt the role of the personnel director and must make a presentation to the chairman of your proposed strategy. He has given you a number of constraints which include the following: you should look for redundancies of around 130 employees (i.e. cut the workforce in South London by at least half); none of those who built up the company must be made redundant; productivity gains must be genuine; and the average payments must not be greater than in a previous exercise elsewhere in the enterprise (£5000 per head) – see appendix below. In particular the Chairman has asked you to produce a report which answers the following questions:

1   What are the advantages and disadvantages of the four options?
2   Will the redundancies be phased or will all people leave at the same time?
3   How will people be chosen? If the voluntary method is used, what will you do about trying to keep the 'best' people or those with valuable skills? If redundancy is compulsory, will seniority or efficiency be the criterion? Will you consult or negotiate with union representatives on the selection criteria?
4   Will redundancy terms be set at the statutory rate? If above this rate, on what basis will they be calculated? Will this be negotiated with the unions?
5   To what extent do you anticipate opposition from the trade unions? What form will this take? Are there conflicts between unions and their members? Will the unions have a view about jobs for the next generation in the locality?
6   What contingencies should you allow for? What of the fears that the plant will close?
7   What methods do you recommend to change working practices and increase productivity? Will the redundancy programme inhibit progress in this direction? Will you negotiate over the changes?
8   What action is to be taken, if any, about the opposition of supervision and line management to any changes in manning levels?

Essential Reading

Mukerjee S (1974) Through No Fault of Their Own, Political and Economic Planning (PEP)
Wood S Dey I (1983) Redundancy, Gower

Additional Reading

Brannen P Batstone E Fatchett D White P (1976) The Worker Directors, Hutchinson (see Chapter 10)
Daniel W W Mukerjee S (1970) Strategies for Displaced Employees, PEP Broadsheet, 36, no. 517
Fox A (1965) The Milton Plan, Institute of Personnel Management
Martin R Fryer R M (1973) Redundancy and Paternalist Capitalism, Allen & Unwin

Appendix

Previous Group Redundancies

Company A   100 redundancies in 1978. No positions identified. Volunteers only, early retirement at 55, no special pensions deal, no volunteers rejected, terms cost £4000 per head. No unions.

Company B 150 redundancies in 1979/80. Positions identified but all were volunteers. Many volunteers rejected. AUEW and TGWU negotiated terms, average cost £5000 per head.

Current Profiles in OEC

Age (years)	M	F	Length of service (years)	M	F
<30	40	25	<2	7	5
30–39	32	33	2–5	25	30
40–49	10	14	6–10	25	23
50–54	10	15	10–20	20	45
55–59	10	20	20+	30	25
60+	5	21			
	—	—		—	—
	107	128		107	128

Types of Employees in OEC

Women Packers and machine operators. Average £3500 p.a. Some are part-time (10 on four hours per day and 15 on six hours per day).

Unskilled Men Storemen, machine setters and feeders. Average £4500 p.a. Approx 25% of these are from ethnic minorities.

Skilled Men Maintenance and tool-room employees. Mobile group (average from three to five years' service) who average £5500 p.a.

Long-service OEC Men Usually skilled or supervisory. Average £6500 p.a.

Office Workers Four women and one man. Average £4700 p.a.

Redundancy Payments Act and Employment Protection Act

On redundancy a lump sum is due to any employee with two years' continuous service.

Lump sum varies with length of service, age and weekly pay. For each complete year of service in which employee was aged 18–21, she/he gets half a week's pay; aged 22–40 gets one week's pay, aged 41–65 (60 if woman) she/he gets 1.5 week's pay. Maximum length of service which can count is 20 years.

Employers are required to consult appropriate trade unions about proposed redundancies and need to disclose reasonabiy full information to unions and employees in writing. This information should include reasons, numbers and descriptions of employees, method of selection and method of implementation.

The union has a right of reply and the employer must consider and reply to any points made.

CASE 17

Management Development: British Rail

John Burgoyne

Organizational Setting

British Rail (BR) is a large organization, particularly in terms of people – 200 000 approximately, of whom 20 000 could be regarded as 'managers'. The organization is also large in terms of cash turnover, equipment, land and property owned, and in numbers of customers.

From a market point of view, the main activities of BR are passenger transport, divided into commuter, intercity and provincial; freight, of which a major element is coal and lesser elements iron and steel; and also a significant general goods transport business, and a parcels business.

There are a number of related activities and organizations: Sealink, hotels, BR Engineering Ltd – all wholly or partially hived off or privatized, and also Travellers Fare – catering on trains and stations.

Like most large organizations, a number of 'logics' underly the differentiation between individuals, roles and departments in the structure of the organization.

'Function' is one such logic. Operators run services; engineers deal with rolling stock; civil engineers look after tracks; signals and telecommunications people deal with the increasingly complicated electronic information and control systems. Many people spend most or all of their careers in these or others of the many 'functions' which exist in BR.

Geographical area provides another 'logic', with regions being the biggest units, some of them still with a strong correspondence to the railway companies which were combined to form BR.

Broad division into market-oriented categories is another important 'logic', and one of increasing significance under the new philosophy of 'sector management'.

Background to the Case

General changes in recent years set the background and context for the management development programme examined in this case study. The organization has become smaller recently, particularly in terms of manpower. One of the more recent structural changes has been the removal of a 'layer' in the geographical logic: regions used to consist of areas which were in turn made up of districts. Now regions are changing or have been changed to a situation in which districts report directly to them. Since the number of districts remains unchanged, this means that regional offices now have many more lines of communication to working units.

Sector management – the market-oriented logic – has been much strengthened in the recent past, as part of a management philosophy to make the organization more like a public sector business and less like an underwritten general public service. The sector management philosophy encompasses the idea of as many separable units as possible operating as cost/profit centres, each trying to maximize its financial efficiency and, where appropriate, buying and selling goods and services from each other. Thus, in theory at least, an operator might 'hire' rolling stock, 'rent' track or pay a fee to use it, and collect revenue by running a service.

Such a philosophy obviously owes much to continuing political and governmental pressure to be more like private industry, and to reduce the PSO (public service obligation – effectively the government subsidy of BR), and hence the direct burden of the railway system on the taxpayer.

The current management development programme has its origins in senior management initiatives to move in these directions. In about 1981 the then existing management development arrangements were reviewed as part of the process of beginning to introduce a new management approach. Existing provision was judged to be inappropriate to the new circumstances, and a new programme formulated. This was done on the basis of 'career graphs', showing the career trajectories of BR managers with seniority grade plotted against age and a view of what management should be like at the different levels. The general aim was seen as the development of a 'business consciousness' more consistent with the approach underlying sector management.

The courses in the new programme ordered for increasing levels of seniority are itemized below.

Basic Management Skills (BMS)

BMS is a course which has evolved from the previous management programme, and which is attended by junior managers. The course has tended to concentrate on basic planning, communications and people management skills. Currently differing forms of it are being tried for the different 'populations' in the grades that it is oriented to – the older managers who are near their career ceiling and have spent much of their careers in supervisory jobs, and younger managers, a few years out of the management trainee schemes, or equivalent, who are likely to move to more senior grades. The programme for the former group currently concentrates more on people management skills, the latter on more general problem-solving.

General Management Programme (GMP)

GMP is a course taught at the BR Staff College by staff provided by a business school. It covers most of the subjects and areas regarded as relevant to management – accounting, organizational behaviour, marketing, economics – and contains a business game and several projects; it also gives participants a chance to take stock of themselves in their work roles. It is a four-week course that runs twice a year for about 30 people. The course has run three times at the time of writing.

Advanced Skill Modules (ASMs)

ASMs are modules conceived in the plan as three separate one-week courses in the areas of finance, personnel and technology. At the time of writing pilot courses on finance and personnel have been run, and a further course in each of these areas is planned, incorporating modifications based on the lessons learnt from the pilot courses. Plans are still being formulated to run a pilot course in the technology area.

The general concept of the ASMs is that they offer participants advanced skills in areas that have not necessarily been their specialism, at a career stage in which they are moving into more general management. In theory, when the full programme of courses is fully operational, ASMs are intended to build on the base laid in the GMP, and to provide a foundation for the next 'level' of course – the Business Management Programme (BMP). At this stage, however, most people attending these programmes have not attended the GMP, and most people going on to the BMP have not attended either ASMs or the GMP. The ASMs are 'bought in' from business schools or management colleges, who are invited to tender for them against a specification.

The Business Management Programme (BMP)

This is a six-week course, run at, and by, a business school. Its general aim is to develop broad general management abilities against a background of awareness of concepts and techniques relevant to management. It is 'educational' and 'developmental' in its intention, rather than skill training. At the moment, because most participants have not been through the GMP, it deals with basic concepts and techniques. The second, and major part of the programme contains a high proportion of projects, including one done 'live' in a non-BR organization, and an array of options which allow the participants to choose a set of areas to study in the light of their individual backgrounds and needs. The BMP has run four times, and aims for about 25 participants on each course.

At the time of writing therefore, the programme, as a set of four levels of course, is largely set up and running, though not in its finally envisaged form, since it will be a number of years before it will be possible for participants in the more senior programmes to have been on the ones for more junior levels.

The Problem

There are three major foci to the problems of the head office team, and one major underlying issue:

1 Initial experience with the programmes suggests a number or issues about course membership, career development and course content which may need attention.
2 Arising from this, and from more strategic considerations, is the question of how, if at all, the programme should be modified, and if it should, how fundamental the change should be?
3 What practical approach to evaluation should be used, and what criteria for effective programmes should be used within this?

The underlying issue concerns how the 'learning' programmes, which are the focus of this case, can, in a practical way, be integrated with career management, personnel policy and corporate policy.

To give some background to the first focus of attention, feedback from the courses has revealed a great variety of activities and experiences amongst all participants but a number of general conclusions stand out.

Some attitude change, towards a 'business consciousness' as outlined at the beginning of the case, has taken place over the periods of the courses, as judged by expressed views in questionnaires and interviews with participants. It is less clear, because the evidence is less accessible, whether such attitude change has been permanent or whether it has translated into action.

There is some evidence that this was taking place slowly anyway, perhaps as a result of both internal structural changes like the introduction of sector management, and the general public awareness that all BR managers have about trends in the organization.

It would appear that more learning/attitude change took place on the courses that happened to coincide with the major railway strike in the summer of 1982, when BR managers came to believe that their industry might change to a degree and at a pace that they had not previously thought likely. However, course providers consider that there is a mild 'resistance' on the part of some participants, to the 'business attitude' and to the ideas and approaches involved in putting it into practice that were taught on the courses. From the participants' point of view, this was seen as the teaching of ideas that were not realistic in the context of the railway industry, or to the latest 'temporary fashion' in management philosophy, the like of which has been seen to come and go in the past. Given that the participants were, in the main, nominated and selected to attend, rather than being there because of their own initiative, there seems to have been a mild effect of 'taking the horse to the water but not being able to make it drink'.

Related to this, there is some evidence of mild influence of the phenomenon that the people who are, in the event, spared for courses tend to be the people who are not in the most critical jobs. It is also apparent that some reversion to type has occurred in the sense that participants have influenced the courses to become slightly more like the pre-1981 courses at the equivalent levels from which the new courses were supposed to be a radical departure. In terms of the individual programmes, conclusions from available feedback are as follows:

As regards the BMS course, the splitting out of the groups at a later career stage from those at an earlier one is useful. The traditional form of the course, focusing mainly on planning, communications and people management skills, is appropriate for the older group. For the younger group there seems to be the choice between focusing on the immediate job skills of people at this level, or beginning the process of more general, and long-term, management education. The former approach seemed to overlap with some of the ending parts of the management trainee scheme; the latter approach seems to encroach on the purposes of GMP. One serious possibility seems to be that this group is in danger of overtraining/educating, and would be best served by being left to accumulate more work experience.

In terms of general reaction and the impressions of everyone concerned, the GMP has been the most successful of the courses in the programme, and the one that has needed least adjustment since its inception. A plausible explanation of this is that the participants have the right amount of experience, and have been away from formal education and development long enough for this general course to be both new and to make sense to them. Some of the parts of this course that are found most stimulating are those that help participants examine their own roles in the light of the ideas presented.

The ASMs are still to a large extent an unknown quantity. The two pilot programmes in finance and personnel were sufficiently problematical in their detail to suggest serious redesign before further testing, while at the same time establishing the importance and relevance of the topics to the people concerned. Study of the finance course, where knowledge is to some extent linear – having one skill being necessary to learning another – led to the posing of the question of whether there actually is a knowledge gap at all, to be filled by an ASM, or whether it is likely to be a temporary measure while people are going on to the BMP without having been on the GMP.

The BMP has evolved significantly, and has two main phases. The first is foundational and, in the long term, may become less important as more participants come who have been through the GMP and some of the ASMs. The second part is more to do with developing broader management skills and understandings. Much of the work is on projects, and in the form of following self-selected options. There is some variation in the way in which participants use this opportunity. Some use it to pursue particular work-related problems that they can envisage for themselves in the future; others use it as a general educational experience, following a broader range of interests which lead to more 'developmental', project-based problems of application.

Concerning the second focal problem, the following points of view, held by the head office team with varying degrees of seriousness and conviction, have surfaced.

The current programme is barely installed, and certainly not fully running. It should be given a fair trial, which is what the management development team is formally committed to doing, in the light of the management development plan agreed by the BR Board. The current priority therefore should be to get the programme to run as well and as smoothly as possible, as is currently planned. Effort should go into the detailed work of making this happen. It is much too soon to be questioning the underlying assumptions, for example, the idea that seniority level is the best basis for differentiating courses. The current programme must be given a fair trial.

Then there is the view that while the above is fundamentally correct, it is already apparent that parts of the existing programme need significant 'fine tuning' and that this should be done.

It is also felt that there is scope for quite significant changes within the existing framework of the programme and its four levels of course. There are many and varied approaches to management education and development, and BR should experiment with a broad range of these within the overall framework of the programme.

Finally, there is the view that the circumstances, culture and needs of BR are changing continuously and rapidly, and to fail to question the underlying structure of the existing programme for several years, in order to 'give it a fair trial', carries the substantial danger of the programme being left behind by events and becoming increasingly irrelevant and inappropriate. Radical alternatives, such as the following, have been suggested for consideration. They are not mutually exclusive and could be combined in a number of ways:

a Do without formal management development altogether.
b Completely decentralize management development; allow different departments and units to make their own arrangements.
c Move to a programme of courses geared to specific topics, issues or techniques, rather than to seniority levels, so that participants from a wide range of levels could attend on a 'need to learn' basis.
d Run short 'saturation' courses (with almost all managers attending the same short course within, say, a 12-month period) on current BR management policy in practice.
e Adopt a centralized 'cafeteria' style of provision – a programme of short courses with places available on demand from individuals and operating units, with the content evolving responsively according to demand. (Places could be free, subsidized, or at the market rate.)
f Put the emphasis on the career/performance appraisal process, and develop this further in terms of the identification, individually, of individuals' short- and long-term development needs, so that BR management development consists mainly of the implementation of these individual plans.

As regards the third focal problem, concerning the evaluation and criteria of effectiveness, there is a debate between two extreme views. The first view is that management development should only be invested in where there is a clear and demonstrable cost–benefit pay-off. The second is that management development is essentially an act of faith, but represents an investment which must be made to build an infrastructure of managerial ability for the future, even if the pay-off is difficult or impossible to assess.

Case Study Tasks

You have been employed as an external consultant to advise BR on its management development programme. Examine and discuss the three issues given earlier: (i) the points arising from initial evaluation; (ii) the current range of options for modifying the programme; (iii) the evaluation approach which might be adopted. In particular you should answer the following question: 'What policy or strategy for the management development programme should those responsible for it work with, and what concepts, models, theories and ideas should it be based on?'

Essential Reading

Easterby-Smith M V P (1981) The evaluation of management education and development: an overview, Personnel Review 10: 2, 28–36
Morris J F Burgoyne J G (1973) Developing Resourceful Managers, Institute of Personnel Management
Schein E H (1978) Career Dynamics, Addison-Wesley

Additional Reading

Handy C B (1976) Understanding Organizations, Penguin
Stewart R (1982) Choices for the Manager: A Guide to Managerial Work and Behaviour, McGraw-Hill

CASE 18

Payment Systems: Mayfly Garments

Dan Gowler and Karen Legge

Organizational Setting

It is in the early 1970s and recession, although always a threat in the garment industry, has yet to hit consumer manufacturing industries with the force of the 1980s. Mayfly Garments Ltd is a medium-sized family firm, still dominated by its founder who arrived in Britain from Europe shortly before the Second World War. The firm, which is non-unionized, employs around 1000 people, mainly on their principal factory site on the outskirts of a thriving town in south-east England. It is vertically integrated in that it dyes yarn, kints cloth for, designs, manufactures, and markets children's clothes of middle range quality. The bulk of production, over 70%, is sold to general department stores and small independent retail outlets, under the firm's own brand label, a household name with a reputation for durability at a reasonable, if not cheap, price. The remaining production is for large retail chains, sold under the retailers' own labels. Lately Mayfly has felt the pinch of increasing competition. On the one hand, supermarket chains, using foreign imports, are undercutting prices on 'bread and butter' lines such as underwear and T-shirts. On the other, 'up-market' children's boutiques, selling fashion garments produced by small, designer-led manufacturers are making in-roads at the top end of this market. Furthermore, the retail chains, also experiencing this competition, are putting ever-increasing pressure on the manufacturing profit margins of 'own label' contracts. Finally Mayfly is finding that the overheads it carries on manufacturing, due to vertical integration, places it at a cost disadvantage in competing with small manufacturing firms working exclusively to contract. This is not helped by the fact that employment in Riverside, the local town, is buoyant and competition for all grades of employee high.

The case study is set within the largest direct labour department, 'the sewing floor', where the repercussions of these competitive pressures are being acutely felt.

Background to the Case

The 'sewing floor' comprises around 200 female machinists, with another 20 or so employed on supervisory or administrative tasks, such as training. About one-sixth of the machinists are part-timers, while all are non-unionized. The machinists are divided into 12 teams of between 15 and 20 operators, depending on the complexity and batch size of the garments being assembled, each supervised by a chargehand. The chargehand's task is mainly administrative – allocating work to machinists and machinists to machines, coping with queries, liaising with cutting, maintenance, work study departments and with the training school – but in slack moments they are expected to 'help out' on the machines. Each chargehand reports to the 'sewing manageress' in charge of the whole sewing floor, who in turn reports to the (male) production manager.

The organization of work within the teams relies on a 'sectionalized flow' rather than the traditional 'make through' approach. In other words, rather than each machinist being assigned all the constituent parts of a garment, with the aim of assembling complete garments, the work is divided into batches involving single operations (e.g. overlocking shoulders) to be performed on specific machines (an overlocking machine). Each operation is then undertaken by one machinist (or sometimes two, depending on cycle time). The team is laid out so that work flows sequentially from the initial to final assembly operations. As each machinist, having completed 'her' operation on a batch of work, then passes it on to the machinist responsible for the next stage in production, the process is characterized by a high degree of interdependence between operations and hence machinists.

A machinist's 'job requirements' can be regarded as comprising three elements: the machine she works; the operation she performs; and the garment she works on. The last element may appear of little significance, but an identical operation, on an identical machine, can involve very different work content, depending upon the size of the garment, the material used, and the number of stages in its production. The major types of machine used by the machinists are five, and there is general agreement between machinists and chargehands that they involve very different levels of skill, and can be ranked in the following order of descending difficulty: (1) lockstitching machines (most difficult); (2) Mauser and Strobel hemming machines; (3) overlocking machines; (4) Reece tabbing machines; (5) Pfaff button/button-holing machines (easiest).

In assessing the amount of skill a job might require, machine, operation and garment must be assessed together. To some extent, of course, there is a clustering in that the most difficult operations are frequently worked on the most difficult machine (e.g. lockstitching a pocket opening), but this is not always the case. The Mauser machine is regarded as one of the most difficult to learn and the most exhausting to work, yet the operations performed on it (straightforward hemming) are relatively simple. Moreover, the operations performed on the overlocking machine vary considerably in the amount of skill required, from 'overlocking shoulders' (a simple operation) to 'overlock insert sleeves' (a difficult one). Equally, a theoretically simple operation (e.g. overlocking sideseams) can be transformed into an extremely testing one, if the material involved is striped and stretchy.

The machinists are paid chiefly on an individually based linear piecework scheme, as is traditionally the case in most of the garment industry. Each batch of work is assigned an allowed time, based on work-study values, which is then converted at the relevant 'standard earnings level' (SEL) per hour. The SEL is fixed at three levels, and sewing operations are assigned to each level according to work-study's assessment of the overall skill required. Machinists reckon that the different earnings levels reflect very inadequately the different levels of skill involved in the different jobs, as only a few pence separate each level. Furthermore, the vast majority of operations, in practice, are paid at the second earnings level. During initial training, or when learning to use a new machine, perform a new operation, or a known operation on a new garment, machinists 'fall back' on to a timework rate, the level of which depends on age, the adult rate being reached at 18 years, followed by small merit increases up to a bar. A machinist returns to piece-work earnings, calculated at the relevant SEL per hour, when the number of garments she produces per hour 'earns' the equivalent of her timework rate per hour. For an adult machinist the timework rate, without merit increases, is about 80% of the second SEL, but for a 16-year-old school leaver it is only about 45%. Management admit that the timework rate, especially for school leavers, is low, but firmly believe that its lowness is necessary to 'encourage' machinists to learn quickly in order to 'get on to piecework'.

While still learning an operation or machine, but having returned to piecework, machinists, at the discretion of their chargehand, may be allowed variable 'training allowances', for variable and ad hoc lengths of time. However, although sometimes used in 'special cases' when earnings fall below the relevant SEL per hour, they are not used indiscriminately to boost a machinist's earnings up to this level if performance remain substantially substandard.

Finally, although in periods of high demand Mayfly's management have experimanted with an evening shift of part-timers, overtime is not worked on principle. Management believe this would undermine the incentive principle of piecework, and freely admit that 'incentives are our Bible'.

The Problem

The Problem in General Terms

In the last six months management have been worried by falling production levels, low quality standards and increased labour turnover on the shop floor. Although ensuing vacancies have been filled, given the competition for labour in Riverside this has not been easy. The personnel officer has admitted that she has often been forced to take on two part-timers in place of one full-timer, and that such full-timers as she can attract tend to be recent immigrants from Pakistan, 'recommended' by relatives already working in the factory. Although the latter are considered good workers, and particularly welcome if they have had previous machining experience in Pakistan, many have a limited understanding of English, which it is feared may lead to training problems, not to mention problems of team integration. Furthermore, chargehands are commenting that morale is low and that erstwhile 'backbone' members of their teams are talking of leaving. They add that they don't blame them – they themselves are continually being 'messed about' and asked to do the impossible. What many machinists seem to agree upon is that the job is now 'not worth the money', and that better terms and conditions can be had elsewhere. Management disagree and point to the fact that vacancies are still being filled, and that the SEL rates are comparable to those offered for similar work in the area. The real problem, they suggest, is that the chargehands are being lax in the organization of the work and are failing to 'get behind the girls'.

A Closer Look at the Problem

In the past year, in response to competition, the firm has embarked on a policy of rapid diversification of the product range into 'fashion' garments. The number of itemized garments (i.e. the number of styles, subdivided into a number of sizes and age groups) has leapt from 1400 to 2000, after a previously gradual increase. Whereas before the diversification management hoped, from one season to the same season in the following year, to carry through a minimum 50% of the styles, 30% with minor modifications, and only 20% new styles, now the situation is reversed. Fifty per cent of the styles in any season are now entirely new, 25% have minor modifications, and only 25% of the styles are from the previous year. Also, the variety of materials (from cotton to all kinds of artificial fabrics) and types of knitted cloth (from interlock to 'skinny-rib') used are similarly increasing. Furthermore, competition has led to greater concern about meeting delivery dates and closer attention is being paid to the control of labour costs, which are perceived to be a decisive element in unit costing.

This combination of factors is having a direct impact on the 'sewing floor'. First, batch sizes now tend to be much smaller and 'long runs' on a garment have become a memory of the past. Secondly, the task of satisfactorily balancing a work team has become more difficult. Work items of differing duration often have to be put together on one team owing to the size of orders and delivery dates. Furthermore, the pattern of work assigned to each team owes more to the priority of delivery dates than to utilizing the existing skills of machinists. Both these outcomes are resulting in negatively reinforcing problems for machinists and chargehands alike.

First, short production runs have resulted in several interrelated problems. Existing standard times are still based on the assumption of long runs, and the procedures for calculating time standards and the SEL into which the estimated times are converted have remain unaltered. But the impact of the learning curve on performance and earnings, given the short production runs, is greatly accentuated. Whereas in the previous year the average machinist had worked at well over standard performance for at least half the production run, now she is often unable to attain even a standard performance before the run is ended, and she is faced with learning, at worst, to handle a new material, operate an unfamiliar machine, or perform an unaccustomed operation on a newly introduced garment. This has meant, besides low piecework earnings, that a disproportionate amount of her time is being paid for at the fall-back timework rate. But not only are earnings perceived to have deteriorated, levels of effort are perceived to have increased. Most machinists consider that the hours spent learning unfamiliar machines and operations and in ironing out the snags of incoming garments involve more 'effort' than working flat out on a familiar operation, garment and machine. Added to this is the irritation involved in coping with the higher percentage of badly cut constituents, needle cutting and machine trouble that accompanies a short-run, as opposed to a long-run garment.

The larger the garment range, the more time studies the production engineering department has to complete. This, machinists complain, has slowed down the alteration of tight estimates and at a time when the effort of learning a job and the frustrations of material and machine trouble are at their greatest, the pay is not only inadequate but unjust. When a tight estimate is finally altered they are not compensated for the garments they have produced 'on the cheap'.

The final straw, the machinists assert, is that inspection is now returning far more batches of work for correction than used to occur. This reworking has to be done in the machinist's own time. Inspection says quality is slipping and blames the chargehands. The chargehands and machinists publicly retort that inspection is now insisting on ridiculous standards and that work that used to be passed is now sent back. (In private chargehands will admit that some of the machinists have become 'a bit slapdash', but have some sympathy for them.) Much of the chargehand's 'spare time' is now spent correcting rejected work in order to 'help the girls out' and to keep to target.

Secondly, the task of satisfactorily balancing a work team is now a nightmare for supervision. As one chargehand put it: 'I tell you these short runs and continued change-ups are a real hassle. And management haven't a clue! Let me give you an example. A month ago we were doing 66/22 and 33/15 shirts. The 66/22 had a lot of lockstitching work – I had four girls on it full-time – but the 33/15 only needed one lockstitcher – it was all overlocking. Given different cycle times I had my lock-stitchers working on one garment, but the overlockers on both. So what happens? The 66/22 finished early, while I was being held up for parts on the 33/15. So they gave me the 41/14 skinny rib. Of course, *that's* nearly all overlocking – it only needs two lockstitchers. What do I do? It wasn't worth getting the 66/22 lockstitchers to learn overlocking on the 33/15, and move the 33/15 overlockers on to the 41/14 because the job was due to end and it wasn't worth the four of them learning just for a couple of weeks. So I put my two best full-timers from the 66/22 lockstitching – Liz and Anne – on to the 41/14 lockstitching jobs and put the other two, Rahat and Pavarti, on to overlocking. Then would you believe it? When the 33/15 ended, a couple of weeks later, they gave me the 41/07 blouse – never mind that the 33/15 had only one lockstitching job and the 41/07 had four! And it's a very short run. Why didn't they give it to me when the 66/22 finished?! That means girls from the 33/15 will also have to work on different machines than they are used to and that means they won't make their money and that means they'll be on to me for training allowances. Great! If I let them have them management will be down on me and, if I don't, they'll leave. Management! When I tell them of the problems that moving girls from job to job causes, they say it's up to me to develop flexible machinists. But when they see the production figures – and you can't expect a girl to reach a good performance if she is being moved around all the time – well, it's a different story then! Now there's always going to be some changes because different garments involve different numbers and types of operations and machines, but you'd think they'd try to give teams jobs as similar as possible to the ones they've done before. But they don't, you know. And these short-cycle overlocking operations on the 41/14! To balance the team someone has to do two per day. It's not fair to put a part-timer on two in an afternoon as she'll never earn her money – anyway Joyce and Maggie would kill me and I've known them since school! If I put a young new girl on with no experience, she'll complain she'll never get her speeds up if she's got to chop and change all day. But what else can I do? If I put her on one of the more difficult jobs she could find herself even worse off and what's more hold up half the team. Then I'll have them all moaning. Thank God, though, that Sharon's prepared to stick with the Mauser – not all girls can take it and I don't know what I'll do when she's had enough (no one can take that monster for ever). But it does mean that I can't really shift her, even though she's good on the lockstitch. And I can't move Kali off the button-holer because with her English I'll never get her on to a more difficult machine and, in any case, it's such a boring job that if I move someone on to it they'll pester to be taken off. And all button-holing jobs have tight rates . . . .'

The sewing manageress added that these problems are getting worse daily due to labour turnover and absenteeism. What is happening is that experienced machinists, fed-up with depressed earnings, are leaving (having first had some afternoons off looking for a new job!). This means, given the sectionalized flow system, that production is disrupted, necessitating 'temporary' redeployment of machinists (in addition to that resulting from the main 'change-ups') to prevent hold-ups. Furthermore, increased labour turnover has accentuated recruitment and training problems. As a result permanent replacements on a team are taking longer to arrive. And, with the short production runs, it is now often the case that by the time a replacement has been trained to do the job of a leaver and assigned to a team, the team can be about to 'change-up' again, and the replacement may need a further period of training – if she hasn't already left Mayfly. 'If only management would do something!' she commented, 'but they just won't listen.'

Case Study Tasks

Imagine you are a consultant brought in to advise management about production problems following the policy of diversification. Consider the questions below, locating your advice within appropriate theoretical frameworks.

Questions 1–2 are appropriate for teaching sessions of 1 or 2 hours. Questions 3–5 will require longer time periods to answer.

1　Do you think the existing wage payment system is inappropriate to the sewing floor? If so, why?
2　How might you redesign the payment system? (Justify suggested changes in

terms of theories about payment system design.)

3 What impact do you anticipate each suggested new payment system will have on

   a machinists' flexibility
   b machinists' output levels
   c product quality
   d machinists' labour turnover and absence
   e the role of the chargehand
   f costs?

4 Management has refused to contemplate any move away from an incentive wage payment system. In the light of this, how would you redesign

   a work organization
   b recruitment and training practices
   c supervisory roles

   in order to improve

   d machinists' morale and motivation
   e sewing floor productivity.

5 Can you suggest any other strategies that might alleviate the problems indentified in this case?

Essential Reading

Lupton T Bowey A M (1983) Wages and Salaries, Gower, Chapter 3
Smith I (1983) The Management of Remuneration, Institute of Personnel Management, Chapter 3

Additional Reading

Bowey A M (1982) Handbook of Salary and Wage Systems, Gower
Gowler D (1970) Socio-cultural influences on the operation of a wage payment system: an exploratory case-study, in Local Labour Markets and Wage Structures, edited by D Robinson, Gower, Chapter 4
Lawler E (1973) Motivation in Work Organizations, Brooks/Cole
Legge K (1974) Remuneration: the problems of selecting and managing wage payment systems, in Administration of Personnel Policies, edited by R Naylor and D Torrington, Gower, Chapter 8
Lupton T Gowler D (1969) Selecting a Wage Payment System, Kogan Page

CASE 19

Equal Opportunities: Champion Oils Ltd

Sylvia Shimmin and Joyce McNally

Organizational Context

Champion Oils Ltd is a medium-sized, wholly-owned subsidiary of a multinational company located in the Midlands. The parent company exercises some control over personnel policies, but pay grade negotiations take place at a domestic level. It manufactures oil- and fats-based products on a system of continuous production. The factory comprises a refining plant, staffed entirely by men, and a production area. One of the major national trade unions has had negotiating rights in the company for over 30 years and effectively a closed shop is in operation. There is a traditional, hierarchical structure of management and supervision.

Background to the Case

The firm employs over 300 people, slightly more men than women. In terms of the jobs they do, the way their work is organized, and the pay they receive, men and women experience work differently.

When the factory went over to 24-hour production to obtain a better return on capital investment, men were taken on to perform operations previously done by women in order to comply with the Factories Acts. Consequently the number and kind of jobs open to women decreased and they were restricted to a limited range of occupations. Women now work as machine operators, packers and cleaners, either full-time on days or part-time on an evening shift. Men are largely engaged, on a three-shift system, in what are considered 'key' areas of the production process, as oil-blenders, tanker-loaders, or in the setting-up and maintenance of operating conditions. A small number of single women able to work shifts are employed as fork-lift truck drivers, a job which is recognized in the company as 'male'; but the distinction between male and female work (as well as male and female pay) has been preserved by the expedient of reserving work on 'higher' trucks for men.

In order to encourage adaptability and mobility in the workforce, employees have access to on-site training in alternative jobs within the company. However, it is acknowledged by the industrial relations manager that this facility is restricted to occupations which, in practice, are available only to men. The trade union at both branch and area level is aware of this contravention of the Sex Discrimination Act but has declined to take active steps to rectify it. The male area organizer of the union points out that men will resist any change in the allocation of 'male' jobs.

The Problem

The Job Evaluation Exercise

Job evaluation (an exercise which purports to determine the relative worth of jobs, and acts as a basis for a remuneration system) was initially introduced into the company in the 1950s, but the scheme had been eroded over time. Narrow pay differentials between job-grades were compensated by incentive bonuses and over-time payments in male areas of work. Wage increases were awarded to different groups of workers, e.g. the men in the refinery, in order to side-step particular industrial relations problems, resulting in an unwieldy, anomalous wage structure bearing no relation to the job-evaluated grade structure. This meant that few employees appreciated the real nature of job evaluation or understood that their jobs had been graded (a situation said to have been encouraged by the parent company which preferred to operate on a secretive basis). In the early 1980s, both manage-ment and union became increasingly dissatisfied with the situation and agreed to a 'rationalization' programme, based on a new job evaluation exercise, which would provide the basis for a revised wage-agreement.

The system of job evaluation adopted by the company's negotiating team of management and union (including one woman on the union side), was a curious form of paired comparison, described by the union's area organizer as 'the brainchild of the industrial relations manager'.

The exercise involved the following procedures: job descriptions for all jobs were provided by departmental managers as the basis for job evaluation. A committee of managers and trade unionists (the Job Evaluation Committee) then selected a small number of 'key' or benchmark jobs which were broken down into component elements or 'job factors' (physical effort; responsibility for safety; responsibility for plant and materials; training and skill requirements; working conditions). Bench-mark jobs were assessed and ranked subjectively according to the extent to which each job factor was thought to be present in the jobs. The remaining jobs were then compared with the ranked benchmark jobs and slotted in at a level deemed to be appropriate. Finally, the entire rank order of jobs was divided into nine grades.

When the boundary lines were drawn between various groups of jobs, an almost clear line of segregation appeared between jobs done by men and those of women, creating male and female grades. With some few exceptions, women's jobs were placed in the lower half of the grade structure and men's jobs in the top half, as in Table 4.

Table 4 Job-grade structure

Job grade	Number of employees	
	Men	Women
1	60	
2	50	
3	17	
4	24	10
5	15	
6		70
7	3	40
8	4	10
9		10
Total	173	140

Participants' Impressions

The current situation in the company and its implications for the future are described below by three people: Edna, the branch secretary of the union; Nigel, the industrial relations (IR) manager responsible for the job evaluation scheme; and Bill, the full-time area organizer of the union.

Edna gives her account first. She is a married woman whose children are grown up and have left home. She has worked at the factory for over 20 years and been secretary of the union there for the last eight. She is the only female member of the branch committee. Her knowledge of the job evaluation scheme is not extensive and, consequently, the information she has imparted to her women members concerning it is of a limited nature. Her understanding of the legislative rights of women in employment is imprecise, but her imagination has recently been fired by a one-day course on women's rights at work, organized by the Equal Opportunities Commission. She considers that her position on the branch committee is an unenviable one; she feels isolated and claims that the male committee members are unwilling to support her efforts to improve the pay and conditions of women. Her own job is that of packer (grade 6).

'When I first worked here, women did most of the jobs. They blended oils [job grade 1] and did the tanker loading [job grade 2]. Men were brought in when we went on to 24-hour working – because of the Factories Acts we couldn't have women on shifts – and these men think they're more entitled to the work than the women. They guard the jobs as *their* jobs and the women are losing out. Like two years ago when we were discussing a productivity scheme; in the first proposals from management they suggested men should stack boxes at the ends of the lines. The branch chairman of the union was quite prepared to go along with the idea and I had to fight a lone battle for the women doing that job. He said: "You don't get my point." I said: "You don't get mine; the women are here now on that job, and you want to take them off and put men on it." He said: "Well, the women will get other work." I said: "What other work? There isn't any round here", and while we argued our two paid officials sat back and kept out of it. Bill [the union's area organizer] and his kind don't help me when it comes to the crunch. I won that round, but lost out completely when Mr Jones [the factory manager] wanted to take women off the dole and put them on a temporary night-shift to meet a sudden demand for production. The men went beserk, insisting that it should at least be 50:50 men and women, and in the end it was all men that were taken on. And when it was time for them to go, as in the agreement, one shop steward tried to get them kept on as holiday reliefs. No wonder Sid [the union branch chairman] is always telling me that one of these days there'll be no women in the factory, only men.

'Last year, when we were promised a new job evaluation scheme, a job evaluation panel was formed to study all jobs. There were four union members and four members of management, with Nigel [the IR manager] in the chair, but he wouldn't have a vote. It was decided in [branch] committee that no branch officers or committee members should be on the panel, perhaps because some men in the refinery said they'd have nothing to do with it if I were elected to it, I don't know. Four names were put forward, unopposed and no women – they didn't want to know; they have this inbuilt sense of inferiority. So we were unrepresented from the start – an all male panel selected the nine benchmark jobs against which to compare everyone else's. Only one woman's job was chosen, the rest were men's, so women's jobs weren't fairly represented. It's sad the management didn't see fit to co-opt a woman to the panel, but they didn't.

'I've no confidence in that panel, which also acts as the appeals committee. They haven't changed anything. I think we've only got the women fork-lift truck drivers on grade 4 because there are men on trucks in that grade. Otherwise I don't think those women would have touched G4. Most women's job decriptions were pathetic – half a sheet of handwritten notes, while the men's were typed on three or four pages. The panel was only given half a day's training by the IR manager and it seems they used the same old job factors which seem to me not to take into account the characteristics of *women's* jobs, like manual dexterity, sustained concentration and effort, immobility, and so on. But I don't know much about the scheme myself. We got one job upgraded, where management had reduced the number of operators from four to three and now to two which means if the machine is running to capacity, each woman will lift 18 tons of product in a day – some weight, that is – but most of the women's appeals on grading got nowhere.

'The women are kicking about the money, because the new scheme has given them no increase – about 80p per week is no sort of rise – whereas the men's job grades 'up' their 'basic' by pounds before they get their shift allowance. What management are going to do is to make a 'red circle' payment to the lower grades [a payment made where, after job evaluation, employees' jobs are placed in a lower grade than the one equivalent to their current wage] to ensure that they get a rise of at least 6%. But that red circle payment is to be eroded, taken back in five stages over five years until it's gone and any newcomer going on those jobs will get the new [lower] rate.

'When they introduced this grading system, I asked Nigel if women could train on the same basis as the men. They [men] come in, they're taught a job and if they're interested and want to learn another job, they just tell the manager. Then, as soon as possible, the manager puts them to train on that second job. Men can learn every job on the floor that way if they so wish, so that when a vacancy occurs they're already qualified to fill it. Nigel denies that he said no when I asked if women could have the same opportunities, but he shows no sign of doing anything about it. One of the directors has said he sees no reason why women shouldn't do any of the jobs being done by men now, but they won't stand a chance if they don't get the same training as the men.'

Nigel, the industrial relations manager, has been with the firm for about seven years. He rejects Edna's claim that the company's policies are discriminatory, and uses her efforts to preserve jobs for women to counter-accuse her of discrimination. He is impatient with the women's criticisms of the job evaluation exercise.

'We had to do something fairly quickly because we'd a demanning exercise to do and we wanted it ready for the wage negotiations in January [a matter of months]. It was understood at the outset that the job evaluation scheme should be jointly managed, so I got the negotiating committee together and went through the approaches we could use. It was understood that paired comparison is not as accurate as, say, the points rating system, but management thought it would lead to fewer arguments and be more acceptable. There's no point in going for a more sophisticated scheme if the workforce isn't ready for it. *How* you grade jobs doesn't matter; what *is* important is a high level of acceptance of the resulting grades.

'The first problem was that not one female would come forward to sit on the panel, although we employ a lot of women here, so we had to make it up as best we could with one representative from the factory, one from the warehouse, one from the yard-gang and one from the refinery.

'We then went through the grading exercise and I think that went quite well. There was little disagreement in assessing the bench-mark jobs and determining the grade boundaries.

'As far as the women are concerned, they did quite well, but Edna accused us of sexism and general fiddling. We started to get a lot of protests from the women who said, "We don't believe in job-grading; what we want is a decent cost-of-living rise." The basic problem is the view that job evaluation is based on nothing but how hard you work, and it's true women on the lines work on a continuous basis. They look around and see men whose jobs are not on a conveyor, but who are using knowledge and skill to keep the process going, and don't appreciate that this is why the men are in higher grades. Most of the women think the machine operators in the refinery are doing simple, button-pushing jobs, not operating a complicated piece of plant containing over 20 tons of oil. I am quite convinced the grade structure isn't biased, but I won't deny that the women are not happy with it.

'There has been discrimination in the past on the basis of who does what job, so we're used to male and female jobs here. Quite honestly, we can't really justify why all the packing is done by women or all the three-shift jobs are occupied by men. I would like to see mixed packing lines and women on some of the more skilled jobs. But it's the union, particularly Edna, that is resistant on this matter. When we went through the demanning exercise last year and more women than men opted for voluntary redundancy she wouldn't hear of men displaced from the refinery transferring to vacancies on the women's lines, but was prepared to see them going down the road. In other words, she perpetuates job segregation without realizing it by fighting to retain women on traditional women's work.'

Unlike Nigel, Bill, the union's area organizer, is convinced the grading scheme is loaded against women. He feels that the conditions under which women are employed are, in a general sense, unjust. However, Bill has seen it all before, and has no expectation of, or practical commitment to, pursuing equality of opportunity for women.

'I said at the outset that my personal view of the scheme is that it is contrary to the Sex Discrimination and Equal Pay Acts. In fact I stated in negotiations that I didn't agree with the way the scheme has been manufactured by management. The job evaluation exercise has given a mirror image of the existing situation with the men in the refinery graded at the top. They've always been pandered to and, being a key area, are in a position to name their own terms. The women, on the other hand, were on a loser from the start because the job evaluation panel was entirely male. After all, women are in the majority in the production area, but we couldn't get one woman to sit on the panel. I felt sure Edna could have persuaded one of the women shop stewards to do so, because they're quite bright; they know what the score is, but we couldn't get any of them to take it on.

'This is a sociological question as much as an industrial one and, frankly, I don't know how to get over it. It's a matter of women's position in society and how you can change attitudes – of both men and women. The mass of the male workers here consider certain jobs to be male preserves which women shall not enter. And certain jobs are female preserves that only women do, like packing and other menial jobs with little skill in them – just like women in this town were, and are, expected to do the menial jobs in the house. Officially the union takes quite a progressive line on equal opportunities, I mean in the form of pious resolutions at conferences, but when you get down to doing anything about it in practice, it's another story.

'There are lots of women at Champion who could do jobs in the refinery, you know, which are far more skilled and rewarding than the ones they're doing now. Some managers agree with us on this, but management's afraid of pushing this issue of training women for the refinery because they're afraid of upsetting the key men there. And there's prejudice on the shop floor against the idea of training for all jobs being available to everyone, irrespective of sex, which is a problem that, sooner or later, both this union and the management are going to have to come to grips with.'

Case Study Tasks

Your task is to examine the terms and conditions of employment of men and women in the company. Identify those aspects of the work situation, including the job evaluation exercise, where men and women are treated differently and decide whether these differences are to women's disadvantage in terms of pay, job status and opportunity. During your discussions on how to improve the position of women in the firm, you should recollect that male employees are, on the whole, against the introduction of equality of pay and opportunity for women; that the union, to date, has not promoted the idea; and that the industrial relations manager largely dismisses the claim that his firm's policies discriminate against female employees. It will help if you divide into small groups to deal with Questions 1–4 then come together to exchange your views and conclusions before proceeding further. The same procedure may be adopted for the remaining questions.

1   a   In what ways does company policy differentiate between male and female employees?

    b   Does company policy place the firm in danger of contravening the Sex Discrimination and Equal Pay Acts? If so, what aspects of company policy are possibly unlawful?

2   What are the effects on women employees of the firm's different treatment of men and women?

3   Job evaluation schemes may be used to introduce and/or perpetuate sex discrimination. Examine the conduct of the job evaluation exercise and identify those aspects which may have led to an underevaluation of women's jobs.

4   Consider the bargaining position of women in the company and offer some explanations as to why, comparatively speaking, women lack collective strength:

    a   reasons stemming from circumstances within the workplace

    b   causes originating in the wider social environment.

5   Identify areas of need and basic information required in order to formulate your 'equal opportunities programme'

    a   within the company

    b   within the localities in which employees reside.

6   What should be the first steps in introducing an equal opportunities programme?

7   Identify the practices and procedures necessary for the implementation of your equality programme.

8   What proposals have you for the monitoring of the equal opportunities programme?

Essential Reading

Equal Opportunities Commission (undated) Guidance on Equal Opportunity Policies and Practices in Employment, free from the Equal Opportunities Commission

Equal Opportunities Commission (undated) Job Evaluation Free of Sex Bias, free from the Equal Opportunities Commission

Morris J (1983) No More Peanuts; An Evaluation of Women's Work, National Council for Civil Liberties

Additional Reading

Aldred C (1981) Women at Work, Pan Books

Beale J (1982) Getting it Together, Pluto Press

Coote A Campbell B (1982) Sweet Freedom: The Struggle for Women's Liberation, Pan Books

Equal Opportunities Commission (undated) Equal Opportunities: A Guide for Employees (and Employers) to the Sex Discrimination Act 1975, free from the Equal Opportunities Commission

Snell M W Glucklich P Povall M (1981) Equal Pay and Opportunities, Department of Employment Research Paper No. 20, HMSO

West J (1982) Work, Women and the Labour Market, Routledge and Kegan Paul

SECTION 3   Industrial Relations

The practice of industrial relations is often characterized in terms of greedy workers, misled by militant shop stewards, pursuing large wage claims. Industrial relations is thus about cash and conflict. Yet this caricature does a disservice both to the people involved and to the system(s) of industrial relations. Although many would argue that power and control, conflict and class struggle are *the* central issues, industrial relations in its broadest terms encompasses the rules, institutions and processes – both formal and informal, structured and unstructured – of employment. Thus, issues within the field of study range from industrial and union democracy, employment law, collective bargaining and the organization of a strike to the interpersonal and individual skills of negotiators.

In the remainder of this book, eight case studies are presented which cover a wide range of industrial relations issues. They are organized broadly from a micro (individual, group) to a macro (organizational, cultural) level of analysis and adopt a variety of theoretical and research perspectives. The cases are: negotiating behaviour; collective bargaining; industrial disputes; a 'lock-out'; strike organization; new technology; participation and communication; and, finally, trade union democracy. Each case is set within the context of British industrial relations. Thus, historical and cultural influences, and legal initiatives, are important determinants of the content, process and outcomes of the cases. Of course, several issues, for example, negotiating behaviour, new technology, industrial disputes (etc.), may be similar across cultures and countries. In addition some of the issues raised will be common to the set of eight cases. Finally, they may also be of interest to the case studies presented in Sections 1 and 2 of the book. The reader is referred to Table 2 in the Introduction for easy reference to these overlaps.

The first case study in this section (Case 20), by Linda Marsh and Richard Graham, examines the negotiation of the terms and conditions of employment between a trade union and an employing organization. The case should be used as a role-playing exercise in order to demonstrate the importance of preparing and planning for negotiations, the actual process and content of discussions, and the social and other skills necessary to negotiate successfully. It is primarily focused at the individual skill and behavioural process levels. Paul Willman (in Case 21) complements this negotiation theme by focusing on collective bargaining processes at a more macro level of analysis. His case presents a description of attempts to negotiate rapid changes in pay, grading and work organization through collective bargaining procedures within a single plant of a multi-plant organization. The case study focuses on the development of a managerial strategy for change, its uneven impact across different occupational groups within the manual workforce and the responses of shop stewards representing these different groups. It illustrates some of the problems which emerge where the prospect of change is associated with job insecurity and the disturbance of relationships between different groups within the workforce.

The next three cases present examples of industrial disputes. Paul Edwards and Hugh Scullion (Case 22) chart the course of one particular dispute. They have argued elsewhere that many disputes never reach the stage of a complete stoppage of work and that, when they do, the majority of strikes are of very short duration. Thus, the large strike is atypical. Consequently, it is important to show, as their case does, how a dispute unfolds over time in a series of unique events. These events may or may not be interrelated and the dispute may or may not result in a stoppage. Moreover, the typical outcome is that disputes are seldom resolved to the mutual benefit of all parties. Their case should be used to consider the following: the reasons governing the actions of the various parties to a dispute as events unfold; the lessons which can be drawn concerning the strategy and tactics employed in a dispute; and the wider implications for ways of handling collective bargaining at workplace level. Paul Routledge (Case 23) similarly considers the key events, actors and issues of an industrial dispute, but this time of the 'big bang' kind. Interestingly, the historical account presented of the 'lock-out' at Times Newspapers Ltd in 1978–9 is informed and enlivened by an insider's view of the dispute (Paul Routledge is Labour Editor of The Times and was Father of the NUJ Chapel at the time of the dispute). Issues central to this case include the use of new technology in Fleet Street, custom and practice and control over work methods, and trade union and managerial power. Finally, John Kelly, Jean Hartley and Nigel Nicholson (Case 24) outline the organization required and the personal involvement necessary to manage and prosecute a major and protracted strike successfully. Their case study is concerned with the 1980 steel strike and, in particular, with intragroup processes, the control and coordination of the strike and strategies for action.

Barry Wilkinson (Case 25) describes what happened to the work of a large number of employees when computer-based 'new' technology was introduced into a factory in the manufacturing sector of industry. The case focuses on changes in: skill distribution and task allocation; working practices; payment levels and the payment–effort bargain; and work-group relationships. His study demonstrates the importance of informal as well as formal bargaining over change, and shows how and why the question of who controls the production process can be the central question with new technology.

The last two cases in this section on industrial relations are both concerned with industrial democracy. Mick Marchington (Case 26) examines employee participation and communication systems. His case focuses, in particular, on the problems and perspectives encountered in operating a system of employee involvement which is connected to a payment system, as well as the communications machinery required for relating company-wide information to the shop floor. Both shop floor and employer expectations and beliefs are highlighted and legal initiatives introduced. In the final case study in the book, Roger Undy (Case 27) continues the theme of democracy in the workplace and also considers the place and influence of legal and state intervention in industrial relations. Undy's case examines union government and union democracy by describing the decision-making processes and structure of the Transport and General Workers' Union (TGWU). Essentially, the question posed is: 'What actually constitutes a democratic trade union?'

CASE 20

Negotiating Behaviour: Micklethwaite Brewery plc

Linda Marsh and Richard Graham

Organizational Setting

This case study concerns a negotiation in the brewing industry about terms and conditions of employment for licensed house managers. The background inform-ation, of which both parties would have equal knowledge, comprises a description of the brewery, the status of the National Association of Licensed House Managers (NALHM) and the licensed house managers within the organization, a detailed outline of terms and conditions currently applying and, finally, details of the current claim by NALHM and the status of the negotiation immediately prior to the next meeting. There are two other sets of information. Each set gives key points govern-ing the approach of each party to the negotiation, the targets and limits they have set themselves on the items being negotiated at present, and any other options they are considering in their efforts to reach an agreement. The negotiators would have ideas about what issues the other party see as key – but could not be certain without checking.

Background to the Case

The Company

The company is the Micklethwaite Brewery plc, a medium-sized brewery based in Manchester, trading mainly in the North of England and the Midlands. The company has 1800 public houses of which some 500 are managed houses. The annual turnover of the company was £200 million in 1982.

A licensed estate is comprised essentially of two categories of premises – tenanted and managed. A tenant is self-employed, and his/her tenure is based on a commercial relationship with the company. This requires the tenant to pay rental for the occupied premises and purchase beer, wines and spirits from the brewery. The company therefore receives wholesale profit. A licensed house manager is both appointed by and directly employed by the company. Terms and conditions of employment are regulated by a collective agreement with the NALHM and the managers' service agreements. The manager orders all supplies from the company, and banks all takings into the company account. The company receives both the wholesale and retail profit, and the manager is paid a salary plus other benefits.

The Negotiating Unit

The NALHM represents the interests of the managers of all managed houses. The brewery agreed sole bargaining rights with the NALHM in February 1972. The forum for negotiations is a joint negotiating committee, which is composed of union delegates, the regional organizer of the NALHM and management representatives. If agreement is not reached in this forum after four meetings the negotiations are referred to the Advisory, Conciliation and Arbitration Service (ACAS). The substantive agreement between the company and the NALHM is effective for 12 months from the 1st January each year.

Current Terms and Conditions

The principle terms and conditions are as follows:

Salary Structure (i) Each of the licensed houses is accorded a grade based on annual turnover. Increased sales over a period of time enables a manager to increase the grading of his/her house. (ii) Grading is agreed by a joint committee (of the NALHM and management). Movement between minimum and maximum in each grade depends upon length of service, five years being the usual time taken to reach the top of the grade. (iii) Turnover bands are upgraded in line with the Retail Price Index in February each year.

The salary structure is shown in Table 5.

Table 5 Salary structure

Grade	Annual turnover (£)	Minimum salary level (including wives' honorarium)
1	0– 80 000	£5400
2	80 000–100 000	£5770
3	100 000–120 000	£6140
4	120 000–140 000	£6510
5	140 000–160 000	£6880
6	160 000–180 000	£7250
7	180 000–200 000	£7620
8	200 000+	£8000

Profit Bonus   Each house has an individual profit and loss account and an annual profit bonus is paid to managers based on 3.5% of net profit. This payment is pensionable and the average annual bonus last year was £900.

Machine Commission   A commission of 10% of the net takings after VAT has been deducted is paid on all machine income (i.e. income from pool tables, fruit machines, video games machines, etc.).

Catering Income   As licensed premises have become increasingly popular eating places, the catering rights are a valuable source of income for the manager and partner/spouse. In return for catering rights the company charges a franchise fee based on gross weekly takings of 5%. The average net profit from catering per managed house in 1983 was £3000.

House Stock Allowance   An allowance is given against stock figures to cover beer handling, manager's entertainment and staff drinks. The allowance ranges from a minimum of £20 up to £35 per week, depending on draught beer sales.

Mileage Allowance   All managers are resident on the premises, although a small amount of travelling is involved on company business, for which an allowance of 20p per mile is paid.

Accommodation   In most cases accommodation is rent and rate free, together with free lighting, heating and water. In addition the company is responsible for the repair and decoration of the living accommodation.

Holidays   Managers receive 24 working days holiday per annum, and in addition they receive double time for each day of statutory holiday worked.

Hours of Employment   Managers are required to work six working days in any one week. The total hours are not formally defined due to the special circumstances of the trade. Managers are required to keep the premises open for business during all the hours permitted by law.

Company Pension   Licensed house managers are members of the company pension scheme, which is recognized to be a good scheme allowing for retirement at 60 years of age.

Wives   Managers' wives receive an honorarium from the company for rendering such assistance as required by her husband. There is no contract of employment and no formal hours. The honorarium is included in the salary scales shown in Table 5. There are a few female managers but none of these have husbands, so the question of a 'husband's honorarium' has not been raised.

Managers' Remuneration Package   The manager's average remuneration therefore consists of a combination of basic salary, profit bonus, machine commission and catering income. The total will depend on the size of the house, its location, etc. The average total salary of a manager in 1983 is shown in Table 6. In addition the company places a value of £1500 per annum on the free accommodation, rates, redecoration, free heating and lighting. They say the total gross value for this based on tax at standard rate is £2142. The average total salary package (not including catering income) for a manager in 1983 (before tax) was therefore £10 542.

Table 6 Average total salary package for a manager in 1983

Salary components	£
Salary	6 500
Profit bonus	900
Machine commission	1 000
Subtotal	8 400
Catering income (less franchise fee)	2 850
Total	11 250

The Problem

Claim Submitted by the NALHM

In October the following claim was submitted to the brewery:

a *Salaries* All salary grades to be raised by £1275 across the board (this represents a 24% increase for the lowest grade, 20% for average grades and 16% for the highest)

b *Unsocial hours* A payment of £1000 per annum to be made in respect of unsocial hours worked by all managers

c *Holidays* Five weeks holiday

d *Machine bonus* Managers to receive 15% of all machine profits

e *Appearance allowance* £520 p.a. to be paid to all managers to help compensate for the cleaning and replacement of clothes

f *Car mileage* The mileage allowance to be raised to 22.5p per mile in respect of all company mileage (to bank, to brewery, etc.)

g *Bank holidays* Managers to be paid at double time and to receive a day off in lieu

h *Christmas Day working* Managers to receive a special allowance of 5% of the day's takings for working Christmas Day

i *Recent draymen's dispute* The calculation of profit bonus to allow for the disruption in supplies caused by the recent draymen's dispute, i.e. managers' bonuses should be calculated on 49 full weeks rather than 52

j *New technology* A new technology payment of £1000 per annum in respect of

     the introduction of new technology such as computerized tills and data links
with head office

k *Increased house stock allowance* An additional £5 per week to be added to
cover drinks bought for customers and bar staff

l *Payment for extended hours* Remuneration to be given for any additional
hours worked beyond normal working hours.

In addition the NALHM indicated that there were a number of other items which it
might wish to raise during negotiations.

    This claim is considerably higher than other claims submitted over the past two
years. The previous negotiation on terms and conditions of employment was
referred to ACAS who found in favour of the management.

Comparability Information

Currently the union claims that managers for some other breweries of a similar size
have better terms and conditions. They also claim that since the last wage rise given
to bar staff, these people have a greater hourly wage rate than the managers. It is the
case that club stewards employed by this brewery have just received a pay award
which puts them ahead of the managers. In April The Financial Times reported that
pay settlements for bar staff were running at 5%.

    Settlement rates in wage negotiations throughout industry generally at the time
of this negotiation were given by the CBI as: 0–5% increase + productivity agreement, 61%; 5–10% increase + productivity agreement, 27%; 10% plus (few having a
productivity agreement), 12%.

    The union claim that in previous negotiations they have accepted a lower than
average award in view of the company's trading position. This is not really disputed
but it should be remembered that some of these awards were a result of arbitration.

Factors Affecting Each Party's View of the Negotiation

The above information is, as stated earlier, common to both parties and provides
the basis of the negotiation. The following pages provide you with information about
other factors affecting each party's approach. Although some of the information
would be known to each party, the items have been written from their own points of
view. In addition to this the management team also have a memorandum from the
chairman of Micklethwaite's.

Micklethwaite Brewery

The following are the key points which would influence the managerial (company)
representatives when carrying out the tasks of preparing for, planning and conducting the negotiation.

Economic Background   Competition within the brewing industry is fierce; there has been a decline in the overall sales volume of beer, although this appears to have bottomed out. In addition, over-capacity amongst the larger breweries is still a major problem. The company is concerned that the larger breweries have made a strong push to penetrate their free house outlets, with some success. It feels unable to compete with the levels of inducements they seem willing to offer.

Micklethwaite's Current Position   Although turnover is up from £200 million to £216 million over the past year, profit margins are falling. Last year the company made £25 million and expect this to rise to only £26 million for the current year. The increased turnover stems largely from investment into new areas of activity such as fast food eating places, not from managed houses. Current levels of profitability are lower than those of some other breweries. Over the past two years the company has transferred 35 managed houses to tenancies. This is a trend which is expected to continue, the degree being dependent largely on the size of the wage settlement with the NALHM. All other major breweries are experiencing the same problems. It is further estimated that agreeing to NALHM's demands would result in 30% of the current managed houses showing a lower return than is acceptable. As a complication many of the houses are in run down areas of the large cities and council estates and are vulnerable to any further downturn in the economy. Finally, it is thought that any industrial action could be disastrous since the company can not afford to lose customers to rival public houses.

Future Prospects   Future prospects show no signs of radical improvement in the short term. It is anticipated that there will be no real increase in volume sales and it is expected that pressure from the competition for free trade outlets will continue. The company currently anticipates the need to inject substantial capital into existing managed and tenanted houses in modernization programmes if they are to remain attractive to customers. Overall, the company feels that it will be difficult to pass on wage settlements to the customer since there is already strong resistance to further price increases: the products are already regarded as being at the top of the range in terms of price. In this context the marketing department anticipate that the maximum possible increase on the price of a pint of beer next year is 3p and even this will cause some loss of volume. It is anticipated that this price increase will produce an extra £7 million of revenue. However, it is unlikely that the total increase in revenue from all sources will exceed £20 million next year. Finally, the company does not expect profits to show any real improvement over this year's projected figures.

Below you will find a memorandum from the company chairman to the company negotiatiors giving his views about the negotiation.

MEMORANDUM

From: Jack Micklethwaite – Chairman

To: Personnel Director
        Tied Trade Director

Subject: The NALHM Claim

I have now studied this claim closely. It is of course impossible to meet these demands, and I am sure they realize that. However, there is no doubt there is a fair amount of feeling amongst our managers that they should get a substantial increase. It looks as if we might have a fight on our hands.

You must not concede this claim. We have to maintain or improve our profits this year, as our major shareholders are getting very impatient with recent results.

On the other hand we can't afford a protracted dispute. Any strike action would cause a serious fall in sales which we just can't afford. And we would probably attract the sort of publicity we can well do without.

We are under severe attack from other breweries for our free house business, and this places an even greater need for secure outlets of our own. In the short term it looks as if any increase in sales volume will have to be achieved through our existing managed and tenanted houses.

I propose therefore that you make every effort to link any pay increase you make to increased sales. This might help us to achieve our objective of increased volume, and reassure our shareholders that we are not giving anything away without getting something in return.

You don't need me to tell you to make sure you have got your act together when you negotiate this agreement. But, I do suggest you have clearly defined areas which you will each deal with.

National Association of Licensed House Managers

The following are the key points which would influence NALHM when carrying out the tasks of planning for, preparing and conducting the negotiation.

Economic Background   (i) Competition within the brewing industry is fierce, there has been a decline in the overall sales of beer, although this appears to have bottomed out. (ii) Over-capacity amongst the larger breweries is still a major problem. (iii) Resistance to price increases is growing and Micklethwaithe's products are already at a premium price. (iv) Inflation is currently at 8% and is predicted to fall to 6% over the next 12 months, though you believe this to be optimistic. (v) Pay rises in other industries are running slightly higher than the rate of inflation. (vi) There is a general feeling of 'over-pubbing' (too many pubs per area per person).

Micklethwaite's Performance Record (i) The year before last Micklethwaite Brewery made a published profit of £25 million on a turnover of £200 million. No profit figures are yet available for last year but turnover was known to be £216 million. It is anticipated that profits will probably be slightly up, but that profit margins will have fallen. (ii) Over the past few years many unprofitable houses have either been sold off or closed down by the breweries. Micklethwaite have many of their houses in the poorer areas of the large conurbations where unemployment is highest. Over the past two years they have transferred 35 managed houses to tenancies. (iii) It is known that other breweries have been taking some free trade outlets away from Micklethwaite over the past 12 months. This makes them more dependent on their tied houses as secure outlets.

NALHM Position Many members of the association feel strongly that their earnings levels have lagged behind over the past few years and do not reflect the long and unsocial hours they have to work. Furthermore, the closures and transfers of houses to tenancies give cause for concern as it reduces the size of NALHM's membership and income. Reductions in membership seem inevitable but need to be kept to a minimum if the association's income and bargaining power are not to be much reduced.

Some managers in the less profitable houses are concerned that they will lose their jobs if the large pay rise is agreed. On the other hand, they are also the people with the lowest earnings level and feel strongly that they should get more. The contrary position is held by managers in the most profitable houses who are the most vociferous in pressing for a large award, as they feel they are not getting a fair deal. While the volume of rhetoric from members has been loud in the call for a large settlement, the NALHM negotiators are not sure how much real support there would be for a real fight. A strike of even a few days would probably result in the loss of the profit bonus for the whole year, or reduce it dramatically. Moreover, any strike action could result in a long-term loss of business as customers may move to other houses.

The NALHM negotiators feel sure that if Micklethwaite are persuaded to settle somewhere near the current demand then a number of managed houses will be transferred to tenancy and the managers made redundant. How many is not known.

The Future There are a number of major changes which could affect NALHM members over the next few years, one of these is the introduction of new technology. The introduction of computerized tills and computer link-ups with the brewery computer is likely to give the breweries much tighter financial control over individual houses. It is believed that this will also place greater demands on NALHM members. The claim for extra payment for accepting new technology reflects those concerns. Additionally, it is believed that there could be a move towards adopting 'continental opening hours' within the next few years. NALHM would like to establish a payment system to cover for this eventuality now, while it is not a major concern to the breweries. The claim for extra payment to cover extended hours is an attempt to establish a precedent for additional payment for any hours worked beyond the normal working hours.

Case Study Tasks

Introduction

The primary focus of this case study is to look at the preparation and planning necessary to result in an agreement that (1) is seen as WIN/WIN by both parties, in that neither feels the other has won at their expense, but both feel they will benefit as a result of the agreement; (2) it is possible to implement successfully. In this context it must be possible to demonstrate *how* the agreement is to be implemented.

If there is time to conduct the negotiation two additional foci for consideration will be (a) how the actual conduct of the negotiation made it easier or more difficult to reach agreement and (b) how the way in which the preparation and planning was conducted made it easier or harder actually to negotiate.

You should remember that all negotiations, those in the area of industrial relations particularly, have implications for future relationships, not only between the parties directly involved, but also for other related groups. Similarly, negotiations are often constrained by past history, the current environment and each party's view of the future. These differences in interpretation of the negotiation's context can have an effect not only upon the negotiation outcome but also in the way it is received by the people the negotiators represent.

The Tasks

Your task will be to take part in a group representing *either* the brewery *or* the NALHM and go through the various stages of preparing for, planning for and possibly carrying out the next negotiation. You should carry out the following set of tasks as a group, bearing in mind the role to which you have been assigned. Each group should only be given information relevant to its own side (e.g. the NALHM or the brewery) if a negotiation session is to be undertaken. You will probably find it helpful to draw yourselves worksheets along the lines of that shown in Table 7, to arrange the material and conclusions you are reaching in a manner that would help you use them efficiently in the negotiation. (Stages 1 and 2 below will require at least an hour.)

Stage 1: Planning the Negotiation

1   (a) List all the negotiable issues as you see them, look widely, try to think of those which are not obvious; (b) add any the other party might raise; (c) add any other issues you may be able to use as levers; (d) assign your priorities; (e) estimate their priorities (i.e. how important is it to achieve your target on each issue; how important are they to the other party?).

2   (a) Discuss and record the following for each issue: (i) the best you can hope for;

Table 7 Suggested worksheet

Negotiable issues	Priorities		Limits			Their target	Cost of concessions	Options and reasons
	Us	Them	Best	Target	Worst			

(ii) your target, i.e. a satisfactory outcome; (iii) the minimum you are prepared to accept and still make a deal; also consider the implications of not reaching agreement. (b) Estimate and record the other party's target for each issue. (c) Check that your limits are as wide as possible – especially on lower priority issues which you can use for trade-offs. (d) Compare the two targets and check that a WIN/WIN outcome is possible – i.e. that there is an overlap between your ranges and your estimate of their target or limits.

3   Where possible, calculate the cost implications of concessions on each issue, e.g. a percentage reduction of 1% in bonus from machine profits means £135 per year.

Stage 2: Preparing for the Negotiation

1   (a) Compare priorities. Remember that wide differences identify areas for trade-offs, i.e. if an issue is not important to you but is to the other party you can give big concessions in return for an issue that is important to you – as long as the other party cannot be certain it is a throw-away issue. (b) Look for creative options on each issue – especially those whose value to them is greater than their cost to you. (c) Put yourself in their shoes – what further options would you raise? (d) With cost/value considerations in mind, plan a broad concession strategy: not just as regards concessions in which you are interested, but also how you will handle concessions they might ask for.

2 (a) Consider all the reasons and arguments you can use to support your case on each issue. (b) Select and note down the two or three arguments per issue which will be most persuasive to the other party. Remember that skilled people advance only one argument at a time. (c) Don't worry if one argument appears several times – if it is powerful it will work. (d) Do not make your case for one issue contingent upon winning another.

Stage 3: Carrying out the Negotiation

1 Prior to the negotiation, spend 5–10 minutes with your partner(s). (a) Agree the role which each of you will take during the negotiation. Make sure that no one has a non-speaking role, for example by dividing up the issues between your-selves equally, agreeing to swop leadership of the team part way through, etc. (b) Try to agree a procedure for interrupting each other during the negotiation, to handle things such as breaking to discuss a new issue or option you'd not planned for, stop your partner(s) giving too much away, etc.

2 Undertake the negotiation. There is a time limit of between 30 minutes and 1 hour. If no agreement is reached the negotiation is referred to ACAS as dead-locked.

Stage 4: Questions for General Review

1 Discuss the following with reference to the literature: (a) the process, content and outcome of negotiations; (b) the skills required for negotiation; (c) the 'real-life' factors both external and internal to an organization which affect negotiation; and (d) the relationships between negotiation, collective bargaining and industrial relations more generally.

2 If the negotiation was carried out: (a) record the terms and conditions of agreement or disagreement; (b) rate (on five-point scales) (i) who won (we/they), (ii) your degree of satisfaction with the terms of the settlement, and (iii) your degree of confidence that the agreement will be smoothly implemented and successful. Discuss these findings. (c) What factors during the planning and preparation phases helped or hindered the negotiation, and how? (d) During the negotiation itself (i) what behaviours or strategies seemed most effective and (ii) what mistakes were made?

Essential Reading

Carlisle J Leary M (1981) Negotiating groups, in Groups at Work, edited by R L Payne and C Cooper, John Wiley, Chapter 7

Rackham N Carlisle J (1978) The effective negotiator, Parts 1 and 2, Journal of European Industrial Training 2: 2–10

Stephenson G M Brotherton C J (1979) Industrial Relations: A Social Psychological Approach, John Wiley, Chapters 6, 8, 10, 13, 14

Additional Reading

Anthony P D (1977) The Conduct of Industrial Relations, Institute of Personnel Management

Barrett B Rhodes E Beishon J (1977) Industrial Relations and the Wider Society, Macmillan

Bazerman M H Lewicki R J (1983) Negotiating in Organizations, Sage Publications

Clegg H A (1979) The Changing System of Industrial Relations in Great Britain, Blackwell

Fisher R Ury W (1981) Getting to Yes, Hutchinson

Karrass C L (1970) The Negotiating Game, World Publishing

Morley I (1981) Negotiation and bargaining, in Social Skills and Work, edited by M Argyle, Methuen

Morley I Stephenson G M (1977) The Social Psychology of Bargaining, George Allen & Unwin

Morley I E Hoskin D M (1984) Decision-making and negotiation, in Social Psychology and Organizational Behaviour, edited by M Gruneberg and T D Wall, John Wiley

Pedler M (1977) Negotiation skills training, Parts 1, 2 and 3. Journal of European Industrial Training 1: 4–6

Warr P B (1973) Psychology and Collective Bargaining, Hutchinson

CASE 21

Collective Bargaining: Car Co.

Paul Willman

Organizational Setting

The South Birmingham works is the largest manufacturing plant within Car Co., a large multiplant operation in the vehicle industry. The plant's business is the manufacture and assembly of passenger cars. Throughout the 1970s Car Co. had experienced a steady contraction of output, from around 1.1 million vehicles in 1971 to under 700 000 in 1979. In addition, it had incurred substantial losses. Employment in the company had also fallen, although over a shorter period, dropping by about 15% between 1974 and 1979, from 208 000 to 177 000.

The causes of this decline had been outlined in several reports produced by outside consultants on the company's performance in the mid-1970s. The company had grown through merger and had not rationalized production: it still produced too many models on too many different sites; there were weaknesses in management organization and quality; there had been a lack of investment in new productive capacity; and there was a history of poor labour relations. However, the two key problem areas were the lack of a good marketable product range, and very low levels of labour productivity.

Car Co. is almost wholly unionized. The company recognizes 11 manual workers' unions, all of which operate closed shops, and have a tradition of local bargaining; in 1976 there were 58 manual bargaining units in the company. All 11 unions are present at the South Birmingham works.

Background to the Case

Following the unfavourable reports on the company's performance, the management decided to launch a new car, codenamed the M2, and to reform its labour relations. The former involved not only a great deal of design work for product innovation, but also a massive investment in automated assembly techniques – such as robotics, automated welding and computer-controlled machining systems – which revolutionized processes of production. The decision was made to produce the M2 at South Birmingham, and purchase and installation of equipment began in 1977.

The decision to reform labour relations involved the centralization of collective bargaining. Historically, the company had relied on local bargaining at plant or department level, which had created a mass of local anomalies in pay and conditions. In addition, it had assisted the growth of a strong shop stewards' organization within the company's plants which was capable of organizing industrial action in support of local claims. In consequence, the company had suffered numerous local disputes and in 1977 was hit by a national stoppage of craftsmen in pursuit of separate negotiating rights to secure adequate pay differentials over production workers and the removal of interplant relativities.

In order to solve its labour relations problems, the company established a participation scheme, based on committees at plant, divisional and company level, which were to involve local representatives in processes of decision making. It also began a 'parity programme' by which plants would move towards equal pay for similar jobs over a two-year period: the programme was to be funded by productivity improvements and based upon a company-wide job evaluation scheme. However, both arms of the labour relations strategy were jeopardized as the company's financial position deteriorated. A new managing director published a corporate plan in 1978 based upon contraction and plant closure: the shop stewards withdrew from participation and strengthened resistance to centralized bargaining. By the beginning of 1979, the framework of management–union relationships was in disrepair and the climate of industrial relations was poor: 1977 and 1978 had been the worst years for strikes in the company's history.

The link between labour relations reform and new product development lay in the discussions of the participation committee based upon the South Birmingham works. At this committee, there was extensive discussion about the new process equipment, the design of the car and the new working practices which would be necessary for both production and maintenance workers. The principal changes envisaged in the working practices were as follows:

a *Team working* Operations within a given production zone were to be organized around a single supervisor; within teams so formed, there was to be little demarcation between the jobs of individual members, and formal progression from material handler to operative to quality controller to maintenance would be possible (see Figure 6). This involved greater labour flexibility and the development of new skills.

b *Two trades maintenance* The essence of the move to two trades maintenance was to be the removal of demarcation between craft skills. Maintenance workers were organized into four distinct trades; machine-tool fitters, millwrights, pipefitters and electricians: all maintenance was organized centrally, and the appropriate trades called to production faults as required. The object was to create two trade groups, mechanical and electrical, and to have teams of two 'on-line', patrolling the machinery.

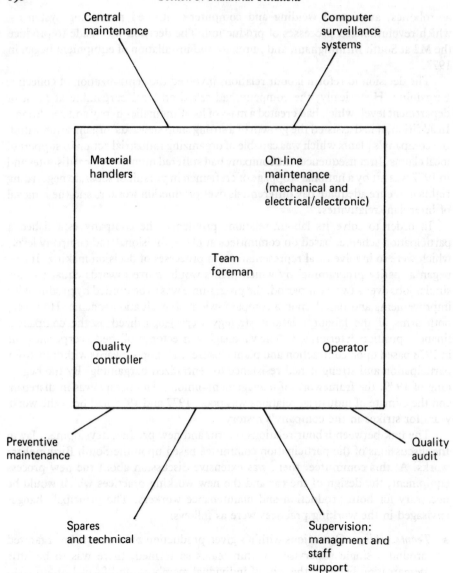

Figure 6 Composition of production teams.

Trade union representatives accepted the need for such changes, but argued that the changes would need to be negotiated according to the terms of existing collective agreements. These negotiations, however, did not begin until the summer of 1979, when the participation scheme had broken down and the collective bargaining climate was extremely sour.

The Problem

The critical factor in these negotiations is that the only common aim is to secure the launch of the M2, which is the key to future profitability and employment. Managers at the South Birmingham works are keen to see the removal of all previous agreements and to have the M2 line operate on their terms, with appropriate manning and working practices: the central issue is to secure high labour productivity. South Birmingham shop stewards wish to preserve traditional arrangements, and want to secure payment for change and a local regrading arrangement to cover team working; craft shop stewards will oppose any attack on craft demarcations. In particular, shop stewards wish to preserve mutuality – the requirement to reach agreement before implementation of change and, in the event of disagreement, to retain the status quo. The South Birmingham procedure runs: 'In the event of any difference arising which cannot immediately be disposed of, then whatever practice or agreement existed prior to the difference shall continue to operate pending a settlement'.

The Bargaining Issues

Management

Goals The key issue for managers is to secure the efficient operation of the new facility. In particular, continuous working is important because the highly automated lines operate at very high speeds: short interruptions, for whatever reason, can be extremely costly. The labour productivity targets set for the M2 are extremely tight, and while the new process equipment reduces the number of *standard hours* per car, the task in bargaining is to provide a system of labour utilization which minimizes *off-standard hours* (see Figure 7). This system provides, through teamwork and two-trades maintenance, for rapid labour response. Although precise estimates are unavailable for the proposed facility, line managers feel that rapid *maintenance* response is by far the more important item. However, this strategy requires the elimination of several current practices.

One key area is mobility of labour: mutuality extends to consultation with stewards over individual employee mobility, but there are also flat vetoes on certain movements, for example between production and maintenance areas.

Constraints These are set mainly by developments elsewhere in Car Co. Because the company has centralized collective bargaining on the basis of a plant-wide job evaluation scheme, two problems arise. First, a local payment for change in the South Birmingham works is ruled out because it raises the spectre of future comparability claims which will frustrate the current parity policy and possibly lead to more local disputes. Secondly, the current company-wide five-grade job evaluation (JE) scheme was the subject of much disagreement *among* workforce representatives and was eventually imposed by the company. It puts most production workers in grade 3 and most craftsmen in grade 1. But it was devised without consideration of the new flexible work patterns on the M2 line. The jobs outlined in Figure 6 must be 'slotted

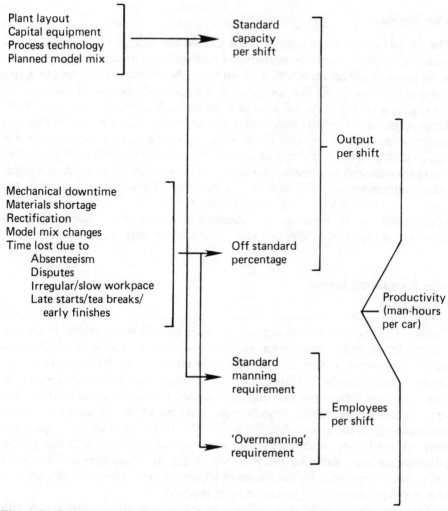

Figure 7 Components of labour productivity in the car industry (derived from Hartley (1981) Figure 4.2).

into' the JE scheme. Once again, the pressure is for all production jobs below supervisor to go into grade 3 to avoid comparability claims. But this frustrates the idea of progression through the team.

The second set of constraints are of rather a different type. The new managing director (MD) has laid renewed emphasis on the 'right to manage', and shown a disposition to remove managers who do not display such qualities. A number of managers who could not get results, particularly in personnel and industrial relations, have moved on. A recent document from the MD states that

'It is managers who have the responsibility for managing, leading and motivating employees and for communicating on company matters . . . shop stewards have the right to represent and to communicate trade union information to their members at the workplace but only within the rules and procedures jointly established . . . . Company action does not depend on their support'.

However, for personnel managers this approach has obvious limitations. Employee cooperation is vital for the success of the M2: high volume, high quality output is the key to success, and this requires relatively high levels of employee motivation. The forthcoming annual review will implement a system of non-negotiable, plant-wide bonuses based upon 'shipped' (i.e. quality assured) output, which could amount to up to 30% of production earnings on high volume lines such as the M2.

Employee Representatives

Goals The key issues for stewards are, firstly, to secure some payment for flexibility and, secondly, to retain some influence on the shop floor to safeguard employees' interests. Car-workers' earnings have fallen from 125% to 104% of the manual earnings average over the last eight years and, although the company is in financial difficulties, the launching of a new product offers the prospect of some bargaining leverage. In particular, the new jobs envisaged within teams are obvious candidates for regrading. However, the issue of shopfloor control is equally important. Centralization of bargaining removed shop stewards' influence over pay, and the new style of management being advocated in the company threatens the long-standing commitment to mutuality.

Within the shop stewards as a group, there are differences of opinion between craft and general workers' shop stewards. General worker representatives strongly resisted centralization as an erosion of local autonomy, but have a relatively open view of working practices on the new line provided that mutuality is retained. Craft shop stewards were very much in favour of centralization because it was part of a package which safeguarded differentials, but proposed to oppose any alteration to craft organization.

Constraints Constraints on shop stewards' behaviour are of five types. The first and most general is that the level of unemployment in the West Midlands is rising: Car Co. has shed a number of jobs in the past few years and plans to shed more. There is considerable pressure from members to safeguard jobs at all costs. This has prompted a second area of concern: three times in the past two years the company has successfully bypassed the normal channel of the National Joint Negotiating Committee to ballot employees directly when agreement on change has not been forthcoming. The bargaining position of shop stewards might be similarly undermined in future, particularly at South Birmingham: both of the old product lines are running down, and the company proposes to select employees for the new lines on the basis of 'good employment records'. Those not transferred may well be declared redundant.

The third constraint concerns the withdrawal of the M2 project and its relocation at the East Birmingham plant. The company has indicated that this plant relocation would be extremely costly at this stage, but that they would consider it as a last resort if the launch of the new model came under threat. East Birmingham will otherwise close in the next two years, and their refusal of this lifeline is unlikely.

The fourth factor to consider is the attitude of unions at national level. Radical contraction, and even closure of Car Co. has been mooted as a possibility if the M2 fails. Not only will this cause substantial job loss at the company, but the West Midlands car components industry will suffer commensurately: some 400 000 jobs are thought to be at risk overall. Although disagreeing amongst themselves on several issues, both the Transport and General Workers' Union and the Amalgamated Union of Engineering Workers are committed to keeping the company open and have put pressure on stewards accordingly.

The fifth constraint is low trust between union and managers. The new MD has recently described the shop stewards as 'the small minority who would like to see the company fail'. The stewards themselves see the MD's aims in terms of contraction and closure.

Case Study Tasks

Imagine you are the leading negotiator on the management side: your responsibility is to secure the work organization necessary for successful operation of the M2 line. The launch itself is *one year* away, but you need to have agreement within six months. In three months' time, the annual pay review arises for the company as a whole. You know, but the union side do not, that the Managing Director's plan is to announce (i) a 10% rise for craftsmen and 5% for other grades (both rises are lower than the rate of inflation); (ii) a generous voluntary redundancy scheme to deal with a further loss of 25 000 jobs over three years. Your objective is successfully to negotiate change. The questions below should be considered.

General

1   What room for manoeuvre do the various constraints leave you?
2   What room do they leave for your opponents?
3   What are the essential and non-essential elements of the company's proposals so far?

Specific

4   How will you integrate any agreement reached here with the annual review?
5   Is there a solution to the problem which is acceptable to craft and general workers?
6   If not, how will you go about implementing change if agreement is not forthcoming?

Essential Reading

Gospel H (1983) Managerial structures and strategies, in Managerial Strategies and Industrial Relations, edited by H Gospel and C Littler, Heinemann, pp. 1–25

Purcell J (1979) A strategy for management control through collective bargaining, in The Control of Work, edited by J Purcell and R Smith, Macmillan

Additional Reading

Batstone E Boraston I Frenkel S (1977) Shopstewards in Action, Blackwell

Beynon H (1973) Working for Ford, Penguin

Hartley J (1981) Management of Vehicle Production, Butterworth

Storey J (1981) The Challenge to Management Control, Hutchinson

CASE 22

Industrial Disputes: Small Metals Factory

P. K. Edwards and Hugh Scullion

Organizational Setting

The Small Metals Factory is a long-established engineering factory, which at the time of the research was owned by a large, multi-plant British company. The company had for several years faced a very difficult economic environment, a declining market share and heavy losses. In an attempt to restore profitability, capacity was being reduced and several plants were closed. The factory thus faced a very uncertain future. Its main role was to supply semifinished components to other plants in the company, and historically it had been subject to large fluctuations in demand over which local management had no control.

Background to the Case

About 650 workers, all of them male, were employed on a variety of tasks involved in the machining and assembly of a range of metal goods. Most worked on day shifts, but night shifts were also operated in a few areas. Most jobs were of the repetitive, routine sort found in metalworking factories: power-press operating, spot and gas welding, assembling of components, and material handling. Direct machine-pacing was, however, rare, with most workers working as individuals or members of small teams on operations on which they could set the speed. Although most work was semiskilled, there was an elite of workers carrying out the most complex tasks associated with the shaping and assembly of metal components. Exactly how much real skill was required in these tasks was a matter of some dispute, with managers and the less skilled grades feeling that the claim to skill reflected history and not current needs. But the claim to skilled status was a crucial feature of the atmosphere of the plant. The skilled workers saw themselves as members of a craft which was not only superior to those who had not gone through an apprenticeship but was also capable of regulating itself without interference from management.

The deeply felt craft tradition was reflected in the plant's union organization. The union which had traditionally dominated the plant was based on the skilled trade, originally limiting itself to time-served members of the trade but slowly opening its ranks to semiskilled workers carrying out ancillary operations such as spot welding and press operation. At the time of the research it covered all workers in the factory engaged in welding, metal shaping and finishing, inspection, and press operation. A general union had entered the factory to organize labourers and other indirect workers, and it had gained a hold over some direct operations such as painting and ancillary operations in the press shop. Demarcation disputes continued to arise over the boundary between the two unions' territories, and there were considerable mutual suspicions. These rivalries were eased somewhat by the existence for some years of a joint union committee (JUC) which considered matters common to the two unions and also the third union in the plant, namely the electricians' union, covering the small number of electricians and their mates in the plant. For all three unions, a pre-entry closed shop had long been in existence, whereby a worker was required to belong to the union organizing the trade in which he was to be employed before he could take up a job.

Both the main unions had sophisticated organizations. The general union had a full-time convener and deputy convener, together with a dozen other stewards, many of whom in practice spent the majority of their time on union business. The other union, which will be called the ex-craft union in view of its development from a craft base, had a more complex structure. It had a central committee with a full-time chairman (who was in practice, but not in name, the convener) together with committees covering each of the main sections of the factory. It had about 30 shop stewards in all, of whom the most influential were the (full-time) senior shop stewards in each section; it was a union rule that these shop stewards must be skilled. The large steward network and the small size of the plant permitted good communications with shopfloor workers. This opportunity was made into a reality by the ex-craft union's tradition of direct democracy: shop committees were elected every three months, there was a weekly mass meeting (always well attended) in each shop, and stewards spent a good deal of their time on the shop floor and not away in offices.

The conduct of industrial relations reflected the considerable degree of control which both unions had built up over the conduct of work. The stewards adhered strongly to traditional ways of doing things: as long as management respected existing agreements they were willing to cooperate in the pursuit of production targets. Notable among the controls developed by the stewards were the following: their ability to control recruitment, such that management needed their agreement to bring in new workers, with consent being given only when the stewards were satisfied that there was sufficient work to go round, and with the recruits then being chosen by management from lists provided by the unions; the establishment of overall manning levels through a process of negotiation in which the stewards generally held the whip hand; the need for managers to secure the stewards' consent before moving workers between tasks; and the working of virtually guaranteed overtime. Management had in the past tolerated these arrangements, and indeed had helped to create them by ceding concessions in return for a steady flow of production and an easy life. Effort levels were thus generally low: the factory operated under a measured daywork system of daily work quotas, which could generally be attained in six hours or less. The atmosphere on the shop floor was not one of conflict or tension. Most workers, stewards, foremen and managers had been in the plant for many years, and they were equally accustomed to traditional arrangements. There were a few ups and downs, but generally speaking the stewards' controls were not openly challenged, there was a sense that things worked well, and there was a comfortable coexistence between the two sides.

A new managment team, comprising the plant manager and the production and personnel managers, had, however, been brought into the plant with the explicit remit of shaking it out of its old ways. The stewards were sceptical. They said that they had seen successive management teams come and go, while they themselves were still there; and they pointed out that the plant had a generally good record of attaining production targets. The plant manager argued, however, that these targets reflected years of inflated manning levels and were no measure of efficient output. His aim was to modernize and rationalize the plant's operations. This included tying the stewards down to clear, written agreements. The stewards were hostile to such agreements, feeling that they were either redundant, in that they wrote down what was already perfectly understood, or dangerous, in that they challenged the position that cooperation with management was a concession which could be withdrawn at will. The new managers treated these arguments with scorn: they questioned the good faith of the stewards, felt that the stewards used their position to delay any change, and argued that any agreement which was reached was worthless because the stewards reserved the right to withdraw cooperation at will. The solution was to establish explicit agreements on managerial rights to which the stewards were committed. Managers stressed that they were not opposed to an influential steward organization as such, but argued that the stewards had to take their responsibilities seriously. In particular, if clear and workable agreements on manning levels and the allocation of work could not be achieved, the future of the plant was in jeopardy because the company would not be willing to send it new work to replace work which was about to cease.

The Problem

Start of the Dispute

Two separate incidents sparked off the dispute. The first concerned rules on the payment of expenses to shop stewards for attending meetings with management outside the plant. The personnel manager was trying to introduce the company-wide procedure which clashed with the local practice. When the new rules were applied the stewards registered their dissatisfaction by using one of their favourite sanctions, a refusal to meet any manager above shop level. Before the issue could be resolved a problem broke out in the inspection department. A special monitoring exercise was taking place, and inspectors had been assigned to it from their normal duties. Absenteeism led to a shortage of inspectors on the goods inward section, and the manager instructed a man to return to his normal job on the section. The man refused because the instruction had not been agreed with the relevant steward, and he was taken off pay.

This action surprised other managers. The personnel manager criticized it: although the instruction to move had been proper, the procedure for warning the worker and advising the stewards before stopping pay had not been followed. Managers felt, however, that to back down would weaken their authority. They therefore defended the initial instruction, and pointed out that complaints about the subsequent actions of the manager of the inspection department could be put through the grievance procedure. They went on to announce that, in view of the stewards' refusal to meet them, unilateral managerial action was unavoidable on certain urgent matters. In particular, work intended for the plant would have to be sent elsewhere.

The action in the inspection department was met by a refusal to do overtime by inspectors, who also banned all mobility between jobs in the department. This meant that each man would stick strictly to his assigned tasks and would not move to any other job. The JUC decided to retain the ban on meetings with management until the threat about new work was lifted and until the inspector who had been taken off pay was paid. The threat was eventually lifted, but the stewards saw the inspector's case as a matter of principle and maintained their position. Managers saw this as simply a pretext. They had been trying to reach an agreement on the introduction of new work, and they felt that the stewards were looking for any excuse to delay negotiations on the agreement.

Escalation

The inspector's mobility ban made life difficult for managers in the main assembly shop. It was exacerbated by the fact that the inspectors' steward in the shop happened to be on the JUC and was frequently away at meetings. The lack of inspection prevented a steady flow of components into the final assembly area, and when the supply of one component ran dry, managers in the shop decided to withhold the earnings of the entire shop for the time that was lost, which amounted to one and a half hours. This action brought the majority of shopfloor workers directly into the dispute for the first time. Stewards and workers alike were convinced that there was a systematic attempt by management to put pressure on them, for why else would pay have been stopped so abruptly? A mass meeting of the assembly shop was held and there was some discussion of an immediate walk-out. But the chief steward of the shop argued convincingly that a walk-out would be exactly what management wanted, and he pointed out that many weapons were available other than anything as crude as an outright stoppage. This was the majority view.

At about the same time as the solidarity of the shop floor was being cemented, divisions appeared in the ranks of management. Foremen became increasingly hostile to the policies of senior management. They felt that the decision to stop pay in the assembly shop simply antagonized workers unnecessarily and made the already difficult task of securing production virtually impossible. They shared the shopfloor view that there were tried and trusted traditions of conducting industrial relations, and that attempts to ride roughshod over custom and practice were unrealistic. Since the time of the stewards' ban on meeting with senior managers, the foremen had been used to deliver messages between the two sides. But they now became so disgruntled with this 'messenger boy' role that they refused to continue to act as intermediaries. They were not, however, a powerful group within management and there were no direct effects on managerial strategy at a higher level.

Senior managers were also considering the implications of the mobility ban. They began to question whether it was satisfactory that the inspection steward could attend JUC meetings as and when he chose without regard to the needs of production. They argued that the stewards had been warned of the consequences of a shortage of components, and thus supported the decision at shop level to stop the pay of the whole shop. In addition, they announced that they would deduct from the inspection steward's wages a sum commensurate with the amount of time he spent at meetings without formal managerial agreement. The JUC saw this as a straightforward case of victimization, and to demonstrate solidarity the whole committee left the plant for half an hour, inviting management to stop their pay too. Managers declined this gambit, however, and continued to insist on meetings to discuss the main issues.

Feelings among the stewards were now running high. Given the history of mutual suspicion between the two main unions, there was a remarkable degree of unity: all stewards saw the managerial actions as part of a general attack on union rights, and as something in which their interests were identical. Managers were aware of this, and of the probability that any attempt to divide the unions would be counterproductive since it would be seen as further evidence of malign intentions. A JUC meeting discussed the imposition of a ban on mobility covering all grades of labour. But the general view was that this would create such disruption that management would have an excuse to lay off large numbers of workers. Indeed, in view of the effect of the inspectors' ban, it was decided that a more flexible policy would be adopted so as to ensure that it did not lead to any more stoppages in the assembly shop.

Neither side wanted to inflame the situation, but they were equally determined not to climb down. Management made the next move by announcing a drastic cut in overtime requirements. This was not, in their view, directly related to the dispute. Instead, it reflected a response to a company exercise monitoring production levels and labour input, and it was essential to the plant's ability to attract new work to be able to demonstrate that it could operate within budgets.

The stewards saw things differently. A 'buffer' of overtime was an established part of the plant's operations, and even in 'normal times' a cut-back would have met opposition. In the current climate the stewards saw the action as a further attempt to escalate the dispute. They felt that they could play the same game, and imposed a total ban on overtime. Following further cases of workers being taken off pay the stewards decided further action was needed. They again considered a total ban on mobility but, fearing lay-offs, rejected it and instead imposed a policy of 'working to the hour'. This meant the strict adherence to hourly production targets. Workers normally worked hard early in the day to create leisure later, and they were willing to 'pull back' any small production losses resulting from minor machine breakdowns. In working to the hour no losses were pulled back. Although imposing no direct financial costs on workers, the practice was not popular with workers since, as they explained, they could not 'get stuck in' but had to spin out their work, thus losing the satisfactions of developing a rhythm, suffering the tedium of working below a comfortable pace, and losing the period of leisure at the end of the shift. Yet they accepted the policy without question, for they knew what the dispute was about and they shared the stewards' distrust of management. When stewards told them that established shopfloor rights were endangered, the workforce had no reason to doubt them. And there were no alternative channels of communication through which management might have presented a different picture.

Working to the hour and the overtime ban gave stewards and workers numerous opportunities to hold up production. With no maintenance work being carried out in overtime, the start of work was often delayed. And stewards now made issues of matters which would normally be accepted. In a typical case a steward insisted that the assembly track be stopped until the area was properly cleaned. The overall effects are hard to estimate, but production in the assembly shop was sometimes 20% below normal.

Management could have threatened a lock-out on the grounds that normal working was impossible. The main constraint on such a course was the plant's relationship with the rest of the company. Since it supplied components to several other factories, an all-out stoppage could rapidly lead to severe difficulties in these factories. More generally, a lengthy dispute would be unlikely to convince the company's planners of the sense of giving important new work to the plant. They attempted to re-establish negotiations by involving the full-time officials of the unions concerned and the divisional personnel manager. A meeting was arranged, but it never took place because two more workers were taken off pay and the stewards refused to allow discussions to proceed. After this failure management used a more aggressive response to the stewards' sanctions. Claiming that overtime was not voluntary but 'semicontractural', they announced that pay would be stopped whenever a loss of production could be attributed to the effects of the overtime ban.

De-escalation

With both sides increasing their sanctions, managers finally persuaded the stewards to have some 'talks about talks'. A new element was introduced when managers pointed to the threat of a major strike (on matters completely separate from the local dispute) elsewhere in the company. They suggested that a long strike could be so costly that it would lead to the closure of several small and marginal plants such as their own and argued that a solution to domestic difficulties was the best way to maximize the plant's chances of staying open. Although sceptical about the closure threat, feeling that they had heard it all before and that managerial plans were fickle and unreliable, the stewards took seriously the possibility that management would use the strike to escalate their own dispute. The plant's main customer was likely to be affected by it, and one of the constraints on management was thus released. There were, indeed, some managers who favoured giving the stewards an ultimatum: resume negotiations or face a lock-out. Others, however, feared the damage that a strike might cause. Divisional management also took a hand by refusing to countenance a lock-out. Managers at this level had to balance several aims, notably concentrating their energies on the larger strike looming elsewhere and maintaining good working relations with the union officials, with whom they had to negotiate in many different contexts and whom they did not want to antagonize by endorsing a deliberate lock-out.

A series of inconclusive meetings, involving divisional managers and officials of the two main unions, took place before the outbreak of the threatened strike in other plants persuaded the stewards to relax the overtime ban, restore full mobility in areas other than inspection, and resume domestic negotiations with management. Managers had also been reviewing the position. The plant had gone through two months of argument and sanctions, and it was felt that industrial relations needed to be put on what one manager termed 'an even keel'. Another inconclusive meeting with divisional managers and full-time union officials led to the matter being 'referred back' to plant level, that is, no agreement could be reached.

Management in the plant finally set up what it termed a court of inquiry to take evidence, with the plant manager acting as the 'independent' chairman. Eventually management offered to reimburse the wages of two of the workers whose pay had been stopped and to suspend disciplinary action against the inspectors' steward for attending union meetings without permission. They did not, however, offer to refund the pay that had been deducted for the time he spent at these meetings. The stewards agreed to this, and all sanctions were lifted. The dispute thus petered out, with several issues, notably the stoppage of pay of several other workers and the conclusion of an agreement on the introduction of new work, remaining unresolved. Neither side had been willing to engage in an all-out confrontation, and there seemed to be little alternative to trying to bury their differences and to return to normal.

Conclusions

The foregoing account has tried to do more than simply describe a complex series of events. It has also offered some explanation of the immediate factors which influenced the key decisions that were taken. The objective in discussing the case is to adopt the standpoints of the key actors and to consider why they acted as they did and what alternatives were open to them. Remember that they were acting with imperfect information; neither side had access to the underlying motivations of the other but had to infer these motivations from observed actions as interpreted through the possibly distorting prism of past experience and accumulated folk wisdoms. Remember also that they did not have the benefit of hindsight: they had to respond to complex and conflicting pressures without knowing what the consequences of a particular response would be.

Case Study Tasks

Questions 1–3 are suitable for short discussions of 1–2 hours; while Questions 4–7 will require longer and more detailed consideration, backed up by appropriate reading.

1   What consequences do you expect the dispute to have had on:
    a   the role of the JUC and interunion relations
    b   the place of foremen in the managerial hierarchy
    c   the attitude of the inspectors' steward who lost pay
    d   the ability of management to introduce change in the future?
2   a   Reconstruct: (i) the stewards' view of managerial strategy; (ii) senior managers' perceptions of the stewards' behaviour.
    b   Attempt a balanced perspective
3   What were the main weaknesses in management's approach?
4   Develop a plan for management to introduce agreements on new working arrangements and the organization of new work.
5   Consider the lessons for other shop steward organizations in relation to:
    a   links between stewards and members
    b   tactics in the deployment of sanctions
    c   the strengths and weaknesses of an organization restricted to one factory.
6   How typical do you think the factory is in terms of the extent of shopfloor power and the availability of sanctions against management?
7   Do you expect the balance of power in this plant will have shifted between the time of the study (1979) and the present?

Essential Reading

Batstone E Boraston I Frenkel S (1978) The Social Organization of Strikes, Blackwell, pp. 13–20, 27–59
Hyman R (1977) Strikes, Fontana–Collins, pp. 11–24, 109–139

Additional Reading

Armstrong P J Goodman J F B Hyman J D (1981) Ideology and Shopfloor Industrial Relations, Croom Helm
Beynon H (1973) Working for Ford, Penguin, pp. 109–150
Clack G (1967) Industrial Relations in a British Car Factory, Cambridge University Press
Clark T Clements L (eds) (1977) Trade Unions under Capitalism, Fontana, pp. 223–287
Gouldner A W (1955) Wildcat Strike, Routledge & Kegan Paul
Hirszowicz M (1981) Industrial Sociology, Martin Robertson, pp. 201–228
Watson T J (1980) Sociology, Work and Industry, Routledge & Kegan Paul, pp. 224–257

CASE 23

A 'Lock-out': Times Newspapers Ltd.

Paul Routledge

Organizational Setting

Times Newspapers Ltd incorporates five publications, namely The Times, its three supplements (Educational, Higher Education and Literary) and The Sunday Times, and is amongst the most famous and prestigious newspaper groups in the world. It operates from Fleet Street, a small concentrated jungle with its own traditions and customs, particularly regarding its trade union organization. The unions figuring large in this case are: SOGAT – the Society of Graphical and Allied Trades, representing publishing room workers, van drivers and circulation representatives; NGA – the National Graphical Association, representing skilled print workers, including compositors, machine managers and readers; NUJ – the self-explanatory National Union of Journalists; and NATSOPA – the National Society of Operative Printers, Graphical and Media Personnel, representing semi-skilled grades and clerical and administrative staff. In all 56 chapels existed at the start of the dispute.

Background to the Case

It is now generally recognized that the 'big bang' theory of industrial relations did not work when it was tried at Times Newspapers Ltd (TNL) in the long, costly and often bitter lock-out of 1978–9. TNL management insisted after the 11.5 month suspension of its five titles that it had achieved 70% of its objectives. Little more than a year later, when The Times, its three supplements and The Sunday Times were put up for sale, it was admitted that industrial disruption had not ceased 'and it has not been possible to operate the new technology on even the most limited basis'.

In the calmer operating climate of today, and with the benefit of the more accurate science of hindsight, it is possible to determine why events did not unfold as management had foreseen and perhaps to draw some general conclusions about the nature of trade union power in the national newspaper industry.

The Problem

To begin more or less at the beginning, the background to the dispute was clearly laid out in a letter to print union general secretaries sent by M J 'Duke' Hussey, managing director and chief executive of Times Newspapers, on 26 April 1978. He complained of 'crippling disputes' which had cost 7.7 million copies of the paper because of unofficial industrial action over a period of just three months.– 20% of total output. Losses due to this action amounted to £1 750 000, equal to the total profit in 1977, which was easily the best year in the company's history.

Hussey told the unions: 'It is not an exaggeration that almost the total working hours of our Board and senior managers are now occupied with trying to prevent disputes, solving disputes and repairing the damage they cause. Virtually no effort is going in to improving the turnover and profitability of the company.' No board of directors – and no responsible trade union official – could stand aside from a crisis of this nature, he argued.

TNL accordingly proposed 'urgent discussions' on four basic company demands: (1) absolute continuity of production; all arbitrary restrictions to be lifted; no unofficial action to prevent publication; (2) negotiation of a new, fast-acting and effective disputes procedure; (3) negotiation of a general wage restructuring based on new technology and computer-based electronic printing systems; (4) a timetable insisting on completion of these negotiations by November 30. If this deadline was not met, publication of the titles would be suspended unilaterally by the company, and staff who had not accepted these terms would be dismissed.

There was another underlying factor, rarely articulated but playing a key role in managerial attitudes: restoration of 'the right to manage'. Hussey let the cat out of the bag in a television interview, saying that Fleet Street had 'allowed situations to develop which it should never have done . . . the right to manage is one of the issues at stake, it is a Fleet Street problem'. As Martin points out, 'management became more committed to new technology as a means of achieving a once-for-all transformation in the company's industrial relations, with an assertion of management's authority' (Martin 1981, p. 255).

As Martin further observes 'Times management was asking for the moon' (Martin 1981, p. 279), and it was not available. The company had chosen to fight on too many fronts. In the first place, the steady shift of power from the centre to the workplace that had been such a feature of trade union development in the 1960s had given further 'clout' to the print union chapels, which were already in a strong position because of the pre-entry closed shop universally operating in the industry. Even if they had wished to, the print union full-time officials could not give *absolute guarantees* of continuity of production.

Secondly, by requiring full use of computerized typesetting – including direct input to the computer by journalists – the company was demanding that the NGA, the most powerful, disciplined and wealthy print union, give up its traditional monopoly of the keyboard. The NGA had watched its counterparts in the USA and West Germany fight, and lose, this battle, with catastrophic consequences in terms of de-skilling and job losses. Joe Wade, general secretary of the NGA, said in an eve-of-conflict message to his members that the rest of Fleet Street, provincial managements and general printing firms were 'waiting like vultures to see the union break its back' at The Times; 'So there is no going back. There can be no surrender. We fight for our union. We fight until we have won.'

And thirdly, the company made the cardinal error of assuming that Times' journalists would behave with their customary moderation and meekly accept the conditions for continuing employment. They did not. On the last day of publication, they voted 142 to 92 to be dismissed along with the printers. It was a passionate debate within the chapel of the National Union of Journalists, fuelled partly by a sense of professional outrage at the management taking the paper off the streets for an indefinite period, and partly by a sense that here was an opportunity to close the earnings gap with The Sunday Times and win greater concessions for operating new technology.

After recovering from the initial shock of this decision, TNL moved swiftly to prevent the break-up of its editorial team. The NUJ negotiated an interim agreement under which journalists 'would not be asked to do work that had not been voluntarily relinquished by another union.' That proviso, which remains in force at the present time, took them out of the firing line but it also had a considerable psychological impact on the company's bargaining position.

Few substantive negotiations had taken place elsewhere by the time the deadline was reached. Only four of the 56 bargaining units had signed deals, covering circulation representatives, maintenance engineers, the Sunday Times NUJ and a handful of building workers. It had taken several months to get all the print union general secretaries into one room, and they then complained that there was insufficient time to conclude agreements before the 30th November. The NGA simply refused to discuss surrendering its control over typesetting, while personal rivalries and chaotic lines of communication in SOGAT and NATSOPA between chapel, branch, region and national leadership sharply diminished the prospects of peace talks.

William Rees-Mogg, editor of The Times and a director of TNL, who supported the lock-out policy, was to complain later:

> 'Negotiation is a process which offers at every stage the opportunity to say "No", regardless of the policy of the Government, regardless of the policy of the trade union movement, regardless of the wishes of the members and regardless of the interests of the members.
>
> 'Our position at The Times is like that of a man at the end of a windswept pier in some cold and out of season seaside resort – perhaps Scarborough in late November. We are confronted with a set of seven rusty and ancient fruit machines. To reach agreements we have to line up three strawberries in each of the fruit machines at the same time.
>
> 'Somehow, heaven knowns how – we have managed to line up three of the strawberries on two of the machines, and we have a couple of strawberries in the third. Of the others, some reject the coin that is put in – however large – while one has a lemon and another has a raspberry rusted permanently in place on the centre of the dial.'

His exasperated comments were colourful but misplaced. The company was asking for too much and usually asking the wrong people – the union general secretaries, rather than the chapels – to deliver it. This policy continued through an abortive two-week postponement of the deadline to the 14th December, during which the then Employment Secretary of the Labour Government, Albert Booth, attempted to bring the warring parties together. The delaying move cost the company £1 million but yielded no settlement, and the first 580 employees who were on two-week notice periods were sacked as the new year came in. Dismissals thereafter continued at the rate of about 100 a week as individual notices expired, and the repetitive experience of people leaving (sometimes accompanied by emotional scenes) inevitably prompted rising resentment on the shop floor. Members of NATSOPA and the NGA voted not to reopen talks with management until all the dismissed employees had been reinstated. An All-Union Liaison Committee bringing together rank and file leaders of the various chapels was formed, supplying a platform for lay officials and further extending the role of the in-house union leaders.

The dispute ran into its fourth month with Albert Booth once again seeking to act as peacemaker. He called on both sides on the 8th March and persuaded the company to re-engage those already dismissed and retain those still on TNL books until the 17th April, a planned date for republication of the titles. The Booth initiative was essentially to win time for realistic negotiations, this time bringing in the chapel leaders. But these talks, too, foundered on the rock of NGA intransigence. The craft printers would agree to a 'back end' system which retained their monopoly of the keyboard. But they would not go to arbitration on the possibility of moving to a 'front end' system giving journalists and tele-ad clerks access to the computer. Les Dixon, president of the NGA, insisted: 'It's a matter of principle and you can't arbitrate on a matter of principle.'

As breakdown came at the Easter weekend, the notices of the 620 NGA men expired and they were dismissed. The union then declared an official dispute, and began paying £40 a week benefit to its members, a sum topped up by the same amount raised in a Fleet Street levy. Later in the dispute, the NGA allowed its members to take work elsewhere, and on several occasions the full authority of its leaders was required to hold its TNL membership together. NATSOPA also found its members work elsewhere in Fleet Street, even where this meant (as it did at the Daily Mirror) displacing temporary staff. The union's undeclared but actual role as a labour exchange for the industry was never more tested, and other national newspaper proprietors found themselves paying the wages of ex-Times employees to whose dismissal they were giving moral support through the Newspaper Publishers' Association, the employers' body for the industry. Like other national newspapers, TNL has for long acquiesced in the system of virtual 'subcontracting' by which the trade unions supply labour and allocate tasks in the production areas.

The temptation to produce some form of newspaper in the run-up to the 1979 general election is thought to have been a major factor in the company's decision, announced on 20th April, to print and publish a European edition of The Times, to circulate exclusively abroad. Journalists were allowed to follow their own conscience in deciding whether to work for it, and after many months of inactivity many did contribute.

The reaction of the print unions was predictably wrathful. It was not long before the 'secret' location – Frankfurt in West Germany – was known. The NGA sent over a national officer to establish contact with the German printing union, IG Druck und Papier, so that the plant could be picketed. Only one edition of the 'Eurotimes' was printed, on the presses of the right-wing Turkish language newspaper Tercumen, close to Frankfurt airport. Pickets had stuffed a petrol-soaked rag into an air vent connected to machine room compressors, and police advised that they could not guarantee safe production of the paper. Amid charges from Rees-Mogg that 'violent and criminal elements' had halted the venture, the NUJ chapel changed its mind and decided that publication of the 'Eurotimes' was an obstacle to a negotiated solution of the dispute. No further editions were printed.

Two more idle months passed before the real breakthrough came in late June over dinner between the NGA leaders and Lord Thomson of Fleet, son of the Canadian entrepreneur who bought The Times from Lord Astor in 1966, adding it to his large portfolio of media investments which already included The Sunday Times. TNL had been a subsidiary of the Thomson organization since 1967, and as such was part of a massive conglomerate with substantial and profitable North Sea oil interests. The Times had consistently turned in a loss, though TNL had in good years made a profit. The large profits of the Thomson organization from oil, travel, publishing and provincial newspapers contributed to a widely held (though eventually erroneous) assumption that even though he did not share his father's attachment to The Times, the new Lord Thomson would not quit ownership of the titles. Conversely, it was also held in some quarters that the oil revenues were being used to break the power of the print unions.

Whatever his motives, Lord Thomson finally agreed to drop the company's insistence on single-key stroking, i.e. to allow the NGA to keep its monopoly of the keyboard. With this obstacle out of the way, negotiations began in earnest.

'Duke' Hussey, flanked by his top managers, attended a meeting of the All-Union Liaison Committee and told the chapel leaders: 'You will find us very flexible. We are newspaper makers, not executioners.' The company conceded that it had missed the signs of change in the balance of power within the unions; that power, it argued, should now be used constructively. Whether TNL had in mind what followed is unlikely; it took four more months to construct a return to work formula, which was the subject of in-fighting between the chapels as each working group scented victory and sought to wring the maximum possible gains from the company. Pay negotiations in the machine room were particularly abrasive, with the NGA machine managers accusing the NATSOPA machine assistants of endangering the peace process by disturbing hallowed differentials.

Within NATSOPA, there was a revolt among the white-collar chapels led by the wily and charismatic Barry Fitzpatrick who objected to what had been signed on their behalf. A clutch of operating agreements for new technology had to be renegotiated, with the chapels once again stamping their authority on the bargaining process. Fitzpatrick had emerged as a key figure in the dispute, leading the rank-and-file Liaison Committee. He is now a full-time national officer of SOGAT 82, into which NATSOPA disappeared through merger. His main rival in NATSOPA–TNL politics, Reg Brady, leader of the Sunday Times machine assistants, left the shop floor by another traditional Fleet Street route: to become an industrial relations executive under the new Murdoch regime.

The negotiations went through a series of broken deadlines, frequently lasting most of the night and pushing the negotiators on both sides 'beyond the limits of physical endurance'. Agreement was reached on the morning of the last day of the 'final, final' ultimatum period; Lord Thomson told waiting newsmen the suspension had been worth it if it secured the long-term future of the papers.

Before the champagne poured by a toastmaster at the front door had disappeared down the printworkers' throats, it was clear that the lock-out had achieved nothing of the kind. The NGA had accepted a back-end system of computerized typesetting, which would cut composing room manning levels by 40% but this had been on offer before the shutdown. Fewer men were to be employed in the machine room, though how many were notional shifts was anybody's guess; this issue also went to an ineffective ACAS investigation. A new disputes procedure had been signed, but it had scarcely been put to the test before the company was back in dispute, this time with the NUJ after refusing to honour an arbitration award. The suspension cost TNL £39 million, and the NGA still had control over the new technology.

The strategy might have worked in the United States, but it did not work in Britain because of the unusually tightly knit nature of the industry, concentrated in a few square miles rather than dispersed in large cities. The print unions' 'labour exchange' had prevented any real privation, and the power of the chapels survived largely intact. In the view of one veteran print union leader, the shutdown 'made no contribution at all to improving relations in Fleet Street'.

However, it did tear away any remaining sentimentality within the Thomson organization parent company towards its difficult dependent. The week-long NUJ strike of autumn 1980 is credited with being the final straw for Lord Thomson, but there were already signs that the firm had decided that The Times was a prestigious luxury which would have to be ditched for the sake of the group as a whole. Under Thomson, Times Newspapers had practically become ungovernable, as his lordship said when the titles were put up for sale on the 23rd October 1980. His continued support for the papers was 'conditional on the overall cooperation of the newspapers' employees, and I have sadly concluded that this cooperation will not be forthcoming under our ownership' (The Times 23rd October 1980.)

It had been a costly love affair with 'the old lady of Printing House Square'. From the formation of Times Newspapers in 1967, more than £70 million was advanced from Thomson sources for investment, working capital and losses incurred. The pretax loss in the year after suspension was £15 million, and TNL had to borrow £22 million from Thomson British Holdings to keep the papers afloat until their eventual sale to the Australian media magnate Rupert Murdoch.

Case Study Tasks

Your main task is to learn some lessons from this piece of history and to develop some new plans for change and for the conduct of industrial relations more generally within Fleet Street.

In particular you should consider either alone, in pairs or in small groups, the questions below.

1 What were the key issues in this dispute?
2 What have the different interest groups gained and lost?
3 If you had been responsible for TNL strategy, would you have handled it differently? What would you have done?
4 If you were the new owner, what would you do now to meet your objectives?
5 If you were responsible for NGA strategy, what would your strategy be for new technology?
6 What is the role of the law in the conduct of industrial relations such as these?
7 Is there a role for third party interventions? What are the advantages and disadvantages?
8 What are the roles of national employer groups and trade unions in planning and implementing change in Fleet Street?

Essential Reading

Martin R (1981) New Technology and Industrial Relations in Fleet Street, Oxford University Press
Sisson K (1975) Industrial Relations in Fleet Street, Blackwell/SSRC

Additional Reading

Cockburn C (1983) New Technology in print: men's work and women's chances, in Information Technology in Manufacturing Processes: Case Studies in Technological Change, edited by G Winch, Rossendale

CASE 24

Strike Organization: Steel Strike

John Kelly, Jean Hartley and Nigel Nicholson

Background to the Case

The UK national steel strike began on the 2nd January 1980 and lasted for 13 weeks. Nearly 150 000 manual and staff steel workers employed in the public (nationalized) sector of the industry came out on strike. The case study focuses on one geographical area of the strike – Rotherham – with about 10 000 strikers. The predominant union was the Iron and Steel Trades Confederation (ISTC) with a national membership of almost 100 000, although most of the other 11 striking unions also had some membership in Rotherham.

The trigger for the strike was a low wage offer made by the company against a background of plant closures and redundancies over the previous five years. The pay offer of approximately 2% was seen as insulting (inflation was running at 17%), and the ISTC Executive issued a strike call, which was followed shortly afterwards by identical decisions by the other unions. Although the company had just announced a further 50 000 redundancies the strike was initiated and prosecuted over the wages issue. There were 12 unions on strike which for national collective bargaining purposes were arranged in four bargaining units. Three of the units were represented in Rotherham. Although each unit negotiated separately, all unions recognized the ISTC as a pacesetter in wage settlements. The ISTC was the main production workers' union, and represented over 50% of the workforce. The remainder were found in the general unions, i.e. the Transport and General Workers' Union (TGWU) and General and Municipal Workers' Union (GMWU) and in the craft unions (AUEW, EETPU, etc.) which were organized into the National Craftsmen's Coordinating Committee (NCCC).

While negotiation over wages was conducted at national level, the responsibility for running the strike was based at local level, in this case Rotherham.

The Problem

The Need for a Strike Organization

In a small or short strike, it may be sufficient for union officials to encourage members simply to withdraw their labour. However, where large numbers of people are involved, an organization becomes highly desirable. A range of activities has to be managed, if control over the environment, both internal and external, is to be achieved. Running the strike organization involved selection of picket targets and provision of support services for pickets such as supplying food and fuel, advising on social security claims, setting up a hardship fund and raising funds. Activities had to be directed towards other groups as well as the strike participants: to opponents of the strike through picketing, as well as to potential sympathizers such as the media, non-striking trade unions and the wider community, who could be useful morally and financially. Figure 8 indicates the range of activities engaged in by the strike committee (RSC).

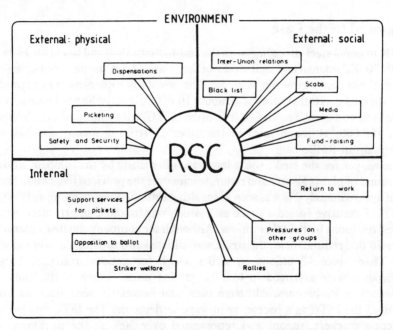

Figure 8   The activities of the Rotherham strike committee (RSC) from Hartley et al. (1983), p. 95).

Establishing a Strike Organization

The British steel industry had a 50 year history of industrial peace and so the majority of steel workers had never participated in a strike and were unsure of what to expect, and of how to organize themselves.

In Rotherham, a temporary organization was established specifically to decide strategy and tactics, and to coordinate strike activities. It shared some properties of the trade union organization from which it arose but was also modified for the circumstances of the strike.

In the month before the strike, the ISTC Joint Works Council, with representatives from all the manual and most of the staff ISTC branches in Rotherham, decided to form the Rotherham Strike Committee (RSC) and elected six of its leading members to it. At its inaugural meeting two days later, the committee had swelled to 13, in order to represent a wider selection of the local branches. During the strike it met daily. It had a chairman, Sam B, and a secretary, Fred T, both from the ISTC. Additional members joined the RSC throughout the strike. When an RSC member was unable to attend he might send a deputy from his branch who might continue to attend. New members also joined where they were responsible for a particular strike function or had particular contacts. For example, members of the picket control function, which was responsible for the activities of pickets, began to attend the RSC regularly after the first month of the strike as picketing became a crucial issue.

In addition to this 'core' of regular RSC attenders, there was a 'periphery' of irregular or temporary attenders. These were strikers who came only for a few meetings or part of a meeting to make unsolicited contributions to the running of the strike by presenting ideas, suggestions or information. They saw their attendance at the committee as wholly legitimate, and a reflection of the committee's permeable membership boundary. As Fred T, the RSC Secretary commented, 'It is always open to people to come in [here] to add their own comments.'

The dominance of the ISTC in the steel industry was reflected in the RSC; the majority of members were ISTC lay officials, with one or two representatives attending daily from each of the other three union groups – TGWU, GMWU and NCCC. The non-ISTC members were involved in their own strike committees but spent a lot of time at the RSC. They were, without exception, experienced and senior lay officials (convenors and executive committee members). But the ethos on the RSC was strongly rank and file such that suggestions from manual ISTC members were far more likely to be accepted than suggestions from non-ISTC members (however experienced) or ISTC staff members.

Figure 9 indicates the formal structure set up in Rotherham to prosecute the strike.

Setting Strike Objectives

The RSC members, especially those in the ISTC, tended to share an outlook on the strike which had a number of interconnected elements and which provided the framework in which strike objectives were set (there were some variations which will be described below). The sense of being victimized by the company and the government gave the RSC a moral certainty about their strike and how they prosecuted it. The belief that they were fighting on behalf of other trade unions may also have raised their expectations about the degree of support and help they would

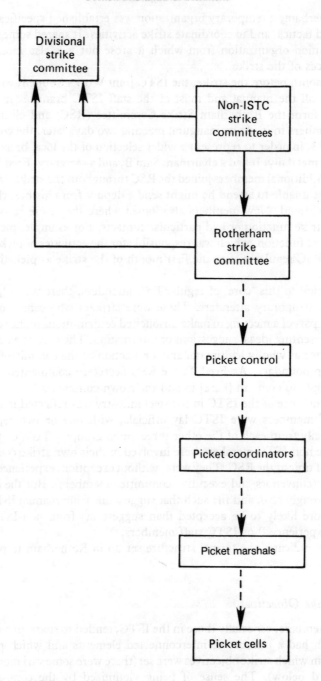

Figure 9 Strike organisation in Rotherham: ——→, send delegates to; – – →, relation of authority.

receive from such unions. The sense of being victims, however, did not make them feel weak or passive: on the contrary, they saw themselves as a strong and powerful strike leadership, a view reinforced by the mass media. Great value was placed by the RSC on being autonomous: the committee perceived itself ready and capable of independent action without national union involvement or permission, and there was also a strong sense of optimism and commitment to the strike.

Prior to the strike, the Rotherham union representatives had no doubts as to the basic goal of the organization: it was to stop all steel movement. Tactics were to be adopted which would be instrumental in achieving this aim. Steel movement and production within the public sector was stopped from the first day, when there was not a single strike-breaker among the striking unions despite the fact that, in line with union rules, the vast majority received no strike pay at all. But the Rotherham steel workers reasoned that to be effective all steel manufacture and use in the country needed to be halted. This meant that private sector steel works, steel stockholders, ports and engineering plants became targets for action. In Rotherham alone there were almost 300 steel producers, users and stockholders, and in the Birmingham area, for which Rotherham was also responsible, over 500 stockholders. The task was a formidable one, and the RSC concentrated its efforts on those companies processing large quantities of steel.

There were two ways of stopping steel movement. The first involved picketing of plants to stop the passage of workers and products; the second was to establish agreements with trade union officals inside plants so that they would curtail or cease production and movement of steel.

The major tactic, favoured especially by the ISTC members of the RSC, was picketing. It absorbed more time and attention in the RSC than any other topic, and its centrality was captured by the words in a document issued by the RSC to strikers: 'the heart and soul of the strike is the picket'.

Picket volunteers had been requested prior to the strike and additional recruits came forward in the first few weeks of the strike. Local pickets were organized into 'cells' of approximately 30 under the command of a picket marshal nominated by the RSC. The marshal was in charge of picket organization in his cell and relayed information between the cell and the strike office. Cells were formed on a geographical rather than union branch basis and consequently most members did not initially know each other. The marshal had discretion over how the cell worked but the target establishment was chosen by the RSC. Local pickets tended to stay on the same target for long periods – some for the duration of the strike. Three RSC members made up Picket Control, operating from the strike office. It was their responsibility to direct cells towards targets, collect information about cell effectiveness, reimburse petrol costs from local and national donations to the strike, and distribute food and fuel. A second type of picket was the flying picket. Organized into bus-loads of 50, again under a marshal, their task was to travel often considerable distances for a 12 hour picket before returning home. Unfamiliar locations, long hours and the likelihood of police confrontation meant that flying picketing tended to attract the younger and more adventurous strikers.

For most strikers, involvement in picketing was a major means of bringing them into contact with the local strike leadership. Picket control and picket marshals were able to relay decisions from the RSC to the membership, as well as providing a channel for information and discussion: about national developments in negotiations, details of picketing and fund-raising successes, help from other unions and so forth. The main alternative sources of information were the weekly union branch meeting or mass meeting, which was inevitably more limited and more formal than the RSC, also the weekly, nation-wide strike newspaper and, of course, the mass media.

The alternative method of stopping steel movement through trade union agreements was argued for by the non-ISTC members of the RSC, who had a wider experience and understanding of the trade union movement beyond the steel industry (since other parts of those unions were located outside steel). The NCCC representative, Tony L, reasoned that stopping steel movement would be difficult to achieve through picketing because of the large number of plants and the need to keep pickets continually on those plants. Inter-union agreements to 'black' steel would be more effective, and he advocated the use of articulate pickets who could encourage sympathy action from the private sector, rather than brow-beating firms into action through large-scale picketing. He was supported by other non-ISTC RSC members. However, this argument was listened to but not generally favoured by the ISTC majority membership of the RSC. So this avenue of action was pursued only sporadically.

Controlling Pickets: Problems of Authority and Militancy

Picketing achieved considerable success in closing down plants in the Rotherham area during the first month of the strike. However, by the end of January, a number of problems were becoming apparent to the RSC in the conduct of local picketing. Picketing the same target for a number of weeks had become routine and dull, so that although cell cohesiveness was high, there had been some reports of 'absenteeism' among cell members. Picketing itself, in the RSC's view, had become slack and less effort was being made by pickets with the now familiar workers and drivers who were crossing the picket lines regularly. In other words, success with a target either came at the beginning as people were persuaded by the pickets, or not at all (since the individual's decision to cross or not to cross the picket line was made early in the strike and was rarely changed). A few pickets were dropping out of their duties altogether and many were reducing the number of hours spent on the lines. Control by the RSC was difficult because cell marshals and pickets enjoyed considerable discretion in their organization. Flying pickets, however, were as vigorous as ever, and their numbers were increasing, as some strikers transferred from the more mundane local picketing.

The deterioration in local picket reliability and effectiveness as perceived by the RSC coincided with mid-strike difficulties at national level. Negotiations became bogged down, and this had a depressing effect on the strikers' morale, which had to be maintained if the strike was to be effective.

The RSC perceived an urgent need to respond to the changing behaviour and mood of the pickets. They linked lack of success in picketing with the perceived decline in striker morale which, they feared, would lead to reduced commitment unless action was taken. The RSC's response to this situation was to propose, agree and organize a series of mass pickets. This entailed the diversion of local and flying pickets for a single day to large, well-known steel plants (target and date kept secret till the date) with the intention of closing the plant through the numerical strength of their mass blockade. Within the RSC, it was argued that a number of advantages would accrue to the strike as a whole from this type of action. The pickets would witness a major victory, which would increase their morale and commitment and reinforce their determination to engage in 'hard picketing' on their return to local duties. The mass action would create a sense of solidarity and cohesiveness which would be valuable in supporting the resolve to stay on strike. Finally, a mass picket would capture media attention in the mid-strike lull, and thereby present the message of strength and steadfastness to the outside world, particularly to the employers and the government. One difficulty for the RSC lay in the limits to their authority. As a trade union organization, the RSC could not 'order' the attendance of pickets but had to 'request' that they attend the mass picket.

The non-ISTC members of the RSC were more restrained in their view of mass pickets. Accepting the difficulties in picketing as defined by the majority of the RSC, they nevertheless saw mass pickets as having only limited effectiveness. They pointed out that mass pickets could fail to close a plant, for example, which could be very damaging to morale, or that it would open again as soon as the mass picket had dispersed. These non-ISTC members reiterated their advocacy of the interunion agreement strategy, established through networks of union contacts.

The staff of Picket Control were obviously in regular contact with many picket marshals and some cell members. Having spent considerable time organizing cells and having borne the brunt of complaints from pickets when arrangements went awry, some of them were reluctant to simply *instruct* strikers to attend a mass picket. Their contact with local picket marshals also led them to believe that disruption to the regularity of cell routine might produce disaffection and cause some to stop picketing. Although sympathetic to the RSC's desire for a flexible picketing organization, they were conscious of the possible costs involved.

Case Study Tasks

Questions 2, 4, 5, 6 and 8 are appropriate for one- or two-hour sessions. Questions 1, 3 and 7 may require a half-day session or could be used as essay titles.

1   As a member of the Rotherham Strike Committee you have been asked to report to a special meeting on ways of improving the effectiveness and commitment of pickets. How would you analyse the difficulties in doing this and what changes would you propose?

2   How would you attempt to increase the numbers actively participating in the strike?

3   In what ways is a temporary strike organization different from most organizations

described in organization theory? In what ways is it similar?

4   What is the impact of hostile intergroup relations between the main protagonists in the strike on the strike's leadership and on member involvement?

5   How would you evaluate the costs and benefits of the picketing strategy chosen by the Rotherham Strike Committee and against what criteria? How would you evaluate alternative strategies, such as negotiation with other trade union representatives?

6   What was the significance of the permeable boundaries of the RSC?

7   How far are the problems faced by the steel strikers similar to or different from those of other striking workers?

8   Legal changes since 1980 (Employment Acts of 1980 and 1982) mean that workers can only picket their own place of work in a trade dispute. Pickets mounted elsewhere (secondary picketing) enjoy no immunity from legal action, and employers faced with secondary picketing can take the individuals concerned to court to obtain damages and an injunction to restrain any further action. In this situation would you advise the ISTC (or any other union) to adopt the same picketing strategy? If not, what are the alternatives?

Essential Reading

Hartley J Kelly J E Nicholson N (1983) Steel Strike, Batsford

Kelly J E Nicholson N (1980) The causation of strikes: a review of some theoretical approaches and the potential contribution of social psychology, Human Relations, 33: 853–883

Additional Reading

Allen V L (1980) The Militancy of British Miners, Moor Press

Batstone E Boraston I Frenkel S (1978) The Social Organization of Strikes, Blackwell

Hiller E T (1969) The Strike (1928), Arno Press

Klandermans B (1984) Mobilization and participation in trade union action, Journal of Occupational Psychology, 57: 107–120

Lane T Roberts K (1971) Strike at Pilkingtons, Fontana

Pitt M (1978) The World on Our Backs: Kent Miners and the 1972 Miner's Strike, Lawrence and Wishart

Pugh D (ed.) (1984) Organization Theory, 2nd edition, Penguin

CASE 25

New Technology: 'RM' Division

Barry Wilkinson

Organizational Setting

'RM' Division belongs to a large manufacturing company employing several thousand workers, although since the 1960s it has operated fairly autonomously from head office. RM is concerned with the precisions moulding of medium to large batches of rubber components, mainly for the automotive industry. Over the last seven years, mainly through rationalization and the upgrading of manufacturing techniques, the workforce has been reduced from 650 to 350. Major decisions on new technology are taken by RM's general manager and technical manager. Their proposals have to be sanctioned by head office, so far always favourably.

Background to the Case

Introducing New Technology

In 1975 RM embarked upon two major new projects. The technical manager said that the primary consideration was to improve the division's competitive position through increasing the quality and reducing the price of products. One innovation was the introduction of injection moulding machines, and the other the introduction of flashless moulding machines. In both cases the machinery came with electronic controls. The new machinery should dramatically increase productivity through increasing the number of rubber components produced with each 'mould' (new machines had a higher capacity than old ones); reducing the cycle times for moulds (they were faster); and reducing process waste, made possible due to the accuracy and consistency offered by electronic control of machines. The new machinery was more expensive than the conventional, though greater capacity and speed easily offset higher costs. Of course, machine breakdown became a more critical problem with more components at stake, and it became more essential that machines be set accurately – an electronic device does not always notice unpredictable variations in materials, etc.

As will become clear, machine operators, process controllers, and work study personnel were in the main occupational groups affected by the new technology. Machine operators were represented by the Amalgamated Union of Engineering Workers (AUEW), and the other two groups by the Technical, Administrative and Supervisory Section of the AUEW (TASS). A closed shop operates at RM.

Management and Union Perceptions of the New Technology

The new machines were introduced gradually from the machine supplier to the shop floor of RM. At first they were placed in a partitioned-off area in the middle of the shop floor. Supervisors and machine operators were slowly introduced to the machinery. At this time managers on the one hand, and shop stewards on the other, were considering how they wished to see the machinery used, and what the costs and benefits might be.

Management had fairly clear ideas on what the new machinery would mean for work organization. The machine operators, previously involved in setting and adjusting machinery, would now simply operate their machines. With electronic process controls guiding most of the machine's movements automatically, this largely meant loading and unloading, pressing the on–off switch, and routine inspection of machine and components. Accordingly operators were given no special training, just on-the-job instruction. The process control department, on the other hand, was to take greater responsibilities, and to be expanded. The work of process control technicians was to become more complex because of more parameters to be accounted for and controlled prior to production runs, and because of the greater precision demanded with faster cycle times. More highly trained technicians were thus recruited. Supervisors and maintenance workers needed some extra training to cope with the new processes, and this was given in conjunction with the machine suppliers. The old moulding machines are to be gradually phased out (except for a few special jobs) over several years as more new machinery is introduced.

Management intended to maintain the existing piecework system for machine operators. In RM the individual bonus provided a significant amount of the pay of operators – often up to 25 or 30% – and (theoretically at least) the degree of effort put in by workers critically affected this portion.

Apart from potential redundancies, the strongest explicit concern of workers and their representatives at this time was that operators *currently employed* should be offered the opportunity to man the new units. Work on the new machines would be far less strenuous, so the union did not want 'outsiders' taking the new work. A shop steward put it like this:

> 'These, flashless and injection, they're a lot lighter work – it's nearly all press buttons – whereas we'd been working on the loose moulding, the heavy stuff, say 10, 15 years . . . you want your blokes to work that [new] machine don't you – pressing a button instead of throwing moulds about. And that's the way we worked it . . . . every person now working in injection and flashless has worked on the heavy moulds.'

The union also wanted a share in the benefits of the productivity increases. RM's manufacturing manager thus complained that '. . . the firm was not only using its most expensive labour in the loose moulders . . . but was also facing demands for a slice of the cake.'

Immediately prior to the introduction of the new technology management had explained to the workforce the basic principle behind automation – 'to compete and survive the company must utilize the most efficient techniques'. Managers were keen to point out that this was never disputed. Yet this basic agreement did not make for smooth and easy negotiations over the sharing of the costs and benefits of the new technology. We will now look in detail at what happened.

The Problem

'Productionization'

Contrary to the popular image sometimes expounded by machine suppliers, virtually all new technology has to go through a process of debugging – of final development and adjustment within the firm to meet its particular needs. During this period, social as well as technical adjustments are made – for instance, to changing work-group relations or changed working hours – often over a long and difficult period. RM's management has coined an appropriate term for this process – 'productionization'.

Management's first problem quickly became evident, and was summed up by the manufacturing manager: 'Development in the production environment meant that the operator would productionize machinery, and rather than management giving production parameters to the operators, the operators would to some extent give them to management.' This meant that machine operators were becoming very familiar with the new technology, performing wider functions than was expected of them – especially the setting of process controls and machine adjustments. Ideally, management would have wished that specialist process control and development staffs establish the new processes, complaining that operators carried over 'bad habits' which were inappropriate on the new machinery. Managers now felt that they had made a mistake in giving workers from the old loose moulding areas the opportunity to work with the new machines, but they had already agreed with the union that 'seniority' (length of service with the firm) would be the primary criterion for selection for work on the new units.

The second major problem, which turned out to be the biggest headache for management, was that of re-establishing piecework rates on the new machinery. Operators might eventually be persuaded to call in the process controller rather than tamper with machine settings, but payment and effort were central and legitimate union concerns.

With the introduction of new machinery, piecework payment was temporarily abandoned until technical problems could be ironed out and everyone become familiar with the new processes. Managers agreed to the union suggestion that, regardless of effort, during productionization operators should be paid 'average earnings' (a sum calculated from the amount they had earned in the previous several months in the old press shop). About six months after the introduction of the first injection moulding machine, management decided it was time to return to piece-work. Operators, however, were enjoying average earnings and resisted this move. It took 12 months to reach an agreement, when management 'bought out' the operators' average earnings by slightly raising, and backdating, the standard hourly payment – to be paid in a lump sum. It was agreed that work on the new machinery should yield a piecework earnings potential equivalent to that on the old loose moulding. The union negotiators also gained a 16% 'relaxation allowance' for operators, to be taken at intervals throughout the working day. These agreements were put to paper in the form of a 'New Technology Agreement'.

But this was not the end of the problem, for with the *mechanics* of the payment–effort bargain at last established, the work study engineers still had to put prices on individual jobs. Of course, operators found themselves in a favourable position. Because of their involvement in productionization, and hence their familiarity with machinery, they could use non-optimum methods for the benefit of the time-study man's watch so that they achieved the best possible piecework rates for subsequent production. It was only two years later (i.e. nearly four years since the introduction of the first electronic machines) that the chief work study engineer felt that 'beating the system' was under control:

'Certainly now, the things that an operator can do to beat the system if you like, are generally now known . . . we now know far more readily the sort of things that they can do. We then either accept that – we'll still pay for that – or we change the method of operation if it's something that has changed on the process.'

Emergent Work Organization

The most striking change in work organization was the transfer of skills and control over the production process from the shop floor to the office. Although machine operators had always been classified as semiskilled, the more experienced among them, together with foremen, had previously been quite expert in setting and adjusting machinery. A few years after the introduction of the electronic machines it was more or less established that machine setting should be carried out by process controllers. Operators only reluctantly gave up any right to tamper with the controls, but the union never saw this as an issue for their concern. This was despite the fact that the strict task division obviously put workers at a disadvantage in negotiating piecework prices.

Divergences from a *strict* division of labour, however, did continue to occur. Management would encourage deviations if they would help production along, and workers would seek them if they would improve piecework performances. For instance, operators would frequently 'twiddle' the injection pressure control to ensure consistent standards. This allowed operators to ensure continuous pro-duction and at the same time meant that process controllers would not have to be called to the shop floor every few minutes to adjust machines.

Operators continued to use any means they could to 'beat the system'. For instance the work study department was currently concerned with the continuing problem of the amount of time booked by operators as 'waiting time' – if waiting time could be booked while the machinery was running then the operator's 'performance' (for piecework calculations) would be higher. A time-study man felt that this possibility was reduced with the new technology:

> '. . .being governed by the machine we can tell how many heats they can do a day – what's the maximum performance they can do . . .. In loose moulding they could [go above that performance] because . . . the faster they go, the more they can do . . .. And you could argue and argue but you couldn't prove that they couldn't do it. But on the electronic machines you know exactly the amount they can do.'

Operators still do 'overbook' but this could now be done only up to a *known maximum* performance.

Operators also reinterpreted the 'system' with regard to the negotiated relaxation allowance. Instead of using the resting time intermittently, as intended by management, many operators would work at full pace for most of their shift, then spend the remaining hour or two relaxing. This was the subject of continuing argument.

We can see then that despite the fact that important aspects of the issues raised by the introduction of new technology were eventually enshrined in a formal New Technology Agreement – redundancy terms, hourly pay, piecework earning potentials, the relaxation allowance, seniority rules – there was none the less a day to day renegotiation of working practices. Managers felt that with the new technology they had gained a tighter control over production, but workers had not given up their contest for that control.

Management Solutions

Although the eventual outcome meant that the management was satisfied overall, the managers saw enough problems with 'productionizing on the shop floor' to be convinced that a separate 'development area' was vital for future innovative projects. By 1981 the new development area was complete, and three major new innovations were being productionized within it. The manufacturing manager was especially pleased that productionizing away from the shop floor would mean that the establishment of working practices and of piecework values would be far less problematic. As machinery comes on to the shop floor, he explained, full-scale production would be immediately possible, and the time-study man would be more expert on work methods than the operator. Workers would now be *told* how to operate equipment, and piece rates would be 'expertly' established. And of course, '. . .once you've negotiated and established a time it's a hell of a job to change that'.

Shopfloor workers (and the researcher!) were not allowed any information on the new products and production technology currently being debugged, on the grounds that a leak of information could at this time prove useful to competitors. However, they were told that many of the large number of remaining loose moulders would be directly affected. The AUEW was resigned to the fact that some redundancies would be involved, and with the recession in manufacturing deepening they felt they would have to try to get the best possible redundancy terms. For the moment they could act on nothing more than this vague information.

Production managers felt they had already benefited from the development area, since all new moulds for new components were coming from there. Thus for the existing electronic machines, operators no longer had the chance to create their own work methods (tooling configuration, task sequences, etc.) each time the product from their machine changed. Methods were already established. However, through the pressure of customer demands the theoretical benefits were not always realized. Thus the chief work study engineer complained that

> '. . . jobs will go out to the production shop in a condition we cannot put a piecework time on – it's not consistent . . . and that ends up then with us paying an average earnings form of payment to operators, and obviously operators, they want piecework really (sic.). . . . But after a few weeks of average earnings they don't want to go back on to piecework. There's a little bit of resistance.'

Whether a little bit more resistance would be forthcoming from workers and their shop stewards when the new processes were introduced was to be seen. Clearly, however, RM's management saw the new development area – the new means of productionization – as a way of further tightening control over the work of operators. Their attempt to 'buy off' this control a few years previously was only partially successful. A redesign of the factory could be even more so.

Finally, an indication of the current bargaining strengths of the parties to the changes might be given by pointing out that, despite the recession, the need to continue to meet customer demands in the face of keen competition meant that management were anxious to avoid a strike. The AUEW, on the other hand, was unsure of its position of strength – RM's parent company had in recent years been known to shut down whole divisions. Hence the parties were each keen to avoid a strike.

Case Study Tasks

Questions 1–3 are appropriate for one- or two-hour sessions. Question 4 is an essay question, whilst the role-playing exercise will require a half-day.

1   a   What were the major changes at RM with regard to skill distribution and task allocation?

     b   Exactly what happened to payment levels and the payment–effort bargain?

     c   What has changed in the work relationships between machine operators and work study engineers, and between machine operators and process controllers?

     d   For each of a–c above, to what degree did the new technology itself determine the changes?

2   If you were appointed general manager of RM, would you wish to make any changes to the way you introduced new technology to the workforce? If no, provide a justification of your position. If yes, what would you try to do about:

     a   the bonus system and the role of work study

b task allocation
c selection and training of operators and process controllers
d the provision of information on new technology to the AUEW
e the 'familiarization' of machine operators with new machines?

3   If you were elected senior shop steward of the AUEW at RM, would you try to change the way you bargained over new technology? If no, justify your position. If yes, what would you try to do about:

a the bonus system
b skill levels of operators and training policy
c provision of information on new technology
d your relationship with TASS?

4   Using the information available in this case (and other information if relevant), discuss the merits and problems within unitarist, pluralist and radical frames of reference with regard to the industrial relations problems encountered with the introduction of new technology. Your answer should include a discussion of the question of managerial prerogatives with regard to technical change.

Role Play

This can be done either before or after the case study tasks. Students will take the role of (i) general management of RM, (ii) the work study department, (iii) the process controllers, and (iv) operators and their shop steward representatives. They should make a thorough assessment of the situation at RM, and then make recommendations or demands concerning the next wave of technology. The role players can then come together and attempt to reach agreement. They should be allowed, if they so desire, to consult one another during the preparation of recommendations. This will allow behind-the-scenes negotiations before the final meeting.

Essential Reading

Braverman H (1974) Labor and Monopoly Capital, Monthly Review Press, Chapter 9
Marchington M (1979) Shopfloor control and industrial relations, in The Control of Work, edited by J Purcell and R Smith, Macmillan, pp. 133–155
Mumford E (1979) The design of work: new approaches and new needs, in Case Studies in Automation Related to the Humanization of Work, edited by J E Rijnsdorp, Pergamon Press, pp. 9–17

Additional Reading

Brown R K (1977) Shopfloor strategies and reactions to change, in The Sociology of Industry, edited by S R Parker R K Brown J Child and M A Smith, George Allen & Unwin, pp. 100–112
Buchanan D A Boddy D (1983) Organizations in the Computer Age, Gower

Fox A (1966) Industrial Sociology and Industrial Relations, HMSO
Friedman A L (1977) Industry and Labour, Macmillan
Goodrich C L (1975) The Frontier of Control, Pluto Press
Hull D (1978) The Shop Steward's Guide to Work Organization, Spokesman
Wilkinson B (1983a) The Shopfloor Politics of New Technology, Heinemann
Wilkinson B (1983b) Technical change and work organization, Industrial Relations
    Journal 14(2): 18–27

CASE 26

Participation and Communication: Kitchenco

Mick Marchington

Organizational Setting

Kitchenco is a manufacturer and assembler of kitchen furniture located in the West Midlands. The company employs some 700 people, of whom 500 work on the shop floor. For simplicity, these employees can be divided into three groups in terms of department and job content; the mills employ 160 people, the vast majority being men who have served an apprenticeship; in assembly there are roughly 200 employees, many of whom are skilled but there is also a considerable minority with no apprenticeship. In this department, there is 25% female employment; all other departments employ about 120 doing maintenance, packing, storage, warehousing, driving and other ancillary jobs. A post-entry union membership agreement is in operation, and on the shop floor there are two unions; the vast majority, including maintenance, are in the Furniture, Timber and Allied Trades Union (FTAT) whilst the 18 HGV drivers are represented by the TGWU. Bargaining takes place at company level, but the company is part of the employers' federation and thus bound to pay rates in line with the national agreement; in fact, Kitchenco pays well above this rate.

The company is part of a furniture products group which is, in itself, a subsidiary of a wider holding company. However, the holding company is prepared to leave industrial relations issues up to individual concerns, and the practices at Kitchenco are not tied in with activity elsewhere. Business is variable in this highly competitive fashion-oriented market, and although Kitchenco is one of the market leaders it only holds about 8% of the market. Order levels vary enormously from week to week, and the whole situation is characterized by insecurity and indeterminancy. The management style of the company is in many ways informal in the sense that managers at different levels meet regularly during the day – which is usually rather hectic to say the least – as well as socially after work. Most of the managers in production are on first name terms with the foremen, shop stewards and a good number of the shopfloor employees. Managers attempt to solve problems quickly, and the idea of 'fire-fighting', 'trouble shooting' and 'working at the sharp end' is paramount to them; not for them to sit in the office developing long-term plans.

Background to the Case

The Participation System

There are two parts to the participation system; one is the Council structure which functions at both company and departmental level, with the latter examining the more parochial or specific issues and thus acting as a filter for the company-wide scheme. This in turn, of course, refers issues back to departmental level as appropriate. The second strand is the financial side of the scheme, which is based solely at company level, and is a value-added system of payment such that earnings of all employees come out of a pool representing the difference between the sales value of output and the costs of supplies, services and materials. The production value added throughout the process is then divided on a fixed percentage basis between wages, salaries, dividends and profits with the fallback of basic wages for all shopfloor employees if the valued added is small. There is a clear and understood link between wages and production ouput.

The system was introduced in order to overhaul the previous payment by results (PBR) scheme and at the same time improve employee commitment to Kitchenco. Regular changes to piecework rates had created a situation of almost constant work study and negotiations, complications over differentials and leapfrogging claims, and this culminated in a series of stoppages, deteriorating productivity and low morale. A team of consultants was called in, and a steering committee of managers and employee representatives set up to assess the merits of the value-added scheme. After several months of periodic discussion, it published proposals covering not only the principles and details for the financial side of the scheme but also the constitution of the council structure. Local and national union officials were involved in this process, and the 'selling' of the scheme also incorporated films and discussion groups. Eventually the proposals were accepted following a shopfloor referendum. The system has now been in operation for five years.

At the monthly meeting, the chair is taken by the works director and the rest of the management team comprises the finance director (who explains the monthly results), the personnel manager (secretary) and four other members of management – usually from production, but occasionally from sales or marketing. The shop floor is represented by 19 members, about half of whom are shop stewards. Some departments took the line that it was best to combine the role of council member with that of steward whereas others felt that it was better to keep them separate; in the mills, for example, a policy decision had been taken to combine the two functions, whilst in assembly the membership had opted for a separation of roles.

Voting is allowed for in the constitution, and that right rests solely with the employee representatives, although it is the chairman who calls for a vote. A wide range of subject matter is dealt with at council, ranging from the chairman's review –

which is concerned with a whole number of general issues – through an analysis of order and production statistics, discussions of job grading or holiday periods, to consideration of social and welfare matters.

Three other issues are important when assessing participation and communications at Kitchenco. First of all, there is some overlap between the council structure and the traditional practice of collective bargaining. Since the council receives the results of the previous month's performance and therefore bonus figures, it is treated very seriously by both employee representatives and the shopfloor constituents. Senior management are also present without exception at the council meeting, so illustrating the high regard they hold for this regulatory mechanism. The shop stewards' committee meets weekly, in works time, and alternates fortnightly between their own private meeting and one with management. The whole atmosphere of these meetings is rather more informal than the council, generally being chaired by a senior production manager. There is some overlap between the subject matter which comes up for discussion at these two meetings.

Secondly, there is a link between the formal bodies and the individual employee at Kitchenco. On the day after the council meeting, management allow time following the mid-morning break for the employee representatives to report back to their constituents and deal with any queries which they may have. On average, these sessions only last 10–15 minutes, although there are occasions when this is extended. Some representatives also like to hold a meeting several days prior to the council in order to pick up any underlying issues which can be brought up at the full session. Minutes are circulated around the factory, but these are not always available quickly, tend to be rather long and often disappear soon after being posted.

Finally, there is no formal mechanism for 'direct' involvement through job enrichment or job design to cover all employees, although there is some informal job rotation on certain packing and warehousing jobs; due to specialization and employee preference, there is little of this in either machining or assembly areas. The company has encouraged employees to become directly involved in other ways, for example by asking them to guide customers or visiting dignitaries around the works or showroom, and talk to them over a buffet. On occasions, an employee may visit a supplier with the works engineer prior to the eventual purchase of a new machine.

The Problem

Presenting Symptoms

As with any system, however, things do not always run smoothly. It was apparent, both from talking with people and from other indicators, that there were problems at Kitchenco. Both managers and employee representatives expressed doubts about the scheme, and criticized the other party for their attitudes or commitment or abilities. A number of key managers all left the company within a short period of time feeling that what had started out as a bold and brave experiment had become immersed in the quagmire of everyday problems, or had regressed to its pre-council days. There was a one-day strike which centred around a failure to consult on the part of management who themselves felt increasingly constrained by the competitive pressures imposed by a tightening product market. The value-added scheme, which had produced high bonus figures over the years, suddenly generated either no or very small payments. For many on the shop floor, who had become used to high bonuses, it was a shock to their expectations and they often blamed other workers whose alleged lack of effort was reducing the value added. There was continuing disenchantment between employees in the different departments who were torn as to whether the council representatives should or should not be restricted solely to shop stewards. And, most important from a communications perspective, there was increasing shop floor apathy and disinterest in the scheme.

Each of the groups involved at Kitchenco obviously had their own rather different solutions to this catalogue of problem areas. For the management team as a whole, there was an acknowledgement that participation had not achieved as much as they had wished for, and an acceptance that they themselves often ended up 'selling' issues to the council representatives rather than engaging in full and fruitful discussion prior to joint decision making. However, they legitimized this non-participation in three ways:

a   By an aggressive reassertion of managerial rights. They felt that they had achieved their current position by virtue of their own abilities, expertise, qualifications or professionalism and, being professionals, could utilize an objectivity in assessing solutions which other sections of the workforce did not possess.

b   By a more defensive demonstration of the inabilities of employee representatives (and sometimes foremen) to make effective decisions due to their *lack* of expertise. Examples were given of times when the representatives failed to grasp a particular point, or countered a management argument by relating an issue back to the detail of their own department. Managers became frustrated when dealing with non-specialists, and were unwilling to delve for ideas that were poorly articulated by the representatives who were often only involved *after* strategic choices had already been made. Consequently, it was hardly surprising that managers characterized their contributions as destructive rather than constructive.

c   By the lack of time for participation due to the rate of change within the environment. Since order levels varied so enormously or priority jobs shifted, there were constant changes to production scheduling. Changes were often made on the spur of the moment, sometimes contrary to a predetermined policy of consultation.

For the purposes of this case study, however, the crucial issue underlying each of these three factors is the extent to which non-participation is either *required* or *legitimized* by reference to market constraints and economic efficiency.

Not surprisingly, the employee representatives saw the problem rather differently. They argued that the lack of realistic participation at Kitchenco reflected a lack of management commitment towards the involvement of employees, and some of them (though not all by any means) became disillusioned with what they felt was a charade at council meetings. There were certainly occasions when the chairman refused to allow, or managed to postpone, a vote which he knew he could lose. One issue, which reappeared at six successive council meetings, was effectively deferred by skilful use of chairmanship and at times blatant use of power. Representatives were urged to re-examine the issue and hold further discussions, and management agreed to circulate more information to the representatives. Eventually when internal dissension amongst the representatives had increased and · cohesion evaporated, the chairman called for a vote and got agreement with the original proposal; the representatives had voted for a solution which they had originally vehemently opposed.

The lack of unity of course was due partly to the mechanism by which representatives were elected to the council, and the continuing disagreement on the part of the workforce as to whether election should or should not be restricted to the shop stewards alone. One possible compromise which attracted greater support on the shop floor was that the council should be expanded such that all shop stewards could be included, but alongside representatives from those areas favouring a separation of roles.

In addition, the value-added payment system itself led to conflict between representatives over regrading or decisions about whether to take on or shed labour. Since the percentage share of the cake is fixed, this means that if more employees are covered by the scheme or there are upgradings, there is correspondingly less bonus for each individual if the production value added does not increase at a similar rate. The opposite happens with redundancies or non-replacements. This merely serves to heighten the tensions between representatives and departments, and between traditional union goals and individual gain.

The employee representatives did acknowledge – in line with management criticism – their own failings and lack of knowledge or ability in certain areas. However, contrary to management, they believed that little had been done to help overcome this deficiency and even claimed that certain managers actually enjoyed confusing them with figures or paperwork. It was rare for the council representatives to take notes at the meetings, and they did show their lack of understanding of the financial aspects of the value-added scheme. Newly elected representatives took a long time to come to grips with the council, a situation that was exacerbated by the lack of a strong leader. This too created problems of unity among the representatives, who were easily outmanoeuvred by management.

The shop floor as a whole had mixed feelings about the system at Kitchenco; whilst they were aware of the problems with the payment scheme, many had worked under the old PBR system, and were much more favourably inclined to the principle of value added. Indeed, a questionnaire survey of the shop floor, undertaken following three successive months of low bonus results, indicated a high degree of satisfaction with the system. Some 80% felt that it was a good or very good system; 85% thought it was an improvement on their previous method of remuneration; and 83% chose this system as the one they would most favour from a list of schemes. About half of them were satisfied because 'it was a good way to earn more money', whilst the other half felt it to be 'a more just and equitable way of sharing rewards'.

They were somewhat more apathetic about the council structure, and many of them either did not know or could not remember much about this side of the representative arrangements. About one in five claimed not to know who their representative on council actually was. Their personal interest in participation was firmly located in task-based issues, although it was clear that their interest in company-wide issues was still desired, not personally, but through their representatives.

All of this, of course, has to be assessed against the objective which each of the various groups had for the system at Kitchenco. For management, these included a desire for greater productivity, a reduced resistance to change and an increased commitment on the part of employees, combined with some vague notion that participation was a good thing in itself; many of them had worked their way up from the shop floor in other companies, and were aware of the lack of involvement afforded to them when they occupied subordinate positions. For the employees and their representatives, there was a desire to help the company become more efficient and profitable, partly due to the obvious financial rewards which this would create but also because of their commitment to Kitchenco as an employer; many of them had worked there for a considerable number of years, and had seen a succession of management teams come and go. Their chances of employment elsewhere within the area were also receding as the labour market tightened. On the part of the representatives, there was an added desire for involvement in order to improve the quality of management decision making.

The Diagnoses

Although all groups were agreed that improvements could be made, there was a range of possible solutions for achieving this. Training, as ever, was a central preoccupation of the solutions; management themselves felt that they needed to become more sensitive to the representatives, and improve their own abilities of persuasion and 'selling'. They also felt that the employee representatives would benefit from a course of study which exposed them to committee skills, decision making techniques and some financial and commercial awareness. They felt that the principles of the value-added scheme needed to be recommunicated to all employees in order to regenerate overall interest in the involvement processes. And, some of them felt that restricting the council to shop stewards alone might overcome the problems of overlap and time-wasting between the council and the stewards' committee. This idea obviously found favour with the shop stewards but not with the council representatives from the assembly area; they were quick to point out that the constitution of the system demanded a referendum of the shop floor before any change could even be considered. The representatives as a whole, whilst keen on training for themselves, felt that more needed to be done to increase management commitment to employee participation and to control the power of the chairman. Some looked for further constitutional changes which would perhaps provide for joint or rotating chairmanship between the works director and the senior steward, or for more control over the agenda or the minutes.

Case Study Tasks

Below, there are a number of questions which relate to the case study you have just read. The first five questions are relatively short, whereas the last three will require more time to be spent on them. At all times, you should bear in mind the practical and financial limitations of any answers which you put forward, and your primary objective is to decide what action should be taken in order to resolve the problems at the company. Think carefully about the theoretical framework within which your actions can be located, and consider both the process and content of any changes you propose.

1   What do you think of the solutions offered by: (a) the management; (b) the shop stewards; (c) the council representatives who are not shop stewards?
2   What is your solution? How will it deal with the problems outlined above?
3   What would be the effect of *your* solution on: (a) efficiency and productivity; (b) union organization; (c) management style?
4   What would you do to make participation more effective within the council meetings?
5   What would you do about: (a) the content and philosophy of training courses for managers; (b) the content and philosophy of training courses for employee representatives; (c) communicating with employees; (d) relating effort to reward?
6   Under Section 1 of the 1982 Employment Act, companies employing 250 people or more are required to indicate within their Annual Statements what action they have taken during the previous financial year in order to introduce, maintain or develop arrangements aimed at: (a) providing *information* to employees on matters of concern; (b) *consulting* employees or their representatives on a regular basis so that their views can be taken into account in making decisions likely to affect their interests; (c) encouraging involvement in company performance through some *financial* scheme; (d) achieving a common financial and economic *awareness* of company performance on the part of employees. Assume that you are the works director, and write about 150 words on this as a basis for the Annual Statement.
7   Assuming that the company wanted to move to a system of sole shop steward representation on the council, how should it go about managing this change in order to increase the chances of success?
8   What do you anticipate would be the wider organizational ramifications of your solution on industrial relations, management development, employee commitment and communications?

Essential Reading

Knight K (1979) Introducing participation, in Putting Participation into Practice, edited by D Guest and K Knight, Gower, pp. 267–286
Marchington M (1980) Problems with participation at work, Personnel Review, 9 (3): 31–38

Ramsay H (1980) Phantom participation: patterns of power and conflict, Industrial Relations Journal, 11 (3): 61–72

Additional Reading

Brannen P (1983) Authority and Participation in Industry, Batsford, pp. 49–65, 116–128

Farnham D Pimlott J (1983) Understanding Industrial Relations, Cassell, pp. 50–70

Guest D Knight K (eds) (1979) Putting Participation into Practice, Gower, pp. 5–18, 287–305

Legge K (1978) Power, Innovation and Problem-solving in Personnel Management, McGraw-Hill, pp. 117–135

Marchington M (1982) Managing Industrial Relations, McGraw-Hill, pp. 35–51, 150–173

Poole M (1975) Workers' Participation in Industry, Routledge & Kegan Paul, pp. 48–84

Thurley K Wood S (eds) (1983) Industrial Relations and Management Strategy, Cambridge University Press, pp. 73–82, 197–224

CASE 27

Trade Union Democracy: Union Government and Union Democracy

Roger Undy

Organizational Setting and Background to the Case

The Government of the TGWU

The Transport and General Workers Union (TGWU) is Britain's largest and most heterogeneous union with, in 1984, some 1 600 000 members dispersed across a wide range of industries. Occupationally it recruits primarily semi- and unskilled manual workers, although it has a significant white collar section of approximately 150 000. During the 1960s and 1970s, partly due to mergers, its membership increased quite sharply from 1 340 000 in 1960 to a peak of 2 000 000 in 1980, followed by a quite sharp drop in membership over the period 1980–4.

Politically the TGWU is affiliated to, and is an influential member of, the Labour Party. In recent years, it has moved to the left politically and adopted a fairly militant industrial posture, particularly in opposing the Conservatives' legislative proposals. Over the years the formal framework of the union's constitution has remained largely unchanged; however, there have been some significant shifts in the informal decision-making process.

The Decision-making Structures and Processes

The government of the TGWU is probably best understood as being composed of two distinct but related channels of decision making: one is the bargaining channel and the other the administrative and general policy-making channel.

Bargaining and the Trade Group Structure The bargaining channel is contained within a trade group structure. There are 14 trade groups in the TGWU and each is similar to an independent industrial union with responsibility, under rule, for dealing with pay, hours and working conditions of the relevant section of membership. For instance, the Agricultural Workers Union, which joined the TGWU in

1982, now forms the core of the TGWU's new agricultural trade group and it will continue to hold its customary annual conference in the TGWU on the same lines as it did before entering the TGWU.

Workers when recruited are therefore allocated to a trade group and made a member of a branch which may be factory or geographically based. If it is factory based, and this is the predominant form of organization, all its members will be in the same trade group. Elections will be held in the branch, by ballot vote, for the purposes of choosing delegates to attend the district or regional trade groups. Indirect elections, normally by show of hands, then take place every two years at district or regional trade groups to elect members of the national trade group committee.

Decisions of the national trade group committees must not conflict with the general policy decisions of the union. Such conflicts are limited by the TGWU's constitution, which provides for a degree of dual membership; i.e. a number of seats on the national executive council are reserved for members elected from the national trade group committees. Of the 35–45 members of the general executive, 14 are trade group representatives indirectly elected by a show of hands vote at each of the 14 national trade group committees. Also, at the next lower tier of general policy decision making – the regional committee – the members are again chosen by a show of hands vote, in this case at the regional trade group or district committee meetings. Thus although the two channels are functionally differentiated into bargaining and non-bargaining activities they are constitutionally related by the dual nature of their membership.

Bargaining Decisions in Practice   The TGWU has not changed its formal structure significantly since its foundation, but it underwent quite radical changes in its informal structure and processes in the 1970s. These changes made it, in some observers' eyes, the 'shop stewards union'. Bargaining decisions were generally decentralized from national to local level and shop stewards encouraged to act independently of the full-time officials. Further, where higher level (e.g. national or company) negotiating bodies were retained, shop stewards were introduced into union negotiating teams and/or decisions were referred back to lay delegate conferences attended by representatives of those directly affected by the proposed agreement. In consequence full-time officials adopted a lower profile in negotiations and became more concerned with relaying information between union and shop stewards and vice versa. They tended in extreme cases to be more like postmen than negotiators. Thus the TGWU ceased to conform with the 'popular bossdom' image associated with the union in the early 1960s.

Attempts by lay activists to cement and formalize this devolutionary trend (by, for example, changing the union's rules to enforce reference-back of agreements) were defeated at the union's policy-making biennial delegate conference. The union leadership therefore retained some discretion over the method used for referring back wage offers and associated strike questions to the membership. Thus, the union leadership remained free to choose the method best suited to the particular circumstances surrounding their negotiations.

In processing bargaining decisions, the TGWU normally refers employers' offers to the members, who vote by a show of hands. A survey of settlements made in 1979–80 showed that 74% of TGWU agreements were referred back to the members for acceptance and a further 8% referred to shop stewards only. Of wage offers surveyed, 56% were determined by show of hands votes, 10% by non-postal ballots, 5% by postal ballot and 3% by some other method. However, the power and engineering trade group, in respect of electricity supply, and also certain sections of the road haulage transport (commercial) trade group provide exceptions to the general use of show of hands votes. Both these groups organized secret postal ballots.

Questions of whether or not the members are willing to take industrial action are normally included in references back when the union is recommending rejection of a 'final' offer.

Administration and General Policy Decisions Decision making in the TGWU's non-bargaining channel is largely determined by reference to the union's rules. The branch acts as the first body at which motions are debated and lay representatives elected. Members voting in the branch by a show of hands, or a ballot, elect representatives to the supreme policy-making body, the 1000 strong biennial delegate conference. In between conferences the 35–40 member general executive council interprets and, when necessary, makes policy. This lay body is elected every two years with all but the 14 trade group representatives being elected by ballot vote at the branch or in the workshop. It is the general executive committee's job to interpret and, when necessary, make policy. However, it devolves much of its responsibility to the eight members of the finance and general purposes committee; a subcommittee of the executive.

Contests for the lay executive (excluding the 14 elected at the national trade group committees) and the post of general secretary attract relatively large numbers of candidates. In 1977 a total of 14 candidates stood for the post of general secretary. A total of 740 460 votes were cast, giving a turnout of approximately 39%. General executive elections may even attract more candidates than those contesting for the general secretaryship. For example, in the 1979–80 elections some regions had 30 candidates standing for two seats. Turnout in these elections varied between 10% and 40% of the regional electorate.

The result of the TGWU elections is, as in virtually all unions, influenced by factors operating independently of the formal decision-making process. But the TGWU elections are not primarily determined by internal party political allegiances. The TGWU does not have nationally organized factions consistently promoting left and right candidates in executive elections. Nor does the TGWU itself issue election addresses for executive elections, although it does in general secretary elections. The ballot paper only provides the voter with limited information including the candidate's name, trade group and the numbers of nominating branches.

In the absence of party political information the candidate's trade group and geographic location have particular significance. If the candidate is employed in a factory or workshop with a large number of TGWU members the chances are that the ballot will be organized at the workplace and result in a relatively high turnout. It is therefore not surprising that the TGWU executive is normally composed of a disproportionate number of members elected from garages, docks and multinational corporations or similar organizations which have large concentrations of TGWU membership in particular regions. The members of the executive, since the devolutionary policies of the 1970s, are mainly drawn from the ranks of senior shopfloor representatives. There is a relatively high turnover of executive members with, in 1978, at least 20 members having less than five years on the committee. The elected general secretary attends but does not vote at the executive. He is elected at the branch or workshop by the whole membership in a ballot vote, and holds office until retirement.

In practice the general secretary plays a much more important role in decision making than the rules would suggest. For example, the devolutionary bargaining policy, referred to above, was initiated by the general secretary. Further, he or she can also dominate the 'platform' of the biennial delegate conference in a manner denied to the ordinary lay executive members. Also, the general secretary can influence significantly the appointment of the union's 500 (approximately) full-time officers and use powers of patronage, regarding future promotions, to considerable effect. Thus, although in rule the conference and general executive have a very powerful influence over the government of the TGWU, at various points in its history it has been dominated by its general secretary.

Overview   The working of the TGWU's two-channel system of government is not dependent on any one simple structure, system of representation or formally pre-described rules. The union's rules largely determine the structures within which decisions are made, but the informal processes have considerable influence on decision making and the choice of representatives. This is particularly noticeable in the bargaining channel where policy and practices rather than written rules shape the government of the TGWU. But in formally separating bargaining and non-bargaining decisions the TGWU clearly runs the risk of fragmenting the union into 14 isolated industrial groups. Thus although this division gives the TGWU some significant advantages – it has been a major factor in attracting merging unions into the TGWU by guaranteeing them a high degree of autonomy – it also threatens the unity of the union.

The TGWU's rules seek to maintain unity in two ways. Firstly, the general secretary, who attends but is not a voting member of the general executive, is given unique prestige within the union by being the only national official elected by the total membership. This allows the general secretary to claim an authority denied to any other official. He or she therefore plays an integrating role in what is a highly differentiated structure. Secondly, by electing a minority of the general executive by indirect elections held at national trade group meetings, the two national levels of decision making are given a common and binding interest. The TGWU's system of government was thus constructed so as to provide both representative processes and effective organization.

Measures to Democratize Unions

Governments in Britain, Australia and the USA have promoted legislation to increase union democracy. Unions themselves have also adopted different methods of decision making associated with improving democracy. For example, as mentioned above, the TGWU devolved bargaining decision making in the 1970s. Also the Amalgamated Union of Engineering Workers, Engineering Section (AUEW(E)) in 1972 and the Electrical, Electronic, Telecommunication and Plumbing Union (EETPU) earlier in the 1960s replaced branch ballots with postal ballots for the purposes of electing their leading full-time officials. The AUEW(E) experienced an increase in turnout of over 100% after introducing postal ballots. The main measures for consideration in this case – the Conservative Government's legislation in 1980 and 1984, initially to encourage and subsequently to enforce secret and, preferably, postal ballots – are therefore not unlike changes initiated by other governments and by some trade unions.

The Conservative Party considered trade unions to be imperfectly democratic. They were in particular concerned with unions' electoral arrangements and especially the relationship between the rank and file and the union leadership. The Conservative Party also argued that trade unions had too much power vis à vis the employer, Parliament and their own membership. In short, the militant union leadership was seen as exploiting its position for its own purposes, which were not identical with those of the ordinary members.

Legislation to increase membership participation in elections and critical decisions by secret ballot was the main means chosen by the Conservative Party to encourage 'responsible' trade unionism. This was promoted by two pieces of legislation. In 1980 the Employment Act and associated regulations encouraged the use of secret postal ballots by offering to subsidize their cost if used to determine a range of specific issues including membership votes on union mergers and rule changes, calling or ending a strike or other industrial action, reference back of employers' offers, and elections to posts held as an employee of the union. This Act had little impact on union behaviour.

Its failure was used to justify the more interventionist measures contained in the 1984 Trade Union Act. In respect of elections it provides members dissatisfied with existing electoral practices the opportunity to use the courts to press for periodic (every five years or less), secret, direct membership elections of national executive members. Official strikes or other sanctions are also made the subject of secret ballots. These are necessary if the union involved is to maintain what immunity it has from civil actions. In the absence of a strike ballot the employer may use the courts to seek injunctions and damages. Finally, the existence of a union's political fund is also made the subject of a membership ballot, at least once every 10 years.

Case Study Tasks

The student's main task is to assess what constitutes a democratic union and to consider the contribution which secret ballots can make to union democracy, using the TGWU as an example of union government. Students could adopt the perspective of union activist, the union general secretary, manager, employer and the Secretary of State for Employment (Conservative or Labour) in answering these questions.

1   Is the TGWU, as described above, a democratic union? (Discuss with reference to different models of union democracy.)
2   How would you improve democracy in the TGWU? For example:

   a   Should all posts be periodically elected by secret postal ballot?
   b   Should the executive be composed of elected full-time officials?
   c   Should political factionalism be encouraged, and if so, how?
   d   Should all reference-back of agreements and all strikes be subject to a postal ballot of the members involved?

3   What would be the effects of your changes on (a) the TGWU's efficiency and (b) the unity of the TGWU?
4   Does legislation which enforces the use of secret postal ballots promote both democracy and moderation? Consider your answer in respect of (a) the union's internal affairs (e.g. (i) elections and (ii) strikes) and (b) the liberal democracy in which unions function.
5   What is your preferred model of union democracy?
6   Advise the Government of the day on how it should act to democratize unions.

Essential Reading

Coates K Topham T (1980) Trade Unions in Britain, Spokesman, Chapter 3 (see pp. 92–93 for a suggested checklist for evaluating union democracy)
Jackson M P (1982) Trade Unions, Longmans, Chapters 4 and 5
Undy R Martin R (1984) Ballots and Trade Union Democracy, Blackwell, particularly Chapter 5

Additional Reading

Clegg H A (1976) Trade Unionism Under Collective Bargaining, Blackwell, Chapter 4
Edelstein J Warner M (1975) Comparative Union Democracy, Allen & Unwin
England J (1981) Shop stewards in Transport House, Industrial Relations Journal 12: 16–29
Goldstein J (1952) The Government of British Unions, Allen & Unwin
Hemmingway J (1978) Conflict and Democracy: Studies in Trade Union Government, Oxford University Press
Herding R (1972) Job Control and Union Structure, Rotterdam University Press
HMSO (1983) Democracy in Trade Unions, Cmnd 8778, HMSO
Hyman R (1975) Industrial Relations: A Marxist Introduction, Macmillan, Chapter 3
Lawrence P R Lorsch J W (1967) Organization and Environment, Harvard University Press

Lipset S M Trow M Coleman J S (1956) Union Democracy, Free Press

McCarthy W E J (ed.) (1984) Trade Unions, Penguin

Undy R Ellis V McCarthy W E J Halmos A M (1981) Change in Trade Unions, Hutchinson

Undy R Martin R (1983) Legislation and the election of union moderates, Employee Relations 5(5): 24–28

AUTHOR INDEX

SUBJECT INDEX

dissociation of, 86
freezing of, 47–8, 56, 57
   depression constant, 56
ion product constant, 87
properties, 47
protolysis, 86
vapour pressure, 48
   lowering of, 48
weight, 17
  units, 17
Weston cell, 307
work:
  energy, 166
  entropy and, 174, 176
  free energy and, 172, 190
  maximum, 176, 190, 308
  pressure-volume, 166, 167
  spontaneous processes, 175, 177
  thermodynamic reversibility and, 190
  units, 15, 309

'useful', 172, 190

yeast carboxylase, 45
yeast hexokinase, 288

zero:
  entropy, 174
  order reaction, 233, 235, 236, 242, 265
  redox potential, 304
  temperature:
    absolute, 18, 24, 174
    centigrade, 48, 304
zwitterion, 129
  of arginine, 137
  aspartic acid, 137
  glutamic acid, 134
  glycine, 130, 131
  histidine, 138
  lysine, 136
  tyrosine, 138